The Lost Executioner

A Story of Comrade Duch and the Khmer Rouge

Nic Dunlop

BLOOMSBURY

LONDON · NEW DELHI · NEW YORK · SYDNEY

First published 2005
This paperback edition published 2010

Copyright © 2005, 2010 by Nic Dunlop

The moral right of the author has been asserted

Bloomsbury Publishing Plc, 50 Bedford Square,
London WC1B 3DP

Bloomsbury Publishing, London, New Delhi, New York and Sydney

A CIP catalogue record for this
book is available from the British Library

ISBN 978 1 4088 0401 8

10 9 8 7 6

Typeset by Hewer Text UK Ltd, Edinburgh
Printed and bound in Great Britain by CPI Group (UK) Ltd, Croydon CR0 4YY

Every reasonable effort has been made to trace the copyright holders
of images reproduced in this book, but if any have been inadvertently
overlooked the publishers would be glad to hear from them, and to make
good in future editions any errors or omissions brought to their attention.

www.bloomsbury.com/nicdunlop

ACKNOWLEDGEMENTS

This book is the result of several years' work in Cambodia, and many people have helped me along the way. Although I cannot name them all I would like to thank the following. In particular Andrew Marshall who tirelessly spent weeks going through the manuscript giving essential criticism and advice, as did Sarah Rooney and Ben Davies. I owe a deep debt of gratitude to them all for their encouragement, support and patience in helping a photographer to write.

I'd also like to thank Bob Maat, David Chandler, Ben Kiernan for reading through the manuscript correcting inaccuracies and giving crucial advice. Stephen Heder for sharing much indispensable material and Alex Linklater whose enthusiasm and patience helped provide the basis for the book. Over the years it was the work, support and encouragement of John Pilger and David Munro as well as the pictures of Philip Jones Griffiths that set me on my course as a photographer.

Thanks too to Nate Thayer for accompanying me on my return to Samlaut, Stuart Isett who also returned with me, Jennifer Adams for her work on an early version. A big thanks to Christine Chaumeau, Arnaud Dubus, Beauphara Thong, Douglas Niven, Chey Sopheara, Chey Phearum, Kalyan Sann and all the staff at Tuol Sleng Museum. Jerry Harmer of APTN, Dominic Faulder, Chean Nariddh Moeun,

Chay Cee Chan, Henri Locard, Bau Chau Doan and Kathleen O'Keefe, Stefan Smith, Dana Langlois, the late Sok Sin, Thet Sambath, Ky Lok, Ouk Ly, Chhang Youk, Men Kimseng, Panh Rithy, Mary Dunbar, John Jackson, Victoria Lukens, Privan Limpanboon, Somying Soontornwong, Therese Caouette, Robin McDowell, Nicolas Revise, John Ryle, Robert Winder, Peter Carey, Geoff Sayer, David and Sophie Appleton, Paul and Helen Davies, Justin and Mischka Byworth, David McKaige and Michael Hayes of the *Phnom Penh Post*, my editors at Bloomsbury Mike Jones and Katherine Greenwood, my agent Robert Kirby, John Hyde and the Fund for Investigative Journalism for their belief in and support for the project.

A special thank you to all the people in Cambodia who took me on often painful journeys through their lives and allowed me to reawaken memories that many would much rather forget. I can only hope that I have justified my intrusion. Some former Khmer Rouge were more open than others but I am sincerely grateful to them all for the time they spent talking with me, particularly In Sopheap.

Above all I owe a deep debt of thanks to my friend Heng Ham Kheng and his family, for his indispensable, wise counsel throughout the turbulent times of recent Cambodian history.

Some of the identities of the people in this book have been changed or altered in order to protect them. Others cannot be named but know who they are – to them I am extremely grateful. I alone am responsible for the opinions and conclusions expressed in these pages. Finally I'd like to thank Pacharin Sinlawan for all her love, support and patience over the years that it took to research and write this book.

For my Mother and Father

and

To the memory of David Munro

A darkness will settle on the people of Cambodia. There will be houses but no people in them, roads but no travellers; the land will be ruled by barbarians with no religion; blood will run so deep as to touch the belly of the elephant. Only the deaf and the mute will survive.

Ancient Cambodian prophecy

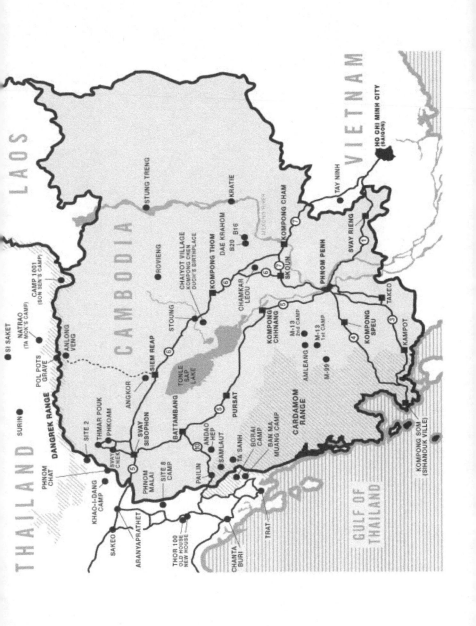

CHRONOLOGY

9th–15th centuries – rise and fall of Khmer Empire centred at the city of Angkor.

1864   Cambodia becomes a French protectorate.

1953   Prince Sihanouk successfully negotiates Cambodia's independence from France.

1965   Sihanouk permits North Vietnamese to establish bases inside Cambodian frontier with South Vietnam, later allowing them to ferry communist supplies through Cambodian territory.

1967   Samlaut uprising.

1969   US secret bombing campaign begins.

1970   March 18 – Lon Nol overthrows Sihanouk in a coup d'état while Sihanouk is abroad.

March 23   Sihanouk, who is now in Bejing, calls his people to rise up. The war between the Khmer Rouge and Lon Nol's government begins in earnest.

April   US and South Vietnamese forces invade

Cambodia from Vietnam to destroy communist bases. They later withdraw.

1973   Illegal US bombing is halted by Congress.

1975   April 17, Lon Nol's republic collapses and Cambodia falls to the Khmer Rouge.

1979   Vietnam invades Cambodia, routing the Khmer Rouge, and occupies most of the country. They install client regime in Phnom Penh – the People's Republic of Kampuchea. Refugee/ resistance camps are set up along the Thai-Cambodian frontier with support from China, Thailand and the West. Khmer Rouge are re-armed and supplied with Western aid.

1982   Sihanouk announces formation of the Coalition Government of Democratic Kampuchea with the Royalists, the remnants of Lon Nol's republic and the Khmer Rouge, who dominate.

1984/5   Vietnamese launch major offensive in attempt to crush the resistance, pushing them into Thailand. The war continues.

1989   Vietnam withdraws from Cambodia. Khmer Rouge capture gem mining town of Pailin.

1991   Paris Peace Accords pave way for the United Nations mission.

1992   Peacekeeping operation begins.

1993   The Khmer Rouge withdraw from process and vow to disrupt election. Royalist Party wins a landslide victory in UN-sponsored elections. The Phnom Penh regime, under Hun Sen, forces a power-sharing arrangement in the new government. UNTAC withdraws. The war with the Khmer Rouge continues.

1994   Khmer Rouge is outlawed as a group.

1996   Ieng Sary, former Khmer Rouge Minister of Foreign Affairs, splits from other Khmer Rouge in exchange for amnesty and brings western Khmer Rouge zones with him.

1997   Pol Pot is tried by his movement in guerrilla base of Anlong Veng. Co-prime minister Hun Sen ousts his Royalist counterpart in a violent coup and fighting erupts between Royalists and government.

1998   Pol Pot dies and Anlong Veng falls to government forces.

1999   Ta Mok, the last of the Khmer Rouge, surrenders and is placed in prison to await trial.

CONTENTS

The photograph of Comrade Duch as Commandant of S-21 that the author carried around in his back pocket, leading him to Duch in 1999 (*Courtesy Tuol Sleng Museum*)

PROLOGUE

THERE IS A photograph that hangs on the wall of an empty building. In it, a man sits behind a table, looking directly ahead, his eyes betraying nothing. He may be smiling, but it's impossible to say. He speaks into a microphone, addressing a meeting of Khmer Rouge cadre who are out of shot. He holds the microphone with spindly fingers. I still look at the picture and wonder what he's saying; whether he's lecturing his staff on the purity of the revolution or perhaps instructing them on how to extract confessions.

It is a crudely reproduced photograph, copied again and again, badly printed and blown up so that all the mid-tones have been obliterated. It has been stained over the years and seems to belong to a part of history long forgotten. The original negative is missing and this is the only single portrait known to exist. There was a time when I shuddered just to look at it. And then I began to carry it with me everywhere I went in Cambodia.

The photograph is of Comrade Duch (pronounced Doik),

commandant of Tuol Sleng prison. As head of the Khmer
Rouge secret police, Duch was personally responsible for
the extermination of perhaps as many as 20,000 men,
women and children. He was the principle link between
Khmer Rouge strategy and the actual mechanics of mass
murder. He was Pol Pot's chief executioner.

On 17 April 1975, Khmer Rouge forces, who had besieged
the capital for months, filed into Phnom Penh and declared
the dawning of a new era; Cambodia was to begin again.
Overnight the Khmer Rouge embarked upon the most radical
revolution the world had ever seen. They evacuated the
towns and cities, forcing people into the countryside, and
mobilised the entire population in their attempt to transform
Cambodia into a rural, classless utopia from which few would
return. They then closed the borders and Cambodia vanished.

'Les Khmers rouges', a term coined by Prince Sihanouk,
were a small group of Paris-educated Cambodian communists who began organising against the government in the
1960s. The United States then launched an illegal bombing
campaign to dislodge North Vietnamese bases and supply
routes inside Cambodia. By the time the bombing was
halted, more than a million Cambodians were either dead
or wounded and almost half the population had become
refugees. Exploiting the devastation in the countryside, the
Khmer Rouge overthrew the US-backed regime in 1975.

Four years later, in 1979, the world woke to scenes of
a second holocaust. Images of skulls and emaciated children
were beamed into living rooms, alerting millions to the
sufferings of the people of Cambodia. The entire population had seemingly disappeared for almost four whole years,
to emerge battered, tortured, starved, and all but destroyed.
A third of the population had died and hundreds of thou-

sands had been executed. Today – a quarter of a century later, and seven years after the death of Pol Pot and the demise of the Khmer Rouge – no-one has yet been held to account for what happened.

I first became aware of Cambodia from a *National Geographic* article in the early 1980s. Along with the photographs from ancient temples in the jungle were images of mass graves that had just been exhumed. What struck me was how fertile and vibrant the countryside looked. Amid this emerald landscape clothes and skulls were mixed in the chocolate earth, as though the countryside had melted in the midday sun to reveal a terrible secret. When the film *The Killing Fields* appeared I must have watched it at least fifteen times at various London cinemas. I would sometimes sneak off to see it on my own for fear of ridicule by my peers, as though I was sliding off to watch porn in Soho. At the same time, I began to take an interest in photography and documentary films about conflict. I read avidly. I scoured the bookshelves of London, hoping to get an idea of the country. I wanted to see what Phnom Penh had looked like before, during and after the Khmer Rouge. I couldn't find anything. It was as if the West had wilfully collaborated with the Khmer Rouge and erased Cambodia from our memories.

For me, Cambodia had become shorthand for all that was wrong in the world. I wanted to understand how a movement that laid claim to a vision of a better world could instead turn people into instruments of overwhelming evil, producing a revolution of unparalleled ferocity. Much of the killing occurred in my lifetime; the secret bombing of Cambodia had begun the year I was born (I have a vague recollection of helicopters on the television), and by the time the Khmer Rouge were in power, rooting out enemies, I was old enough to be one of their victims.

Who were these faceless perpetrators? Like the word 'terrorist' the term Khmer Rouge had become so overused that it had ceased to hold any meaning for me, as though they had simply emerged from the flames of the US bombing. Eventually, in the summer of 1989, at the age of nineteen, I left art school for Cambodia to find out for myself. I later moved to Bangkok as a photographer and made frequent trips to the country. I never believed that I would get so close to an answer.

In early 1997, I travelled out to Svay Rieng province, part of the 'Eastern Zone' under the Khmer Rouge. It was here that the killing took on a fury unmatched in the rest of the country. Hundreds of thousands perished here and the countryside is littered with mass graves.

The evening was drawing in and the cool breeze rustled the sugar palms that towered above as I followed an old farmer along the dyke. The sun was easing its way down behind the trees ahead, bathing the scene in a golden light. He stopped at an intersection of paddy fields and crouched in front of a small puddle. I did the same, enclosed by a sea of green rice shoots.

The farmer began recounting the scene immediately after the Vietnamese army had driven out the Khmer Rouge. He described how he and others pulled nineteen corpses out of the puddle in front of us. 'It was deeper then,' he said. Further on there were more; men, women both young and old. 'We could smell the bodies,' he told me. 'That's how we found them.' The Khmer Rouge had used the pagoda as a prison, destroying it before they fled. 'And they led people to be killed over there,' he said, pointing to a pile of rubble on the other side of the field.

I sat and nodded in silence. I remember thinking how I couldn't feel anything and yet I could almost see a film reel flick images past the old man's eyes, recalled from some secret place in his memory, as he recounted his experiences. 'At night,' he said, 'I can still hear their screams.'

The farmer could see it right there in front of him and all I could think of was how beautiful the scene was and how guilty I felt for thinking that. Over the years travelling through Cambodia I would make pilgrimages to countless local Khmer Rouge execution sites whenever I could. All these visits seemed to do was remind me that, although we occupy the same world, we live in separate universes. The chasm of understanding was as wide as ever.

Tuol Sleng, a former secondary school or *lycée*, sits in the heart of the capital, Phnom Penh. After their victory, the Khmer Rouge converted the buildings into a secret facility, code-named 'S-21', with Comrade Duch as commandant. In keeping with the Khmer Rouge obsession with absolute secrecy, prisoners would arrive at the gates of the prison, often at night, in the deserted Cambodian capital. Here they were tortured to confess to their 'crimes'. They were accused of working as spies for the KGB, the Vietnamese, the CIA and, in some cases, all three. Afterwards they were taken out of the city and executed. Of the 20,000 who passed through Tuol Sleng's gates, seven survived.

The prison is now a museum where thousands of mug shots of Comrade Duch's victims are displayed in the same rooms they were tortured in. The Khmer Rouge, like the Nazis, were meticulous in their record-keeping and thousands of documents and negatives have survived. Names and ages, even height and weight, were recorded.

Over the past sixteen years, on almost every trip I made

to Cambodia I wound up at Tuol Sleng, drawn to it by the idea that it might yield answers to some of the questions that stalked my mind. There, I would pore over the archives and the thousands of photographs of victims in an attempt to make sense of what had happened to them. The photographs bear silent testimony to the sufferings of the Cambodian people and it was these images that haunted me. For me, they had become a permanent reminder of the world's impotence, of our collective guilt in failing to prevent the crime of genocide.

As commandant of Tuol Sleng, Comrade Duch presided over the mechanics of the Khmer Rouge genocide, and was a key witness to it. He was present at many of the interrogations at Tuol Sleng, where a wide variety of torture methods were employed. They ranged from electrical shocks and the pulling out of toenails, to severe beatings and near drownings. His testimony in a trial of former Khmer Rouge leaders would be crucial in upholding the overwhelming evidence that exists of mass murder. The documents kept at the former prison are clear evidence of his guilt, with notations written in his hand ordering executions and details of gruesome methods of interrogation. In one memo a guard asks Duch what to do with nine boys and girls held at the prison who were accused of being traitors. Duch has scrawled across it, 'kill every last one'.

There were many rumours of Duch's whereabouts: that he had been killed during one of the many purges of Khmer Rouge ranks; that he was working under a pseudonym for an aid agency in northern Cambodia. He had not been photographed for more than twenty years, and he had never spoken about his role in the killing. It seemed that Duch, like so many others who were responsible for the Cambodian holocaust, had vanished. But with the civil war coming to an end in 1998, and new parts of the country opening up every month, I thought I'd show his photograph to Cambodians I met to see if anyone recognised him. Even if by some incredible coincidence someone did, I knew they would be reluctant to speak. He was a terrifying figure even among the Khmer Rouge. As a fighting force, the Khmer Rouge no longer existed, but former members were everywhere: as government officials, army generals, village leaders. As one Cambodian put it, 'They are all around us; we live among the tigers.'

Over many years working as a photographer in Cambodia it became clear to me that if we were ever to understand the Cambodian holocaust, and bring any measure of justice, finding Duch and others like him was vital. Duch was the most important witness to those dark years and could shed light on a highly secretive period in his country's history. And I wanted to know what it was that had turned a seemingly ordinary man from one of the poorer parts of Cambodia into one of the worst mass murderers of the twentieth century.

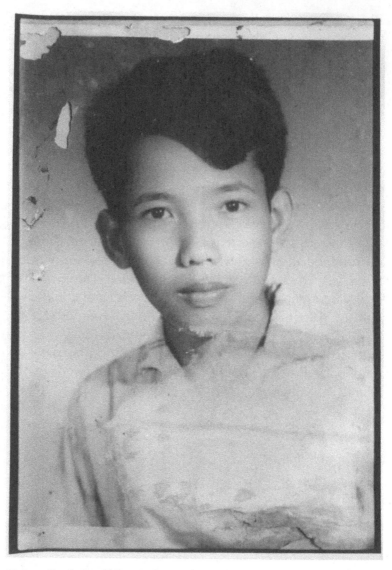

Kaing Guek Eav (Comrade Duch) at the age of about seventeen
(Photographer unknown)

PART I

Kaing Guek Eav

CHAPTER 1

'Better to destroy ten innocent people than let one enemy go free'

In MARCH 1999, I hitched a ride with a mine-clearance organisation into a former Khmer Rouge zone.

We left Battambang early in the morning and began our journey down Route 10, one of the most fought-over stretches in Cambodia. After an hour of bouncing over spine-jarring roads, past hills that soared like cathedrals from the flat rice plains, we turned left at a junction and all signs of civilisation vanished. There were no houses, no people, no fields. The road was new.

Here the road threaded deep into the mountainous forest close to the Thai border and our ultimate destination: the former Khmer Rouge district of Samlaut. This was the last area to have ceased hostilities with the Cambodian government after more than thirty years of almost continuous upheaval. Samlaut had been the first place to rise up against the government in the late 1960s. And it was here, in June 1998, that the Khmer Rouge finally laid down their weapons, bringing the conflict full cycle and opening the area up to outsiders. Although the war was over, and the Khmer Rouge defunct, the same local leaders remained in control. But the ghosts of the past were still far from laid.

The jeep jerked to a halt at a military checkpoint marking the start of former Khmer Rouge territory. Shacks of recently returned refugees were huddled in the trees along the side of the road. Young soldiers in government uniforms carried AK-47s and stared impassively at us and, despite our smiles, remained sullen but let us through.

Samlaut had been an area of conflict since the 1960s when a peasant uprising was brutally crushed. Often considered the birthplace of the Khmer Rouge revolution, the area had now arrived at a tense peace. Uniformed Khmer Rouge soldiers mingled with civilians who had returned from refugee camps in Thailand and had begun to rebuild their homes and lives in an area that was heavily mined. It was a bleak part of the country. Dry jungle, denuded forest and neglected farmland bore witness to the years of war.

The mine-clearance team I was travelling with had arranged to meet the leaders in the area to discuss the removal of ordinance and hundreds of thousands of mines that lay waiting in the rich soil all around. While the meeting was taking place, I wandered over to a group of people lying in hammocks beside the district office and begun talking to a Khmer Rouge amputee. A short, wiry man appeared wearing a white T-shirt emblazoned with the initials ARC (American Refugee Committee). Shaking my hand he politely introduced himself in perfect English as Hang Pin. He told me that he had been a schoolteacher specialising in mathematics and that he had originally come from Phnom Penh and had recently worked in a refugee camp on the Thai border. He had worked with American aid organisations since 1997. He took a keen interest in my Leica and, using this opportunity to photograph the people in the group, I caught him in the frame. Large ears, bad teeth, cropped hair – he had aged a little, but the likeness to the photograph tucked in my back pocket was unmistakable. Hang Pin was Comrade Duch.

For twenty years no-one knew what had happened to Comrade Duch. He had left Phnom Penh with the rest of the Khmer Rouge when the Vietnamese invaded in 1979. On that same day, the 7th of January, a Vietnamese photographer crossed Monivong Bridge and entered the deserted city of Phnom Penh. Ho Van Tay had followed the Vietnamese 7th Division Armoured Corps that led the attack into Cambodia on Christmas Day 1978. An experienced journalist, Van Tay had covered the war against the Americans as a combat photographer and cameraman and had walked the entire length of the Ho Chi Minh trail, an extremely hazardous journey that took him three months to complete. He had been wounded in the leg during a US bombing raid and had filmed the liberation of Saigon in 1975.

Resistance was light. The Khmer Rouge defence collapsed under the weight of the Vietnamese onslaught. The night before, the division commander had asked Van Tay if he wanted to accompany him to Phnom Penh. They were still some hundred kilometres from the capital and Van Tay had expected the fighting to be heavy and protracted. He had known the Khmer Rouge before and, like many of his fellow countrymen, admired them for being formidable fighters.

'Are you joking?' he asked in disbelief.

The battle-hardened Vietnamese troops had never

thought that the Khmer Rouge would give way so easily and many expected that the worst was yet to come, that Phnom Penh would be the place where the Khmer Rouge would make their stand.

'No,' the division commander replied. 'This is for real, we're going to take Phnom Penh.'

Clambering on top of an old American armoured personnel carrier he perched himself among sixteen other heavily armed soldiers. The column rumbled its way through the night, arriving on the outskirts of the city at dawn. Cambodian and Vietnamese scouts had gone on in ahead. They waited. They could hear the sound of small-arms fire and the occasional boom of cannon, the echoes rolling through the streets to where they sat. Then, when the news came in over the radios that the city had been liberated, the main Vietnamese regular forces went in. What they found stunned them.

For three years, eight months and twenty days Phnom Penh, under the Khmer Rouge, had remained a ghost town. Having evacuated the entire population at gunpoint as part of their vision to radically restructure Cambodian society, the city, save for a few thousand Khmer Rouge, became nothing more than an empty shell.

The central Monivong Boulevard became a vast deserted canyon where nothing stirred in the tropical heat. Its buildings had been painted white, but the back streets were scattered with the debris of looted buildings. Untamed gardens had begun to reclaim the empty houses. Chairs, pots, sewing machines, mattresses and old family photographs lay scattered about in the vacant buildings and deserted streets. Just after the Khmer Rouge had been driven from power, one of the first western journalists to visit Cambodia had walked the entire length of Monivong

Boulevard in the early morning, the same distance as from Hyde Park to Clapham Common. He didn't see a single soul. The Khmer Rouge had blown up the national bank before their departure and now thousands of useless banknotes fluttered through the vacant streets. The same journalist came across a chequebook on the bank's counter made out to 'cash' and dated 17 April 1975, exactly as its owner had left it almost four years before.

Street and shop signs had been painted out and cars were swept into huge piles along with dishwashers, fridges and other electronic appliances considered reactionary by the Khmer Rouge. There they sat among the weeds, rusting quietly in the scorching heat, no longer of use in the new society. Elsewhere telephones that had been ripped out of buildings from all over the city had been dumped in a large pile, doused with gasoline and set alight, leaving a blackened mass of melted plastic.

This was the scene that greeted Ho Van Tay when his country's Soviet-built T-55 tanks clattered into the silent city.

The sun was already high in the sky as the column thundered along the empty boulevards, their bewildered troops at the ready. 'It was completely quiet,' Van Tay recalled. 'They didn't find anything. The Khmer Rouge had fled, they had just run away.' Little did he realise that pairs of eyes were following their movements from the deserted buildings on either side of them. The grass was growing wild and coconuts lay where they had fallen in the middle of the streets. Armed with a 16mm camera and a Pentax, he shot scenes of the tanks arriving and the flag being raised. He then returned to Ho Chi Minh City with his scoop.

Van Tay delivered his material to his editor in Ho Chi

Minh City and returned to Phnom Penh that same night. The traffic was heavy. Passing thousands of troops and columns of tanks, he arrived early the following morning. He filmed Khmer Rouge prisoners who had been captured and rounded up by the Vietnamese and their Cambodian allies, the vast majority of them children. 'There were at least 2,000 that I saw and we had to feed them – they were very malnourished.' They had been captured on the way to Phnom Penh and brought to a holding place in the city centre. Most of them were under fourteen years old and a large proportion were young girls. Many were so small that they couldn't even carry their own AK-47s. Their fatigues were far too big for them. It was as though the Khmer Rouge army had somehow shrunk in the face of the Vietnamese invasion. Some older cadres were in their twenties, but most had fled, leaving an army of confused and frightened children to defend the country.

That same day, at about noon, accompanied by his editor, Van Tay drove through the city in an old US army jeep, looking for things to film. In one area he came across a series of shop houses containing bizarre stockpiles of items. The first contained a neatly stacked mountain of shoes that reached the ceiling – but only the left shoe. Next to it there was another shop that contained thousands of right shoes. A whole row of shops contained sewing machines that had been placed on top of one another. Next to it was another containing stacks of cooking pots, another with chairs and another filled with tables. Then, as Van Tay drove along the road from the Olympic stadium back towards the Independence monument, he passed through an invisible cloud of the most formidable stench. 'I had smelt this smell before,' he said. 'It was very heavy in the air – not animal, but human. I can still smell it now.'

Van Tay and his colleagues followed the stench through what had been a well-to-do neighbourhood, passing large villas as they continued through the streets. 'The closer we got, the worse it became,' he said. Eventually they came to a corrugated-iron wall crowned with coils of razor wire. A sign above the entrance read, 'Ecole Première de Tuol Sleng'. He prised the gate open and climbed through. They found themselves in the back yard of what had been a large schoolhouse. Rats scattered as they approached. Ahead was a metal-framed structure with a corrugated-iron roof and behind it four imposing grey buildings. Pots and chairs and sewing machines lay scattered about. Clothing hung from washing lines and several hammocks were suspended between the trees. It was clear that those who had once occupied the compound had left in a terrible panic.

The balconies of the buildings were covered in a netting of barbed wire; the former play area had recently been ploughed. Inside the rooms they found typewriters, telephones, photographs and office equipment, all of it hastily abandoned. Drawers had been left open and thousands of documents were scattered about. Bullets littered the floor next to a Chinese radio set. In another room they discovered hundreds of stacked fetters and padlocks that hung on nails with numbers next to them. Beside them lay a spilled bag of lime. Lying on tables were instruments of torture – whips, saws, axes, hoes and batons. Van Tay found busts of Pol Pot and a series of portraits that had been painted from photographs. One of the paintings depicted a particularly demonic-looking Pol Pot barking into a microphone. He crept up the stairs to the second floor of one of the buildings. 'There were flies everywhere,' he said.

More papers were scattered about amid tufts of hair and

large, inch-deep pools of semi-dried blood. Peering through the window, he saw the source of the stench: corpses in varying stages of decomposition, chained to iron bedsteads. There were perhaps twenty or thirty bodies in different rooms – men, women, children – 'but it was impossible to tell their ages as they were so decomposed and swollen'. Van Tay had to clamber over some of them. Vermin ran everywhere. The victims had been hit on the head with a shovel, their skulls exploding on impact. 'Some of the heads had been completely destroyed,' he said. Careful not to disturb anything he tiptoed around the rooms. 'There was a popping sound from the maggots under my feet.'

Gingerly, he made his way through the four buildings, taking pictures as he went. 'My hands were shaking, I was so afraid.' The last of the day's light was beginning to fade as they made their way out. Passing through the gate, Van Tay and his crew discovered four children, including a month-old baby, all of them extremely sick and malnourished. They hurried off in their jeep to seek medical attention and to inform the authorities of what they had found. The Khmer Rouge's darkest secret was about to be exposed to the outside world.

When I first arrived at Tuol Sleng in 1989 the buildings were empty save for a few guides who smiled and waved me in at the entrance. I walked straight to the first building that photographer Ho Van Tay had approached ten years before and, like him, peered inside. There in the room was a bed frame, some faded clothing, an old US army ammunition box and a table and chair. Below the bed was what looked like a large pool of dried blood. The authorities had hung one of Ho Van Tay's photographs on the wall. Taken in 1979, it showed the same room with the same bed. The only difference was the distinct outline of a corpse, its hand outstretched.

Tuol Svay Prey, the district in Phnom Penh where the prison is located, roughly translates as 'The Hill of the Poison Fruit Tree'. *Tuol* means hillock. *Sleng*, depending on the context, means either 'bearing guilt' or 'the enemy of disease'; *Sleng* is also the name of a tree with extremely poisonous fruit. To the Khmer Rouge the prisoners at Tuol Sleng were known as *Neak thos* or 'guilty persons'. To a handful of people assigned work nearby in the same section of the city, it was known simply as *konlaenh choul min dael chenh:* the place where people go in but never come out.

The occupying Vietnamese had transformed the prison into a museum, which opened a year after the liberation of the city. Situated in what had been a residential area, it comprised four three-storey buildings in a single compound. Beyond, there had been an execution ground and several mass graves. The whole area was sealed by an electrified fence and a corrugated-iron wall. The ground floor of building 'A' was where interrogations had taken place and where high-ranking prisoners were confined. The ground floors of buildings 'B' and 'C' had been converted into holdings for other important prisoners. They had been divided into cells with crude brick and cement partitions. Large holes had been smashed in the original walls by the Khmer Rouge to form a crude corridor linking the rooms to one another. Some of the cells contained shackles, a plate and an old US ammunition box used as a latrine, as if awaiting the next prisoner.

Outside sat two large empty pots under what looked like an exercise frame. The pots had once been filled with water into which prisoners had been forced. Then their wrists were lashed to the frame, they were hauled up and suspended in the air, dislocating their arms – a method known as 'the rope' in medieval Europe.

Inside building 'B' there was a glass cabinet that held a large pile of clothing stripped from prisoners. Geckos which had made their homes among the rags scattered for cover as I walked past. Beside the pile were various instruments of torture: a hoe, a whip, several shovels, as well as manacles and chains. There was a box that had once housed scorpions and other poisonous insects used in torture sessions. On the other floors the rooms had held prisoners in mass detention. They were stripped and made to lie down on the floor and held together by a large iron fetter. Outside, the prison regulations had been translated by the Vietnamese from a blackboard for the benefit of visitors. I stood in front of the signboard and read them. It was the only place in the museum where the Khmer Rouge spoke directly to you.

THE SECURITY REGULATIONS

1.   You must answer accordingly to my questions. Don't turn them away.
2.   Don't try to hide the facts by making pretexts this and that; you strictly prohibited to contest me.
3.   Don't be a fool for you are a chap who dare thwart the revolution.
4.   You must immediately answer my questions without wasting time to reflect.
5.   Don't tell me either about your little wrong doings or the essence of the revolution.
6.   While getting lashes or electrification you must not cry at all.

7.   Do nothing, sit still and wait for my orders. If there is no order keep quiet; when I tell you to do something, you must do it right away without protesting.
8.   Don't make pretexts about Kampuchea Krom in order to hide your jaw of traitor.
9.   If you don't follow all the above rules, you shall get many lashes of the electric wire.
10. If you disobey any point of my regulations, you shall get either ten lashes or five shocks of the electric discharge.

Inside, the photographs of the prisoners were put on display by the Vietnamese curators. Thousands of faces adorned the walls. There they were, as they had arrived at the prison – men, women, children, Muslims, Christians, ethnic minorities and a handful of foreigners. In some, the prisoners had attempted to smile as if the Khmer Rouge might take pity and somehow spare them. Others looked traumatised and some had received blows, their faces bloodied and swollen. Each person was tagged by a number. One shirtless boy had his number pinned on to the skin of his chest.

Looking at the photographs on the walls was a dizzying experience. As the prisoners looked at you they created a false intimacy and yet the repetition of so many faces stripped the prisoners of their individuality. My eyes darted around trying to find something that would allow me to comprehend what was in front of me. There were so many of them. Not until you walk through the empty corridors of Tuol Sleng does Stalin's idiom that one death is a tragedy – a million a statistic, take on a terrifying potency. This was the only lasting trace that these people had ever walked on this earth before being 'smashed to bits', as the guards routinely reported to Duch. I could feel their eyes follow me. I realised I was seeing the world according to the faceless *Angka* or the 'Organisation' as the Khmer Rouge leadership called itself. When the victims looked back they were looking at their tormentors. Confronted with the enormity of what had happened, how was one to react?

I began to take photographs of the photographs. The last room displayed photographs of the mass graves found in various parts of the country, showing exhumed remains and mushroom-like skulls laid out in neat rows by the hundreds, whitened by the tropical sun. One survivor had been commissioned to depict Khmer Rouge atrocities in crude paintings which hung in the last few classrooms of the fourth block. They showed women being whipped and people being lowered into barrels of water. There was a large map of the country fashioned out of varnished human skulls from the mass graves found in the compound. And there, among other photographs, was one of the director of the prison, Comrade Duch.

I waited self-consciously in each room for the ghosts of the victims to talk to me. Walking down the empty corridors I thought I would leave with some deep question answered, or a newfound value, as though there was some great moral purpose in me being there. I tiptoed around, awkwardly taking photographs. The next room was the same and so was the one after it. Outside, storm clouds began to gather. I returned to the balcony to make my way to the next building and the heavens opened. The downpour was so heavy that I found myself trapped in the building. I could feel the panic rise within me.

One photograph stood out. I had seen it reproduced in books before. It was of a young mother cradling her baby.

She sat there in front of the lens expressionless, resigned to her fate. Her baby lay sleeping in her arms. Her hair was a bob in the uniform Khmer Rouge style and her shirt was the standard black worn by everyone. A placard hung around her neck. On it was the date: 14 May 1978, and the number 462. Her name, I later found out, was Chan Kim Srun, her revolutionary name Saang. She was the wife of a senior Khmer Rouge cadre from the ministry of foreign affairs. Her eyes were swollen from crying.

I wondered what it was Kim Srun had seen that day – if she had any sense of what lay in store for her and her child. Was there something in her eyes that could tell us that she knew she was about to die?

'Better to destroy ten innocent people than let one enemy go free' ran a Khmer Rouge slogan. Because of the lack of information displayed at the museum we often assume that the prisoners of Tuol Sleng were innocent victims; the terror in the faces elicits a response of pity from the viewer. The popular image of the Khmer Rouge in the West was of young, fanatical murderers in black pyjamas, wielding guns. What is not immediately apparent to most visitors to the prison is that Tuol Sleng was created for rooting out enemies from *within* the party. The majority of prisoners were from the Khmer Rouge's own ranks. This adds an unwelcome moral complication: among the photographs that I now faced there were interrogators as well as guards from the prison itself, Khmer Rouge who suddenly found their roles reversed during the many purges. The upside-down world of Tuol Sleng blurred the distinction between the guilty and the innocent.

Despite attempting to eradicate the past and found a new Cambodia, the Khmer Rouge were shaped by it. They sometimes referred to the past as a kind of memory sickness to which they were the cure. It was as though, as one writer has noted, people were killed simply for remembering a different world from the one the Khmer Rouge were trying to create. In their obsession with rooting out enemies and 'cleansing' the nation, death became the only purification.

It seemed no accident that Tuol Sleng had been a school. All over the country teaching and learning centres, pagodas and schoolhouses became places for 're-education', often a Khmer Rouge euphemism for execution. Many senior cadres had been teachers. The principal purpose of the prison became the principal irony: by setting out to eradicate all trace of these 'enemies', the Khmer Rouge had unwittingly preserved their memory permanently, through documents and photographs.

And one of these photographs had led me to Duch.

CHAPTER 2

The Burden of Angkor

CAMBODIA IS AN easy place to romanticise. From the vine-draped temples of the ancient Angkorian empire, remnants of Cambodia's glorious past, to the forested Cardamom mountains and the Great Lake, it conforms to the clichéd postcard image of an eastern Garden of Eden. Its towns and cities, mapped out by the French, are spacious tree-lined boulevards with large villas of fading yellow stucco. Roughly the size of England and Wales, it is centred around the Tonle Sap or Great Lake, a vast expanse of water that stretches over a thousand square miles. The lake is surrounded by a green patchwork quilt of paddy fields fenced in by sugar palms. The land seems so apparently abundant in food that the Chinese even coined a saying, 'as rich as Cambodia'. From the lake's southern shores, the plain gradually sweeps up to the Cardamoms, disappearing into the leaden monsoon clouds. To the north, the Dangrek range forms a natural frontier with Thailand. Cutting the country in half is the mighty Mekong River.

Angkor was the capital of one of south-east Asia's greatest empires, which once stretched from south Vietnam to Burma, and covered much of the Malay Peninsula. Tourists in Cambodia today are taken first to Angkor, then to Tuol Sleng, two strange apparent opposites as a basic itinerary for a holiday-maker. The lost kingdom of Angkor represented the peak of Khmer civilisation, while the brutality of Tuol Sleng represented the extreme perversity of power. In fact, the two places have more in common than one might think. Both were created at the cost of thousands of lives by regimes of institutionalised brutality. But the parallels don't end there.

Angkor's greatness depended on rice production, grown for centuries in the rich alluvial soil surrounding the Great Lake. The temple complex itself included large reservoirs, or *baray*, whose true purpose is still disputed. Many believe they were used for irrigation, even though there are no irrigation canals leading to the surrounding fields. It was with this mistaken belief that the Khmer Rouge ordered the construction of large dams and irrigation canals, projects on which hundreds of thousands of people died. Angkor was an inspiration and a symbol of the nation's potential. As Pol Pot had said in 1976, 'If our people can build Angkor, then they can do anything.'

Despite their attempts to rewrite history, the Khmer Rouge made constant references to Angkor: in speeches and broadcasts, even in their national anthem. King Jayavarman VII was the only Angkorian king the Khmer Rouge ever praised. Jayavarman – *jaya* means victorious, *varman* means protector – greatly expanded the empire, building more temples and edifices than any of his predecessors. He has often been referred to by historians as a megalomaniac. Like Pol Pot he mobilised the entire population and employed slave labour for the realisation of his vision.

The gates of the great walled city of Angkor Thom are carved with stone faces, believed to modelled on Jayavarman's, gazing down upon the mortals below. Each face bears an enigmatic smile. At another Angkorian temple, the Bayon, more than a hundred more faces adorn each of its towers. Wherever you turn at least one pair of eyes follows you. The faces represented the all-knowing, all-seeing god King as he kept watch over his subjects. The Khmer Rouge used to say that 'The Organisation sees all'. The faces of the Bayon appear on Khmer Rouge bank notes, which were printed but never issued. Black-clad peasants can be seen transplanting rice next to an image of one of these faces.

Jayavarman imposed upon his subjects Mahayana Buddhism, which followers believed was the universal way to salvation. Merit was made by doing works for the greater good and it was perhaps an unconscious echo of Mahayana which found expression under the guise of communist theory. Mahayana believed that only by following this example could people reach true liberation. Theravada Buddhism by contrast, which arrived later and dominates today, believed salvation was to be attained through rituals and ceremonies for the individual.

The centrepiece of this once powerful nation is the magnificent Angkor Wat complex built in the twelfth century. As tall as Notre-Dame cathedral, it is the largest religious monument in the world. Its five towers rising above the surrounding jungle canopy are visible for miles. These silhouetted towers have been used by successive Cambodian regimes to adorn their flags, including the Khmer Rouge.

Like the Khmer Rouge when they were in power, Cambodians today constantly look to the past. While Angkor is a source of great pride, it is also a burden. It is both a celebration of Cambodia's past greatness and a reminder of its subsequent decline – a symbol of a deep national insecurity when the empire was overrun by Cambodia's traditional foes – the Thais and the Vietnamese.

The majority of Cambodia's settlements were situated along rivers and waterways that snaked their way across the plains. Houses were shaded from the searing heat by the stately fruit trees that grew tall along the lush banks. Village life had changed little over the centuries and, although beautiful, it was an unforgiving landscape and life was hard. The heavy tasks were carried out by water buffalo. The roads – really nothing more than tracks – became potholed quagmires in the rainy season, only adding to the isolation of rural life. Behind the villages were well-irrigated paddy fields that spread towards the horizon, petering out into the uncultivated land beyond. But it was these arid swathes of the country that constituted the majority of Cambodia's agricultural potential, and it went untended. The farmers relied on unpredictable monsoon weather rains for their family's survival.

Kompong Thom sits in the centre of Cambodia. This sparsely populated province is bound by thick forests to the north, dissolving into the swampy shores of the Great Lake to the south. The provincial capital, which goes by the same name, is marooned in a sea of paddy fields.

Strategically located, Kompong Thom province was fiercely contested by the Khmer Rouge and government forces in the early 1970s. All along Route 6, the only road linking it with Phnom Penh, battles raged, with thousands of government troops routed by the Khmer Rouge and their allies, the North Vietnamese. The province had been devastated by B-52 bombers sent on the secret orders of Nixon and Kissinger, a campaign of destruction which the Khmer Rouge would exploit. Kompong Thom was also the birthplace of Pol Pot and Comrade Duch.

Duch was born Kaing Geuk Eav on 17 November 1942 in a hut on the banks of the River Stoung. The eldest and only son of a family of five, both his mother and father were Chinese Khmers and had lived their entire lives in the village. The family was poor. By the time Duch was born, Cambodia had begun its steady economic decline, with large landowners driving farmers into a vicious spiral of debt. Many Cambodians had become slaves in their own land, a humiliating position for the descendants of the Angkorian empire.

When Duch was nine years old, a dispute over land forced the family to move to a plot left by Duch's great-grandmother, where the family house now stands. Their fortunes changed when Duch's father, Kaing Ky, got a job as a clerk with a local Chinese fishery company. He was hired because he spoke Chinese, but the work was seasonal and he could never put money aside. To supplement their income his mother, Siew, sold orange cakes and fried bananas in the market. Their neighbours regarded Duch's family as honest and hard-working people who helped others in need.

The young Duch began studying in the next village at the Po Andeth ('floating banyan') school, a small wooden building shaded by a pagoda. Every day, along with the other village children, Duch made the ten-minute walk from his home along a sandy pathway to school and back. He then moved to Kompong Chen primary school next door. There, his teacher Ke Kim Huot was a popular figure who often gave money to the poorer students so that they could continue their studies. It is almost certain Ke Kim Huot later helped Duch go on to study in Phnom Penh. Duch continued to progress well at his studies, passing all his exams with ease.

Duch grew up in an isolated world bound by tradition and stifling codes of conduct. Most peasants were deeply conservative, and had been for centuries. Strong attachments remained with the family and there was deep reverence for the traditional way of life. The pillars of Khmer life – the nation, the *Sangha* and the King – remained absolute and, for the most part, the people accepted their lot.

Before the French colonised the country in the nineteenth century, the King was at the top of the social scale; below him were his various officials, and at the bottom were the villagers. The *Sangha* bound these worlds together and the authority of the monks, like the King, was beyond question. The King had arrived at his position from accumulation of good karma in previous lives and he ruled 'like an axe from heaven'. He was largely a reclusive figure, and like the spirits and gods, was revered as a god King by his people. As with the legend of King Arthur, the King and the land were inseparable, the fortunes of both inextricably linked. Life, for most rural folk, was precarious. Beyond the village were evil spirits, animals and marauding bandits and other unseen dangers. Outsiders were viewed with suspicion. As in Buddhist teachings, humans were imperfect and in need of guidance and protection. Alone they were helpless and vulnerable and it was considered safer to remain as part of a group. A strict hierarchy was maintained through a patron–client system. People were expected to serve those in authority and those in authority expected to be served. Outside of the family, alliances were formed and it was believed that 'The rich must protect the poor, just as clothes protect the body.' To have a patron meant having protection.

In 2002, I visited Duch's old home. It was a modest but substantial house, perched on stilts and shaded by mango, longan and palm trees. The shutters had recently been painted blue. The walls were a greying white of mud-and-wattle and the exposed beams gave it an almost mock-Tudor appearance. The air was thick with the scent of jasmine and wood smoke mixed with pig dung. The house had a steep, rather ostentatious concrete staircase suggesting that Duch's family had been, by local standards, a family of some means.

There was nobody in, but the door was open. A man in his early thirties then appeared and immediately I could see the family resemblance: it was Duch's nephew. His mother was now living in Siem Reap, further to the west, the nephew said, and he was looking after the house. (Duch's father survived the war and the Khmer Rouge but died of natural causes in the mid-eighties). With a smile he invited me in and leaving our shoes at the foot of the staircase we climbed the steps. The interior was dark and musty, I had to wait for my eyes to adjust after the intense glare of the sun outside. The nephew, pulling out some mats to sit on, served some lukewarm Chinese tea. The house was dirty and unlived in. There was an old Singer sewing machine in the main room where guests would have been received and meals eaten. The teak floor – worn smooth over the years by thousands of footsteps – felt cool beneath my bare feet. Burnt stubs of incense protruded from a bowl in a traditional Chinese shrine set above the door. Propped up against the back of the cabinet behind the grimy glass sat a framed black-and-white photograph of a wedding. Dead insects had imprinted themselves on the paper in between the glass and the image. About thirty people were stiffly lined up, blank expressions on their faces as they stared out at me from the cabinet.

The photograph had been taken at the foot of the stairs that I had just climbed. It could have been taken yesterday – the house had changed little. All those seated had been told to place their hands on their knees as though on their best behaviour. A cluster of people, clearly not part of the group, possibly cooks, sat in the open window relaxed and smiling in sharp contrast to those below. The photographer had used flash to illuminate the scene. I scanned the faces for Duch, but he was nowhere to be seen. I had attended Khmer weddings before and had noticed how the occasion was taken over by the incessant need to document every moment as if the whole ceremony were laid on for the purpose of having it photographed. It was as though the photographs were needed to somehow legitimise the proceedings. Before the days of machine printing, people could only afford one formal portrait. It was a serious business and in the resulting photographs people looked solemn and self-conscious, as though they were attending a funeral and not a wedding. This photograph was no different.

Next to it lay a formal portrait of a teenager. It was Duch at about seventeen. Part of the image had been eaten away by white ants and the bottom had rotted in the humidity. It didn't detract from the smooth-skinned, neat, almost angelic youth under the glass. It was the first time that I had seen an image of him without his Khmer Rouge uniform. Unsmiling, hair carefully combed, his eyes were focused somewhere in the distance beyond my right shoulder, past the chipped frame that now contained it. The image embodied a certain idealism, as these kind of studio photographs of young teenagers often do. It had survived all the years of upheaval.

I drove on to Siem Reap to find Duch's mother. It grew dark, and the world narrowed to the LandCruiser's headlight beams and the potholes they illuminated. Three years before, it would have been impossible to take this route. Then the night belonged to the Khmer Rouge. Now the road was deserted. I strained to make out the houses in the trees, but they were concealed in darkness.

After driving for hours, the glow of Siem Reap appeared on the horizon. Taxis overladen with goods and people hurtled past at frightening speeds. After the countryside, where life had changed little since medieval times, arriving in Siem Reap left me in a daze. There were brightly lit internet cafés, hotels, chic restaurants housed in old colonial buildings and noisy karaoke lounges.

Duch's mother lived with her daughter and granddaughter in a small shack down a Siem Reap alley. When I arrived Kaing Kim Siew was cradling her great-granddaughter in a hammock in the corner, while Duch's sister was busy in the kitchen.

It was an awkward encounter for me, and a deeply uncomfortable one for them. They knew I had come to talk about Duch. Once she had relaxed a little, his mother recalled an obedient but earnest son. She described how Duch's father made the boy a tiny boat and dragged him around the house in it. This was his favourite game. As a young boy, Duch often accompanied her to the market or to visit relatives nearby. But, at the age of three, Duch fell sick. 'I was frightened, very frightened,' she recalled. 'He was my only son.'

Cambodia had a high infant mortality rate and medicines were scarce. Most people relied on traditional healing and distrusted modern drugs, which they couldn't in any case afford. Life expectancy for most didn't extend much beyond forty-five years. Diseases such as malaria, tuberculosis, polio and dysentery were widespread. Drinking water came from wells and had to be boiled to avoid a multitude of parasites and diseases. Hence Duch's mother's terror when he fell sick.

As he grew older he helped his parents around the home. 'Because he was the oldest,' said his mother, 'I used to call him to help when I had no time.' Every day, after school, he went to fetch water from the river and watered all the trees and plants in the garden. The family grew and sold vegetables and fruit. Duch also chopped firewood and helped his mother prepare food, and sometimes helped his father with his accounts. He spent most of his free time at home – an intense, rather lonely figure who preferred books to the company of others. Maths books were his favourite, but he also read Khmer and French literature. 'Even when he went to work like this, he would bring a book and when he felt tired, he'd stop and read,' said his mother. She described a serious boy who rarely smiled and hardly ever laughed. But nor was he without humour. His sister recalled him dancing the *Ram Khbach*, a traditional Khmer dance, and sending the entire family into fits of laughter.

His three other sisters attended school but, as tradition dictated in poorer families, the eldest stayed at home to help run the household. 'He was very sorry for me,' said Kim Hiep, 'because I was the only one who never had the benefit of an education, so I was the "ignorant" sister.' She began to work as a seamstress to help pay off family debts. 'We were poor,' said his mother. 'Life was terribly difficult.'

The photograph I had found at the house in Stoung had shown Kim Hiep's wedding in 1969. Duch was not in the picture. He was serving an unspecified sentence for his communist activities at the time, in a prison near Phnom Penh called Prey Sar. Later, when the Khmer Rouge took power, the same prison was to come under his direct control as commandant of S-21.

Kim Hiep's marriage only lasted eight years. By the end of Pol Pot's reign, Kim Hiep's husband and most of those in the photograph were among the two million missing. Even friends and family from the Khmer Rouge's upper echelons weren't spared. Nearly a quarter of a century later, she still had no idea what had happened to her husband. He had been arrested in 1977 somewhere in Kompong Thom and sent to Phnom Penh. Later a former executioner from Tuol Sleng told me that he had been taken to the prison and executed.

Looking at the other houses along Stoung's riverbank, there was little to distinguish Duch's home from the others. To their neighbours and relatives they were much the same as everyone else. They were *tomada* – ordinary. But their large wooden house with its tiled roof was a far cry from the impoverished hovels that made up much of rural Cambodia – and they had even owned a small plot of land. But here in the village there was nothing remarkable about them. Nor was the fact that Duch spent his time alone, separate from other children, considered strange. And perhaps that was all there was to it, that Duch really was a recluse. He was studious, polite and unremarkable

– or perhaps remarkable in his lack of distinction. There was only one side of him that ever found expression and that was the bookish loner who rarely emerged from his parent's home.

Traditionally in Cambodia, the family was all-important and much stock was placed upon outward appearances, particularly among the ethnic Chinese. Clearly Duch's mother and sister were anxious to preserve the appearance of a harmonious family, concealing any discord that may have existed with all the formal decorum of the wedding photograph. The more time I spent with them the more I sensed a protective fence being weaved before me, unsure as they were of my intentions. Duch would have been well aware of the expectations of his family and of the importance of his position within it. Later, like many Khmer Rouge cadres, his Chinese-Khmer lineage would set him apart from the ranks of ethnic Khmers that the revolution claimed to champion. As an outsider, he might have felt trapped by his own limitations on one side and his family's ambition on the other. With his academic ability, he was perfect material for a cadre of a revolution.

His mother and sister knew something of his role during the Khmer Rouge but how much was difficult to say. And they certainly weren't going to tell me. They naturally wanted to discourage further investigation by painting a flawless image of him. The family had invested all their hopes in Duch. No doubt they were also protecting themselves from that painful time and from what the family favourite had become. It was as though they were holding the photograph of the schoolboy up to me, using it to protect themselves and the image of the family. I could sense their confusion. They remembered a son and brother; not the executioner of S-21.

CHAPTER 3

The Good Khmer Rouge

I T WAS THE rainy season in Bangkok and the downpour had been thudding on the roofs of the city for days. Leaping the black puddles and negotiating the labyrinthine lanes between the vendors, I followed my companion. Sokheang had been with the Khmer Rouge for almost twenty years and I was finding it difficult to keep up with him. He was known as a *Ranakse*, or a 'front' person – a general term for Khmer Rouge without rank. At fifty-eight, Sokheang possessed a taut energy that, combined with his nimble movements and spiky hair, made it easy to believe that he was twenty years younger. Before returning to Cambodia he had a final errand to run. His youngest son had assigned him the important task of purchasing a Manchester United T-shirt, with clear instructions on colour, size and style. He was determined not to return empty-handed. For hours we traipsed around the shops and stalls and I began to wonder if we were going to have any success. Undeterred he carried on.

Sokheang had come from Phnom Penh to have his

regular medical check-up as he had been complaining of dizziness and insomnia for some time now. His doctor couldn't find anything physically wrong with him, but had given him a large shopping bag of assorted pills. In the streets near his hospital we found stalls of T-shirts by the dozen. Within seconds he had pulled one out and saved the trip.

In some respects Sokheang was similar to Duch. They were both from the same province, their parents were of Chinese extraction, they were the eldest in the family and they were among the brightest at school. They attended the same *lycée* in Kompong Thom before continuing their studies in Phnom Penh. And they had both joined the Khmer Rouge. But that was where their similarities ended. By the time Sokheang became involved with the movement as a student in Paris, Duch was already a seasoned killer in the jungle.

For ten years now, Sokheang has worked as a human-rights investigator. The pressure from his job is intense and involves investigating abuses and giving help wherever appropriate. During a coup in 1997, corpses were found in various locations around the capital, murdered mostly by government death squads. On numerous occasions he was called out to investigate. Once his office was informed of a killing that had taken place in a rubber plantation some distance from the capital. Sokheang and his boss eventually found the exact spot, dug and recovered the corpse of a man in his late-forties. He had been shot in the head. There were also signs of torture. Sokheang interviewed plantation workers nearby who told him that they had seen a vehicle arrive at dusk and a short while later they had heard a gunshot.

It was dangerous work and, although Sokheang had

never been threatened, he knew the risks. One colleague was hospitalised after being beaten by government thugs and other colleagues had been threatened at gunpoint.

As a former Khmer Rouge, the irony of being a human-rights worker was not lost on him either; he had once teased a friend of mine by introducing himself by saying, 'Can you believe that? A Khmer Rouge working for human rights?' The more I got to know him the more I liked him. He was sincere, inquisitive, stubbornly principled and extremely generous. We became friends.

Sokheang had been defined by his time with the Khmer Rouge and he talked of little else. When I stayed in his home in Phnom Penh, there were times when I would have to go for walks alone, just to break from the discussion. He was tormented by his past. He never talked about it with his children, all of whom had been born in Khmer Rouge camps.

Sokheang was born in a small village not far from Kompong Thom town, in the opposite direction to Duch's. He described his family as 'lower-middle-class peasants'. His father was a local businessman who ran a small shop in the village, selling everything from pencils to cooking oil. He also bought rice from the farmers to sell on to the merchants in Phnom Penh and lent money at rates that the farmers could afford. He was regarded as fair and easy-going and was respected among the people.

Sokheang's father – unlike Duch's – had never owned their home. When the war broke out, his village was completely destroyed. The family then fled to Phnom Penh, where Sokheang was already enrolled as a student. He was then awarded a scholarship to study in Paris. Despite his reticence, his family insisted that he go. It was the last time that he was to see his father. From Paris, Sokheang went on to China before coming back to Khmer Rouge Cambodia. He wasn't permitted to return to his family. It was not until 1992, twenty-one years later, that he finally managed to separate from the Khmer Rouge and be reunited with his mother. By then not only had his father died, but three of his brothers had been killed.

Sokheang now lived with his wife and children in a shop house in the centre of Phnom Penh. The tiled sitting room was spotlessly clean with high ceilings and bare walls. In one corner an enormous television sat with a video. In the other were two bookshelves with an assortment of French and English books and various papers. Whenever I visited him in Phnom Penh and after his family had gone to bed we would spend the rest of the evening sitting chatting about the past on his balcony, a pouch of Samson mild tobacco and cheap Thai beer as company. The sounds of children playing and the thump of the construction site next door had by then calmed down as Phnom Penh grew weary of the day and people retired from the heat and the dust. We sat there for hours, illuminated by a fluorescent strip light, a layer of insects gathered at our feet. Sihanouk had once accused the Khmer Rouge of being *les révolutionnaires de salon*. In his honour, Sokheang had christened his balcony *le salon*.

One evening, I asked Sokheang about his own schooling in Kompong Thom, thinking that he might be able to fill the gaps in Duch's story as a young boy in the 1940s and 50s. Sokheang, although a year younger, had attended primary school at the same time. Like the monks chanting their Pali mantras, learning by rote was the accepted method of education just as in English schools of the time. 'In geography,' he recalled, 'we would have to learn the size of the country, the population, the agricultural produce, et cetera. And we would get called up to recite it to the rest of the class.' The accuracy of this recitation was the measure of a successful student. 'Knowledge,' said Sokheang, 'was the storage of facts.'

Primary schoolteachers, like the monks in the temple, were severe and were not to be questioned. Following their orders was the only way to avoid trouble. 'Beating was an accepted form of tutoring,' said Sokheang, as were whippings and canings. Author Someth May remembered his first teacher as 'a real monster' who, when he tired of beating his students, would entrust the job to his favourite pupil.

Despite such austere methods Sokheang considered himself fortunate. 'All the teachers were very conscientious, they wanted their students to learn. So even though they beat us, we never complained.' Some discussion was permitted in literature classes, but there was never any question of directly confronting your teacher, who probably knew no other way to command respect. In the West, respect is generally earned. In Asia it is more often assumed.

Teachers traditionally held an important place in Khmer society. The term for teacher in Khmer is *Loke Kru*, a term that can also be applied to magicians, medicine men and fortune-tellers, all of whom are revered by society. *Kru* means *guru* and in this respect they were similar to the monks in the *wat*. Cambodian Buddhism was a colourful cocktail of Brahmanism, animism and ancient mysticism. Some of these monks were believed to possess supernatural powers and able to converse with the dead. Previously, children throughout Cambodia had studied at the pagoda. They were taught by the monks, many of whom were poorly educated, and whose basic qualification was that they could read and write. The reverence in which the older generation held the monks was typified by the adage: 'I give you my whole child. Teach him everything you know. You set the rules. Whatever you do is up to you. I need only the skin and bones.'

This respect was reinforced by the traditional literature that Sokheang and Duch were taught, which encouraged a fatalistic conformity. As one proverb says, 'Do not reject the crooked road and do not automatically take the straight one; instead, take the one travelled by the ancestors.'

For most Khmers, moral guidance and instruction was given by the monks in the local temple, often in the form of ancient fables. The *Gatiloke*, literally 'the way of morality', is a collection of stories handed down through the centuries by word of mouth. They were a mixture Buddhism and ancient folklore and were tales of wisdom, justice and compassion, warning against the dangers of greed, lust and magic. The *Gatiloke* was taught to both Sokheang and Duch.

One folk story from the western province of Battambang tells the tale of Phnom Sampeou, a block of limestone that sits on the surrounding plain and resembles a galleon on a still sea of green fields. During 'the UN time' I would, on occasion, climb its steps to escape the madness that circled the plains below and sit on the summit next to sheer precipices with their spectacular views of the surrounding countryside. At dusk, a continuous black line of bats would snake their way across the sky from the caves that riddled the hill.

The word *sampeou* roughly translates as sailing boat or junk. A story called 'The Girl Who Let Down Her Hair' describes the birth of the hill.

One version tells how a wealthy young man, following the advice of a respected hermit, married a woman called

Rumsay Sok. As a wedding gift, the young man gave his new wife a magical gold hairpin. But soon after their marriage the young man fell in love with another woman who bore him a child. They decided to elope together on a boat, but his angry wife sent a fierce crocodile in pursuit. As the crocodile approached the boat, the young man threw a cage of chickens into the water to distract it, but to no avail. He then threw a cage of ducks, but still the crocodile pursued them. Then Rumsay Sok's magical hairpin fell from her head and hit the water, which dried up and the boat was stranded. Rumsay Sok caught up with the two lovers and took back her husband. She then slowly tortured the woman to death, cut off her head and placed it on a bamboo stake, scattering the rest of her remains across the plain below. The crocodile died on one mountain and the couple were left on Phnom Sampeou.

It was one of many stories that warned of the dire consequences of ignoring the advice of holy men and, by extension, the karmic forces that kept the universe in check.

Another story which comes from the *Gatiloke*, the *Tbal Kdoong*, warned of the dangers of setting oneself apart from the rest. A *tbal kdoong* is a rice pestle common in villages throughout Cambodia. It looks rather like a seesaw with a hammer at the end. It was usually operated by women, who used their body weight to lift it like a lever at one end and then dropped it on to the rice bowl at the other, ridding the rice of husks.

The story tells of a rich young widow who lived on the edge of a village. Her baby had fallen sick. A scoundrel dressed as a monk, who had planned to rob the widow, arrived outside her house. She told him of her sick child and begged for his help. The scoundrel told her that there was a demon holding on to the baby that was causing the illness. He told her to perform a rite to get rid of the demon and restore the baby's health. After preparing an altar to make offerings he instructed her to place the baby in the bowl of the rice pestle beneath the hammer. He then told her to stand on the other end. That way it would scare the demon away and cure her child. She did as she was told while he went into the house to fetch incense. He then robbed her of all her riches and ran away. Stuck on the pestle unable to move she called out for help but because her house was on the edge of the village no-one heard her cries as everyone was working in the rice fields. She could do nothing until people returned home from work and by then the scoundrel was long gone.

In the *Gatiloke*, as these stories illustrate, people rarely lived happily ever after. It reinforced a deeply rooted belief in a preordained life, a time-honoured acceptance of the status quo, which provided a useful means of social control to numerous regimes – including, ultimately, the Khmer Rouge.

Like Duch, Sokheang regularly came top of his class, therefore avoiding getting smacked or beaten. Unlike in the West, where pupils are often derided by others for being 'teacher's pet', Khmer pupils competed for their teacher's attention. As a favourite, Sokheang was often dispatched to buy a bowl of mandarin oranges for his teacher's breakfast. 'I was happy to do it,' smiled Sokheang. 'He always gave me one or two to eat as well.'

Apart from the radio, Duch would have had little contact with the outside world and few distractions. Travelling film-projection teams did go from village to village, erecting giant screens across the road or in a public space, often in the grounds of the *wat*. As a small boy Sokheang would often attend. The people sat on matting spread out below.

Entire families, including young children, stayed up late to watch these magical images dance above them.

Before the main film, like trailers, the executions were shown. These were of the Khmer Serei, or free Khmer, a band of anti-Sihanouk rebels. 'I saw it two or three times,' said Sokheang, shaking his head. The sentence was carried out just before sunrise. 'There were about twelve people with carbines or rifles and among them there was one without a bullet. This was to let the executioners believe that they might be innocent of the killing. The prisoner was blindfolded and his hands tied behind his back. The executioners stood a dozen metres away and waited for the order from a commander. They fired at the same time.'

Traditionally, executions were far more elaborate. The blindfolded prisoner would be made to kneel at the edge of a freshly dug pit. A red flower was placed over the prisoner's ear. Then the executioner would perform a ceremonial dance around the condemned, known as a *srangapen*. He would then raise the sword in front, as if to kill, but a second executioner behind the prisoner was the one who actually carried out the sentence. The body was thrown in the pit and covered with earth and the head placed on a stake for all to see. Ritualised killings such as these were recorded as late as the 1940s.

The tide had yet to turn against the left, who were for the most part tolerated. But the executions sent a powerful message from Sihanouk's government and it was clear what would happen if people questioned the established order and took matters into their own hands.

In the 1950s Sihanouk began modernising Cambodia's education system, which had been utterly neglected under French colonial rule. All over the country new secondary schools or *lycées* were constructed and competition for places became intense. Kompong Thom was no exception. In one of the first years of its opening there were 700 candidates for just 200 places. Duch, aged fourteen, was one of the chosen few.

At the *lycée*, Duch continued to excel. Once a month he returned home to visit his family, making the five-hour journey by bicycle. There were no dormitories for the students, so Duch lived with an elderly couple who ran a small noodle stall near the *lycée*. He received free accommodation in exchange for helping prepare the noodles and cleaning the house. His family sent him a small rice ration and he cooked his own food. He spent his free time reading and studying. Ambitious, driven and keen to please his family, he threw himself into his studies. One contemporary later remarked, 'He fixated on studying almost to the point of sickness.'

While his peers played volleyball, Duch preferred the company of his books. He organised a study group with other children to improve on classwork and prepare for exams. One member of the group, a woman called Sou Sath, still lives in Kompong Thom. She was a childhood friend of Sokheang's and had grown up in the same village. One morning, during the hot season in 2003, Sokheang, Sath and I sat in the shade of the large tamarind trees of the *lycée*, as Sath recalled her former study partner.

'He was the brightest in the group,' she said, 'always very helpful and understanding. He liked to read a lot, so he understood a great deal. We always explained the lessons to one another and he was generous with what he knew.' He was an earnest boy and 'hungry for knowledge'. He was known throughout the school for his academic achievements, but was never particularly popular. He made a point of treating her and the other girl in the group as equals and encouraged them to be strong in their beliefs and endeavours. 'He treated everyone the same and he wanted me to be strong, like a man.' Otherwise, unlike most of the boys of his age, he never took much interest in girls, she said.

One member of the study group was a Chinese-Vietnamese boy of the same age, called Ho Ngie. Like Duch, Ho later joined the Khmer Rouge but was killed in 1970, the first year of the war. Often they would be seen together walking the two kilometres with their bicycles to the government information department opposite the market. There they would read the papers and, when the government officers weren't looking, tear out stories. He and Duch, said Sath, became inseparable.

It was at this time that his interest in communism began to take root, most likely at the encouragement of his former primary-school teacher, Ke Kim Huot, who was transferred to the *lycée* in 1958. According to Sath, Duch spent much of his time at his house. Kim Huot was a passionate anti-monarchist who believed that the only way to free the peasantry from the notorious corruption of a Royalist government was through the creation of a popular republic. Instead of reverting to the ancient fables in the *Gatiloke*, he provided Duch with a new framework and vocabulary to interpret the world around him. Duch would have read in the papers of liberation movements throughout the world. Mao Tse-tung had yet to unleash the Cultural Revolution, but there would have been much talk about events in China. The Great Leap Forward, based on Mao's belief that human willpower and effort could overcome all obstacles, was in full swing. This went against traditional karmic teachings in Cambodia and would have been an attractive alternative to a young idealist acutely aware of the inequalities in society. After study group, Duch sometimes escorted Sath to her home, railing against feudalism, the monarchy, the rich and the current system for exploiting the people.

When Sihanouk implemented his plan to improve the education system the traditional learning places moved from the vicinity of the *wat* to the newly constructed schools and *lycées* that had been built all over the country. With many monks collecting alms in cash, building ornate temples or wearing silk robes, some people had already begun to regard the *Sangha* as corrupt. By contrast the new generation of teachers wore simple clothing and often lived a rudimentary life, denying themselves many comforts in the process. The shift in respect for the monks had begun as a new cohort of enlightened teachers emerged.

Like many other teachers, Kim Huot looked after his favourite and poorer pupils by giving them food and free accommodation as well as extra lessons. It was a practical way of moulding impressionable young boys and girls. To be poor in Cambodia was shameful, something to conceal. Ke Kim Huot's students must have been intoxicated by the attention lavished upon them. Here was a man of learning, a respected figure in the community, treating them with kindness and talking to them about such notions as 'equality', 'liberty' and 'justice'. Duch's close relationship with his teacher and mentor was to continue for many years. In 1967 they both joined the Communist Party of Kampuchea (Cambodia).

Sokheang arrived at Kompong Thom *lycée* a year after Duch. From a young age Sokheang – also a reserved and studious boy – was acutely aware of being different from his peers. 'At school I would look on as other friends played in the courtyard, but I rarely participated,' he said.

'I don't know why.' Like Duch, Sokheang had been introduced to French literature and particularly liked the progressive works of Victor Hugo, Voltaire and Rousseau, as well
as Molière and Montaigne. He also studied Khmer literature. The *lycée* teachers were different from those at primary
level and were generally popular. With a half-serious expression Sokheang told me that there was no need for the
harsh discipline of the primary schools because by then,
he said, they had been 'beaten into shape'. At the end of
each year a ceremony for the best students from each class
was held. Sokheang won every year without fail. The
governor of the province and other local dignitaries would
come and give out prizes. 'We were proud,' said Sokhcang.
To be a student was to be part of a new elite.

Encouraged by his teachers Sokheang too began to think
of the society around him and the problems people faced
on a national scale. 'I began to reflect and see what was
happening in society,' he said. They talked of the corruption and nepotism in the government and explained how
it caused the poverty all around them. Although aware,
Sokheang was a long way from the revolutionary Duch
was fast becoming. Despite being sympathetic to the leftist
cause, Sokheang wanted to study agriculture, become a
professor and contribute something practical towards his
country's development. He also saw this route as the only
way to avoid the nepotism and cronyism he saw all around
him. 'I hated corruption, at the same time I was also afraid
that I could fall into its trap,' he said. 'I never gave a single
penny to any law-enforcement people,' he went on, his
palms in front of his chest. 'If I broke the law, like going
through a red light, I preferred to pay the fine, but not a
bribe – one can say that I'm extremist,' he laughed, 'even
now.' Sokheang, like many of his contemporaries, admired

figures like Khieu Samphan and Hu Nim who later emerged
as leaders in the Khmer Rouge. What made them different
to other government officials, he said, were the choices
they made, influencing people by example. 'If they wanted
to have a motorbike they could've had one – they chose
not to.'

Sokheang first experienced corruption at the age of
sixteen, when his uncle sent him to the birth-registration
department to make a copy of his son's birth certificate.
He gave him 500 riel to give to the officer in charge. 'Why
is there a need to give anything?' thought Sokheang. 'This
is his job.' He decided not to hand it over. So, at the
department, the official made him wait . . . for hours.
Sokheang sat patiently outside the office, determined not
to pay. Finally, the official agreed and when he returned
with the copy he gave the money back to his surprised
uncle. 'This,' said Sokheang with a mock frown, his finger
in the air, 'was the first time that I fought against corruption.'

Yet the corruption rarely directly affected pupils like
Sokheang and Duch. They seldom suffered the harsh injustices of the poor, upon whom the police and bureaucrats
preyed. They were keen to set themselves apart from the
rest and described themselves as 'intellectuals' and therefore part of a new and special grouping. 'Intellectual'
carried gravitas. What it really identified was those whose
education went beyond the teaching of the temple. Most
of the police were of limited education and wary that some
among the students were sons and daughters of prominent
businessmen and local people of rank. The pupils were
aware of the position they held and became bolder in their
opposition. 'The police didn't dare to confront us,' said
Sokheang.

*   *   *

Sokheang had known Duch at Kompong Thom Lycée, but only from a distance. Duch was studious, recalled Sokheang, but 'most students were'. What set Duch apart from the others was his interest in political developments. He was a favourite among the teachers and already something of a leader – the kind of student that others went to for help with their studies.

By 1960, most Khmers of school age were offered the chance to become literate. This created many more students than the country had use for. Before Sihanouk's reforms, having a secondary education would have guaranteed a job in the government. But not any more. The reforms had produced an educated elite whose prospects were bleak. The dislocated youth who had left their villages to go to these *lycées* had broken from the traditional life of their families and felt an increasing detachment from the world of their parents. And yet they found themselves held back by a culture of cronyism and corruption unwilling to accommodate them. The new school system, free of a tainted *Sangha*, was creating the perfect framework for communism to spread.

It would take several years and a 6,000-mile journey before Sokheang became directly involved in the movement, and by then he believed that he had no choice but to join the Khmer Rouge. Duch's interest in leftist politics was well known by those already in the *lycée*. Recalled Sokheang, 'People used to characterise him as "a progressive,"' or left wing. 'At that time, they weren't called Khmer Rouge,' said Sokheang, 'but everybody knew.'

Nor was it an accident that many former *lycée* students and teachers would become the vanguard of the Khmer Rouge. Most of the leaders had been teachers, as were many of the staff at Tuol Sleng; they had played a crucial role in politicising a generation of students. Yet for revolutionaries like Duch, concerns for the poor and the injustices in society, seem to have been largely theoretical. Their discussion had been garnered from books rather than from critical thinking or original observations of their own. Much of the criticism seemed to have been fuelled by frustration. Genuine discussion and questioning were not a part of the culture. As in Tuol Sleng: you were either 'right' or you were 'wrong'. And like the 'bad' pupils in primary school who had to be beaten, the 'wrong' at Tuol Sleng had to be killed.

Sokheang's natural-science teacher at the *lycée* was a tall, almost albino man called Mam Nay who later took the *nom de guerre* Chan. Sokheang remembered him as a good and gentle teacher, distinguished from the others by a severe case of eczema. He played sports, wearing long sleeves and trousers, no matter how hot the weather. He was also more than 170cm tall; a giant in Cambodia. After Sokheang had left Kompong Thom, Chan became principal at a college further to the east and became very active in politics. It was the time of China's Cultural Revolution and, like Duch, the outspoken Chan had become active in spreading the word among the students and the teachers at every opportunity. 'He put Chinese revolutionary posters on the walls of the classrooms, distributed books on Mao and Lenin,' said Sokheang.

Years later, after the Khmer Rouge victory, Sokheang's cousin bumped into Chan on a deserted Phnom Penh street. Chan had been arrested for his activism and thrown into the same prison as Duch in the sixties, where the two had become friends. Chan later became Duch's deputy and the chief interrogator, considered even among the other guards as one of S-21's most terrifying cadres. Sokheang's cousin asked the former teacher what he was doing now. 'I catch pigs,' Chan replied.

By attempting to modernise Cambodia's educational system, Sihanouk had created breeding grounds for a revolution that would depose him as head of state, imprison him and send the country back to the Stone Age. Many members of the royal family were arrested and brought to Comrade Duch and executed.

In 1977, Duch's *lycée* teacher Ke Kim Huot was dragged through the gates of Tuol Sleng. After several months of savage torture – which Duch might have overseen or even participated in – he too was put to death.

CHAPTER 4

'The tree grows in the rural areas, but the fruit goes to the towns'

IN 1961, DUCH PASSED the Brevet d'Etudes Secondaire de Première Cycle, which brought him to the same educational level as French students of the same age. He was fifteen. He then went on to Siem Reap to attend the Lycée Suryavarman II, where he passed the first part of his baccalaureate. This took most students two years to complete, but Duch passed his in one – a rare achievement. The same year he was offered a place in the prestigious Lycée Sisowath in Phnom Penh, specialising in mathematics. It was here, among the boulevards of flame trees and yellow stucco walls of the *lycée*, that he successfully passed the second part of his baccalaureate, coming second in the entire country.

Arriving in the capital in 1962, Duch would have witnessed at first hand the widening gap between town and country. Many peasants distrusted the wealthier city people and officials, whom they saw as corrupt and often outright hostile to the poor. Historian Michael Vickery recalled how officials on weekend picnics, entertaining guests, would stop in a village, drop in on a house and ask the owner to kill a chicken and prepare a meal. A request from an official was as good as an order. The official would then impress his guest with the traditional hospitality and relative prosperity of Cambodia's farmers. It was not thought of as an imposition.

All discontent was internalised. Open displays of anger were generally suppressed and frowned upon. The taxes the peasants paid went to the city, as did their produce. The Khmer Rouge later exploited this resentment. As Cambodia's leading leftist, Hou Yuon, wrote, 'The tree grows in the rural areas, but the fruit goes to the towns.'

Like many students, Duch lived for free at a riverside temple, Wat Ounalom, not far from the Royal Palace. As he became more and more drawn into political activism his visits home decreased. Ke Kim Huot, his old teacher, had since moved to teach at a *lycée* south of Phnom Penh. It is likely that he supported Duch financially. To a young country boy in his late teens Phnom Penh must have conformed to much of what Duch had been told. And self-conscious, as undoubtedly he was, he would have been all too aware that his background excluded him from much of what Phnom Penh had to offer.

Duch wanted to become a professor of maths. He fell in love with Kim, Ho Ngie's sister, the friend with whom he had studied the newspapers. Together they began to study maths at the University of Phnom Penh. The families were in agreement over the match and they got engaged. But for reasons that are unclear the engagement was broken off and Duch concentrated on becoming a teacher.

In 1964, following in Ke Kim Huot's footsteps, Duch began studying for his teaching certificate at the Institut de Pédagogie, a stone's throw from his Phnom Penh *lycée*. The institute was a cradle of activism and the director was a Paris-educated mathematician called Son Sen. He fled the capital that year to join Pol Pot in Cambodia's infant Communist Party as a member of the central committee. Later Son Sen emerged as Defence Minister of the Khmer Rouge and Duch's immediate superior when Duch became commandant of Tuol Sleng. According to one former Khmer Rouge, Duch was introduced to the Communist Party of Kampuchea by a man named Chhay Kim Hour, a professor at the institute. He was head of a communist cell in the capital. Chhay Kim Hour took Duch under his wing, giving him training sessions and educating him about the party. They became close.

About fifteen years later, just before the Khmer Rouge regime collapsed, Chhay Kim Hour, like Ke Kim Huot before him, arrived blindfolded at the gates of Tuol Sleng. He was taken in by Duch, his former protégé, and executed.

By the time Duch was studying to become a teacher, Cambodia was growing increasingly unstable. Despite its putatively neutral status, the country's leader, Prince Sihanouk, was busily trying to keep Cambodia from being dragged into the escalating conflict in neighbouring Vietnam. He was wary of US influence and began cultivating a closer relationship with China. (He later severed diplomatic relations with America completely, greatly alarming Cambodia's powerful elite.) Privately he believed that the Vietnamese would win the war and had secretly allowed the North Vietnamese army and Viet Cong to ferry supplies down the Ho Chi Minh trail and from Cambodia's port at Kompong Som. By doing so he thought that Cambodia would be spared the ravages of war. It was a dangerous gamble that would prove disastrous for Cambodia.

Nicknamed 'the playboy prince', Norodom Sihanouk saw himself as father of the nation, referring to his people as '*mes enfants*'. During his frequent trips around the country, clamouring crowds would line the roads at the prospect of seeing him and some would travel great distances just to be able to touch the ground where he had trodden. He was intelligent, calculating, erratic, charismatic, passionate, hysterical and incredibly vain. He was also an unpredictable political animal and a shrewd negotiator, as he had proven in his dealings with the French when they granted full independence to Cambodia in 1953.

While he travelled the countryside, cultivating this populist image, his deputy Lon Nol jailed, tortured and murdered opponents to his government. The crackdown fuelled the resentment. Many student activists and teachers were arrested and imprisoned. Among those who fled to the jungle was a schoolteacher called Saloth Sar who was later to take the *nom de guerre* Pol Pot. He hailed from a relatively prosperous farming family in Kompong Thom, fifty kilometres from Duch's home. Possibly because of his connections to the royal household in Phnom Penh, Pol Pot had been awarded a scholarship to study electrical engineering in Paris in 1949. There, along with Son Sen, Ieng Sary and Khieu Samphan, he became active in left-wing politics and joined the French Communist Party. This group later formed the core of the Khmer Rouge leader-ship. Pol Pot failed to pass his exams and returned to Cambodia to work as a teacher in Phnom Penh. In 1963, fearing arrest by Sihanouk's police, he escaped to the jungle. He then spent two years in a Vietnamese army base in the jungles of the north-east before visiting Hanoi and then China in 1966. He then returned to Cambodia. In the remote forests there he drew some of the inspiration for his vision of a classless state from the tribal people who lived without money, property or markets. Many of them were to become his most trusted bodyguards. It was not until the Khmer Rouge victory in 1975 that Pol Pot was announced as prime minister of Democratic Kampuchea.

To Sihanouk, students and teachers were considered threats. Although not necessarily communists, many saw themselves as 'liberals' or 'progressives'. As far as Lon Nol was concerned, there was no middle ground. Sihanouk didn't disapprove of Lon Nol's heavy-handed measures, unless of course it was in his interest to do so. There were frequent demonstrations in the capital and many were imprisoned. Others, like Duch's former mentor Ke Kim Huot, escaped to the forest, as the police became more and more aggressive in their pursuit of these *Khmers rouges*. 'There was much pressure from the government – everybody was red,' one former student said, as the situation between the two camps became more and more polarised. In the countryside too the repression began to be felt.

In 1963, in an attempt to placate the left, Sihanouk began to nationalise export and import trade along with banks and distilleries, arguing that Cambodia should rely on its own resources. Sihanouk had taken this idea of self-sufficiency and nationalisation from two leading left-wing politicians Khieu Samphan and Hou Youn who were still part of his administration. He said he wasn't going to allow Cambodia to be seen as a client state of the United States, that enough trade was already in the hands of foreigners.

More than ninety per cent of the population lived in the countryside and made their living from agriculture. As the state squeezed the peasantry and took control of the rice exports, resentment deepened. The North Vietnamese army and the National Liberation Front, or Viet Cong, began buying rice directly from the farmers at far higher prices than the state. By 1966, more than a third of the entire rice harvest was sold illegally on the black market. Bit by bit Sihanouk's government's control of the countryside was beginning to wane. More heavy-handed measures were required to prevent the farmers from selling their rice to the Viet Cong.

On 28 August 1965, Duch got his teaching certificate and was posted to a *lycée* in Skoun, a small town in Kompong Cham. Located at the intersection of three national highways, Skoun was the traditional stop for an early lunch for those going overland to Angkor. Little more than a series of shop houses facing a market, Skoun is still famous for a dish called *A Ping*, a kind of giant forest spider the size of an outstretched hand which is barbecued black and sold by young girls with electric smiles who press their faces against car windows, balancing large plates of these things on their heads.

Arriving at the *lycée* on his battered Chinese bicycle, the new maths teacher quickly made an impression. With his shirt outside his trousers and his scruffy looks, Duch wasn't their idea of a Phnom Penh graduate. To Meak Meurn, a former pupil, now himself a teacher at the *lycée*, Duch was 'a very strange professor'. In Cambodia, people of more humble beginnings did their best to conceal their poverty and took pride in looking smart. Yet here was the *lycée*'s most qualified teacher, who was well paid but preferred to dress simply and ride a bicycle to school instead of a car or scooter. He was also a chain-smoker, puffing his way through several packets a day. He shared a house in the town with the headmaster and his bedroom was a mess of scattered papers and books about Mao, Engels and Marx.

But he was a good teacher, earnest yet committed and well liked, particularly among the poorer pupils. Meurn remembered him as 'a very patient and very gentle professor', who worked extremely hard and who never punished his pupils. He fed the poorer ones and offered lodgings, just as his own teacher had done. During classes, he was meticulous and particular. As another former pupil recalled, 'He was known for the precision of his lectures as if he were copying texts from his mind on to the board.'

He rarely relaxed or socialised. While the other teachers enjoyed parties and festivals where they would dance and drink, Duch stayed behind to show Chinese propaganda films that described pest control in the countryside to demonstrate how the parasites, like the ruling classes, fed off the hard work of the people. Often, after classes, he would tell Chinese morality tales that carried political overtones. He even tested them on Maoist theory, handing out leaflets at the end that, according to Meurn, 'taught us to hate the Prince's feudalist regime and the capitalist regime'. It wasn't all theoretical. Meurn described how Duch organised his students to help the farmers build up the paddy embankments and initiate labour classes to assist the peasantry. They learned quickly under his guidance. 'He tried to teach other students to help the poor and less fortunate in the countryside,' said Meurn. 'He was the only one like this.'

These young recruits had become devoted followers. 'He was well educated and his views were of a high level,' said Meurn. By now, Duch was a committed communist and his grooming of the poorer students was designed with one sole purpose in mind: to prepare the ground for revolution. And the time was fast approaching.

Not far from Skoun, in the rubber plantations of Chamkar Leou, the Khmer Rouge had a large base. This might explain why Duch was able to continue his communist agitating so openly for as long as he did. The local authorities might have been cautious about moving against people like him, fearing it could upset the balance and lead to open conflict in the area. Kompong Cham and Kompong Thom were known bastions of Khmer Rouge support and further beyond to the east was the North Vietnamese army. Duch was also a graduate of the Institut de Pédagogie, where to be openly leftist wasn't considered unusual. As Meurn said, 'we respected different views.'

Then Duch learned that his friend and comrade Chhay Kim Huor had been arrested with ten others in Phnom Penh while handing out leaflets denouncing Lon Nol as a traitor. Chhay Kim Hour was imprisoned without trial for a year. It is almost certain that he had been Duch's main contact and liaison officer.

By this time, explained Sou Sath of his Kompong Thom study group, Duch had become *Monuh Daach-chat* a term the Khmer Rouge used to refer to a loyalist who would sacrifice anything for the movement. The random and cruel nature of the various crackdowns resulting in the arrest of so many of his friends would have convinced him of the evils of the current regime. Sath was by now married and living in Kompong Thom with her husband. She was teaching at a primary school and, like many of her colleagues, had become a communist sympathiser. Duch used to give them information when he came to town. He carried a copy of Mao's little red book in his pocket, along with a larger one entitled *The Lectures of Mao Tse-tung*. They met discreetly at her house, where he would distribute books and pamphlets among her colleagues and hold discussions about philosophy and Maoist theory.

In 1966, the same year that Pol Pot visited China, Mao Tse Tung unleashed the Cultural Revolution. In order to put an end to 'revisionism', young radicals and Red Guards began accusing many top party and government officials of failing to follow original communist principles, branding them 'counter-revolutionaries'. Nothing was sacred enough to be spared by these mobs as they rampaged through the country. Universities and schools were shut down; intellectuals, artists and writers were humiliated and, in some cases, killed. Thousands were sent to the countryside to be re-educated through hard labour, self-criticism and study sessions. Temples were ransacked and monasteries disbanded, books were burned and any reminders of China's feudal past destroyed. This constant revolution unleashed forces that proved almost unstoppable. The army was then called in and began its own reign of terror and thousands were killed. They began the Campaign to Purify Class Ranks carried out by Thought Propaganda Teams. Anyone with a suspect background such as a university education was sent to be re-educated.

No other single movement was to have such a profound influence on the Khmer Rouge who, once in power, took the fanaticism of the Cultural Revolution a stage further.

Back in Kompong Thom, Duch had become a passionate advocate of the revolutionary cause. At meetings he gesticulated wildly as he spoke. He constantly railed against Sihanouk and his government, said Sath. She saw he had become a man of 'rigid principle'. But there was no doubting his sincerity. His speeches were peppered with communist jargon about 'the feudalists', and the 'proletariat'. He was persuasive and charismatic and had become adept at holding people's attention, winning people's trust regardless of age or social standing. For Sath, 'He was the sort of person who liked to be listened to more than the other way round.'

Sath was unsure of Duch's position within the Khmer Rouge. Most people then did not know of the existence of the Communist Party of Kampuchea. It had been obscured by the broad brush stroke when Sihanouk coined the name for the left, *Les Khmers rouges*. However, she was certain he was taking his orders from someone. Duch was in charge of distributing books and information to people in the area, to friends and colleagues, in order to spread the word. They had a network, she said, and could operate quite easily, 'because all the people were sympathetic to their ideas'. Duch had become head of a communist cell in Skoun and Kompong Thom with orders to convert and recruit. But it is still unclear what his position was or who he answered to.

By now, Duch was being closely monitored by the local authorities. It was only a matter of time before they came after him, as he must have known. The situation all over the country had reached crisis point. The divisions between the left and the pro-American right and the widespread disenchantment with the government had created a potentially explosive situation.

In 1967, the touch paper was lit. On the other side of the country from Duch, in the district of Samlaut, the government forced a number of peasants off their land and built a sugar refinery. The peasants were angered by the lack of compensation, and their increasingly desperate position made for a tense situation. Then the government sent in troops to collect taxes and ensure that the peasants sold all their surplus rice to the government and not to the Vietnamese. One contingent of soldiers was too forceful and the villagers fought back, killing two of them. Shortly afterwards a local garrison was overrun and arms were taken as the whole area rose up.

The Khmer Rouge took their cue. All over the country similar unrest was being reported. Sihanouk, who was abroad, wanted the uprising crushed, and he wasn't particularly bothered how. Lon Nol seized the opportunity to move against the left and quell all dissent. Villages were burned and thousands were killed. Heads were mounted on stakes outside Battambang. Trucks filled with more heads were reportedly brought to Phnom Penh so that Lon Nol could see that his orders were being carried out.

Despite growing discontentment and hardship across the countryside, the Khmer Rouge still had neither the support nor the means to launch all-out war against Sihanouk's regime. They were probably caught off guard by Samlaut but, realising the importance of what was happening, claimed the uprising as their own. Duch's loyalty to the Khmer Rouge already bordered on the fanatical. Suddenly, he found himself on the front line. He sent a group of his loyal, poorer students to distribute leaflets in Kompong Cham town. The leaflets called for the overthrow of the 'fascist regime in Phnom Penh'. They described Sihanouk's government as corrupt, oppressive and feudalistic, and called for the people to 'rise up'. Three of his students were arrested and jailed by Sihanouk's police.

When news of the arrests reached Duch, he realised that he was a wanted man. Disguising himself as a farmer he went into hiding, or so his students thought. In fact, he went to the Khmer Rouge base in nearby Chamkar Loeu, where at the recommendation of Chhay Kim Hour, he was accepted as a full member of the Communist Party of Kampuchea.

However there was another reason for him to disappear. According to Sath, he owed a lot of money from playing *Tontin*, and his creditors had reported him to the police. *Tontin* is a rotating credit scheme between friends where each member of the group puts an equal amount of money into a kitty. They then take it in turns to borrow the total and repay it. Sath couldn't understand it – it seemed so out of character. Duch was generally a cautious man. She didn't know how much money had been involved; 'I just knew that he played *Tontin* to collect money to help the revolutionary forces. When it was time to pay back the money, he didn't have any and he escaped into the jungle to Chamkar Loeu.'

Whatever the real story, a few months later Duch was arrested by the authorities. He was then jailed in Kompong Cham before being transferred to the Central Prison in Phnom Penh and then to Prey Sar, the main holding centre for political prisoners just outside the capital. There, along with hundreds of others, he was held without trial for the next two years. He was thrown in the same cell as Norng Soun, the editor of the left-wing paper *Prachachon*, and Mam Nay or Chan.

Sihanouk, retuned home, realised he needed to curb Lon Nol's increasing power and distance himself from the repression, and demanded his deputy's resignation. He then accused the two remaining prominent leftists in Phnom Penh, Khieu Samphan and Hou Youn, of leading the uprising. They then disappeared, believed murdered by Sihanouk's death squads. In Phnom Penh, 15,000 people came out to demonstrate their support for the two men and a state of emergency was declared. Although he later distanced himself from the crushing of the uprising in Samlaut, Sihanouk said that he 'read somewhere that 10,000 died'.

The leftist opposition of the schools and centres of study and the grievances of the peasantry were beginning to converge. The picture-postcard image of an abundant, peaceful land, created largely by the French, was beginning to unravel. Ironically, it was this idealised image of Cambodia that the Khmer Rouge would attempt to create. But, in order to launch a revolution with the full backing of the peasantry, a major cataclysm was needed.

CHAPTER 5

'Brothers and sisters, go to the jungle and join the guerrillas'

I HAD ARRIVED early but the table soon filled. It was Sunday afternoon in Phnom Penh and Sokheang's wife, Veng Heng, had prepared Chinese noodles and fish curry with fresh bean sprouts, shallots and bitter cabbage. We sat perched on our seats, chopsticks in hand, as she placed the large dishes in front of us. As Sokheang poured me a glass of beer he turned to me, grinning, 'You see, just like Paris.' Farmers, a princess, a diplomat, ex-students, teachers – almost all of Sokheang's friends were former Khmer Rouge. Sokheang was enjoying his Sunday afternoon, rushing about, tending to his guests.

I sat beside a woman in her late-fifties with a gentle expression and wavy, greying hair. She talked of Sokheang as a younger brother. She leaned over and in an almost conspiratorial tone said, 'He keeps good memories from that time,' meaning the 1960s. 'We all do.' Before the war, Phnom Penh had been a beautiful place, she said. It conformed to all the notions of an idyllic oriental kingdom.

'The 1960s were a wonderful time. We had the Beatles, Ray Charles . . .' She talked about the students and how they had all remained close friends through all the hardships that followed.

Concerned that I wasn't eating enough, she filled my bowl with a second helping of noodles. 'We always talk about Pol Pot though,' she went on. 'Whenever we get together we're always reminded of the absence of our friends.' She pointed to a man with a shock of silver hair on the other end of the table. 'Ho was a friend of my little brother,' she said. 'He reminds me of him.' The little brother had died during 'the Pol Pot time'.

'He once told me,' she said, referring to Sokheang, '"you can talk about the Khmer Rouge, but you can't cry."'

'Why not?' I asked.

She paused. 'Because there would be no stopping.'

Ong Thong Hoeung, the man at the far end of the table, had joined the Khmer Rouge in Paris. Known as Ho, he now lived in Belgium and had returned with his daughter for a few weeks to visit friends and family. Sophinie had been born in the forest of Kompong Cham in 1978 just before the Khmer Rouge collapse. It was her first trip back since she had left with her family as refugees. After the fall of the Khmer Rouge, Ho was the first to spirit out confessions from Tuol Sleng to the West as evidence of Khmer Rouge atrocities.

He was a slight figure with a handsome face and intelligent eyes. Like Sokheang, like nearly all the people around the table, Ho had not endured the harsh years leading up to the Khmer Rouge's takeover. He had been in Paris as a student. But growing up in a small village in Kandal province, he had always possessed a strong sense of social justice, always aware of the inequalities he saw around him. There the rich had everything, and the poor had nothing.

As a young student in Phnom Penh Ho, like many of his contemporaries, had been attracted to what he called 'the progressives', led by Khieu Samphan. There he saw the Cambodian bourgeoisie for the first time. 'They spoke in French at home and they had maids who were little more than slaves,' he said. 'They behaved like foreigners.' Nepotism reigned. Qualified graduates, including many of Ho's friends, were sidelined by less capable ones whose father was related to their employer. The only jobs were in the administration and they were mostly accounted for by the sons and daughters of the rich and powerful.

When Ho arrived as a young student in Paris in 1965, the wealth and grandeur of the city stunned him. 'I became angry and frustrated with the regime in Phnom Penh. It seemed to me that Cambodia was backward.' He began to question the world that he had known all his life – how the elite hadn't done anything for the people and how the lives of farmers had degenerated. 'I was shocked because we're very proud of the temples of Angkor, but when I looked at the sculpture and the tools that they used, they were the same as the ones they use today,' he said. 'So I began to read books and I met students both French and foreign. When I was in Cambodia we didn't have access to so much information. I didn't have many books; I began to read extracts of Jean-Jacques Rousseau. And all the injustices in Cambodia I felt we had to fight. Like Rousseau I saw that "man was born free, and everywhere he is in chains". So in Paris, I met with other progressives and started to read Marx and Tolstoy and Gorky. I didn't understand much Marx, but I particularly liked Gorky.'

He spent a lot of time with new friends from Brazil,

Mexico, Peru, Cameroon, Senegal, but mainly from former French colonies. 'I envied their freedom,' he said. The more they talked the more he realised the commonality of their experience. That was the time that he began to form what he described as 'a political conscience'. 'I came to the conclusion that the problem was political so we must fight to change it. The atmosphere in Paris was very exciting, very free. We used to distribute leaflets denouncing imperialism and against capitalism,' he said. He defined himself as a 'progressive' – not a communist. 'I began meeting with Americans like Noam Chomsky and Laura Summers.' The atmosphere was euphoric. 'It felt like a new world. It felt like everything was possible and the freedom of oppressed people could become reality.' His confidence was bolstered by the common views of others from disparate parts of the world. 'I was very surprised to find American and French friends and it encouraged me. It was the first time that I found a genuine comradeship between people, it was very emotional – the best time of my life.'

After the May 1968 demonstrations in Paris, he joined the Khmer Rouge and, like Sokheang, returned to Cambodia after the Khmer Rouge had seized power. By the end of Pol Pot's rule, Ho's father and four of his eight siblings were dead and most of his extended family had been wiped out. When I asked him the total he looked down and shook his head. 'It was so many . . .' he said. 'Perhaps as many as 200 people.'

On 11 February 1969, a decision was made in the US that was to condemn Cambodia to ruin. A secret breakfast meeting was held at the Pentagon where it was agreed that the US air force would bomb Vietnamese targets inside Cambodia. Approved by Nixon and Kissinger, the plan went ahead to bomb a neutral country without the knowledge of Congress or the American public.

'Operation Breakfast' was to take the form of a series of B-52 air strikes inside the border with the aim of dislodging and destroying the central headquarters of the North Vietnamese army and the Viet Cong forces, thus buying time for the US troop withdrawal from South Vietnam. This was then extended to what became known as 'the Menu' operation, which included targets 'Dinner', 'Snack', 'Supper', 'Dessert' and 'Lunch'. However, instead of the desired effect of driving the Vietnamese communists inside Vietnam, they moved deeper into Cambodia. And so did the bombing.

Ten years before, a US government report had described Cambodia as a country populated by a superstitious, 'docile and passive people', whose world was restricted to village, temple and forest and who, 'could not be counted on to act in any positive way for the benefit of US aims and policies'. Cambodia had become the 'sideshow' to the US war against Vietnam as Nixon and Kissinger launched their illegal assault on the country's populated heartland. To Nixon and Kissinger and the others involved, Cambodians weren't even abstractions – they simply didn't exist.

'I used to watch them – they flew very high,' said Sou Sorn, who had gone to Sokheang's primary school in Kompong Thom. The bombs fell on the village cooperative first and then the market; she heard the whistle, then the explosions. Sou Sorn, like the others, took cover in the small shelters that had been built before the bombing eventually drove her from the village. For the US military, Cambodia was now a 'free-fire zone' where everything was a legitimate target.

'I was terrified,' she said. The whole place had been

ignited by napalm. While Sokheang was safely studying in Phnom Penh, his village had quite simply been wiped out.

Flying high above the cataclysm they wrought below them, the pilots were further insulated from the destruction by the language of a high-tech war: 'soft targets', 'anti-personnel', 'objectives'. A 'soft target' could be people or buildings like Sokheang's village primary school, which was completely erased.

'I can't recognise anything,' said Sokheang as we walked down the road past the sprawling market. He stopped for a moment, his hand on his hip, the other rubbing the back of his head. 'It's all new. I can't even work out where my home was.' Groups of people were making their way home. The village looked as though it had always been there. The wooden houses sat on their stilts hugged by the lush vegetation that surrounded them. The grass verges had been neatly shaved by lolling buffalo. Sokheang's house had disappeared early on, burned by napalm and then obliterated by wave after wave of bombing sorties. Sokheang's village had been right in the middle of one of the most contested areas during the early part of the war. The Khmer Rouge had a base nearby and bombing had been unrelenting. Often North Vietnamese troops would file through, together with smaller groups of Khmer Rouge. The only landmark he could identify was the bridge on the road to Kompong Thom.

A single B-52 carries a payload of 10,000 pounds. From an altitude of 30,000 feet the belly of these enormous planes would open and their deadly cargo would fall in ladders, carving up whatever lay on the ground below. Often the planes would be hidden by cloud; all that could be seen were the advancing lines of explosions. By 'carpet bombing,' like this, the squadron's strike pattern would saturate the area, blasting furrows for a mile and a half, as though the landscape had been torn up with a giant plough. In many areas the lines of these craters are still visible from the air.

We wandered further along the road and walked up to a man sitting on a plastic chair in front of a house. He was repairing a piece of machinery when we arrived, his hands covered in black grease, a thick pair of glasses tied to his head with elastic. The man, Pech Chin Sreng, described how the ground shook. 'If we were near, we had to protect ourselves like this' – he gripped his hands on either shoulder to hug himself – 'and lie down on the ground.' He pointed to a large grassy hollow just behind us, and another, across the road. This had been the closest encounter. Approximately nine metres across and five metres deep in the ground was a crater from a bomb dropped by a B-52 more than thirty years ago. Luckily he had managed to get to the bunker in time. The explosion made his ears ring for days afterwards.

Other planes came regularly, usually T-28's with napalm. They would always arrive after the Vietnamese troops had moved on. The troops knew of a T-28 attack in advance from the whirr of spotter planes high above. The villagers cowered in metre-deep slit trenches piled with logs and earth, little protection against such sustained attacks, whose payloads ignited everything and sucked the air from people's lungs.

One time Chin Sreng had been caught out in the fields when an AC-47 gunship circled above him. Nicknamed 'Spooky', it was a cumbersome propeller plane equipped with three large machine guns that fired 6,000 rounds per minute, saturating the surrounding area with lead. It began firing at him, the large bullets kicking up the dirt less than three metres from where he stood. He managed to escape unscathed. By the end, he was one of the few people left in the village. The rest had either fled or had been killed. They tried to do their best to tend their land. 'I was so angry with the Americans and the Vietnamese!' he said. 'Everything was destroyed – it was a time of indescribable suffering.'

In 1994, I visited a temple not far from Sokheang's village where the Mines Advisory Group were working. MAG, a UK-based charity, was clearing the area of mines and unexploded ordinance so that farmers could return to till their land. The whole district was a former battle area. MAG's advisers, former British servicemen, oversaw Cambodian teams that worked the ground. When a mine had been located, it was destroyed in *situ*. But here the problem wasn't landmines.

Working in old, overgrown trenches and paddy dykes, in temperatures in excess of thirty degrees centigrade, their metal detectors squealed away at the high metal content in the ground. Everything had to be treated as a potential mine and work was painfully slow. They were sifting through the years of shrapnel, looking for orbs of steel the size of tennis balls. These were cluster bombs, known as 'bombies' or in military speak, an 'area denial sub-munition'. Hundreds of thousands had been dropped during the US war. When a cluster bomb is released from the plane, the propeller on the end unscrews the cigar-shaped canister and releases 650 of these small balls. The arming device is then activated and works its way down the inside of the ball. If it doesn't work its way down the whole way it can land without detonating. Children have been known to take them home. When a bomblet detonates, some 200,000 steel fragments will be propelled, at ballistic speed,

over an area the size of several football fields, creating a
deadly killing zone. These white-hot shards literally shred
the body of those in the area. Some bomblets contained
metal barbed darts that would pin people to the ground.
A B-52 could drop 25,000 of these bomblets on a single
bombing run. They also have a dud rate of up to thirty
per cent. Many remain dormant in the ground for years
until they are disturbed, becoming more unstable. For a
new generation who have never known war, the countryside can be a dangerous place to play. Cambodia is
littered with the debris of war and every month a deadly
harvest is reaped.

I was told by MAG to keep to the well-trodden paths
and warned of potential dangers along the way. Other
teams were working further beyond the village on the edge
of the fields. I passed through an opening in a dyke fenced
in by branches and guarded by large sugar palms. The
field had dried out and a dark puddle sat in the middle.
MAG had marked the location of the debris to be destroyed.
As I got closer, I could see a bomblet that had been in
the earth for some time. It was a beautiful rusty, earthen
colour and looked rather like a flint ball, the size of a
clenched fist.

As I looked down at this thing I realised the difference
between being here and in a mined area. There was always
a degree of predictability about mines and minefields.
These bomblets were scattered all over the area completely
indiscriminately and were far more unstable than the plastic
mines I had become familiar with.

By the time Congress halted the B-52 strikes in 1973, more
than two million bombs and other ordinance had rained
down on Cambodian fields and villages. More than a million

people had been killed or wounded and two-thirds of the country's draught animals had died. Almost half the population, including Sokheang's family, had been uprooted and had fled to the towns.

For the Khmer Rouge and the peasantry this unprovoked attack demonstrated the absolute evil of the United States. As the CIA later reported, the Khmer Rouge 'were using the damage caused by B-52 strikes as the main theme of their propaganda'. By exploiting the peasant's misery and identifying the people in the cities as the enemy, their ranks began to swell. More and more saw the Khmer Rouge as patriots. They were idealistic, driven and fiercely disciplined. They talked of a promised land, a new beginning as great as the time of Angkor and more and more began to heed their call.

In Stoung, Kaing Kim Hiep, Duch's sister, recalled for me her panicked rush to the bunkers with her eldest child clasped to her chest. The bombers came at different times and pounded the area for hours. 'We were forever in the shelters,' she said. While the family endured the terror of indiscriminate air attacks, Duch was in prison and knew little of the horror of the US bombing campaign. His family were shocked when they heard of his arrest. His mother went straight to Skoun to try and find him. If she had known before, she would have stopped him, as she put it, from 'playing politics'. 'We felt devastated,' she said. 'We didn't know the reason behind it.'

His mother then travelled to Prey Sar accompanied by his eldest sister. Despite their fears they found him in good health and good spirits. They continued to visit him for the regulation fifteen minutes once a week, bringing him fresh fish and fruit. They didn't dare ask why he had been jailed: the prison staff kept a close eye on them. Duch told his mother not to worry, that he was fine, that he was being treated well.

But was he? The police routinely abused prisoners and torture was considered normal practice. His prison experiences might well provide some insight into his incarnation as the commandant of Tuol Sleng.

'Do you think he was tortured?' I asked his mother.

There was an awkward silence.

'I worried about this *a lot*,' she said. 'I dared not ask.'

I turned to his sister, Kim Hiep. 'It's possible,' she said after a while. 'We thought about it a lot.'

There is no record to confirm whether Duch was tortured in prison. But the methods later employed in Tuol Sleng certainly suggest that he had some knowledge of the process used in Cambodian prisons.

This 'minor tradition of torture', as one survivor called it, was centuries old. In the time of Angkor, corporal punishment usually involved the amputation of a hand or a foot or even a nose. Notions of guilt and innocence were loosely defined and those arrested were automatically assumed to be guilty. At the turn of the nineteenth century, the whole process of arrest, confinement and punishment was characterised by severe torture and the methods employed no less brutal than those used by the Khmer Rouge. When a suspect was arrested and didn't confess immediately, he or she would be slapped on the face with a *pean* – a circular piece of hard wood with a handle similar to a table tennis bat. One strike with this would dislodge several teeth. If this didn't work then a *kumneap slasloeng* was used. This was a wooden lever that operated on the same principle as a press and was placed on the temple. It was then gradually tightened until the prisoner confessed or fell unconscious. Innocent people with nothing to confess were tortured until their eyeballs popped out.

Another punishment for prisoners was the *chongkuang tradak*, or stork's knees, still commonly used today in Burma. Two iron shackles were placed around the ankles with a longer piece running between. Another piece ran from the joint to the waist where the prisoner had to tie it up or hold it with his hand in order to move, usually with great difficulty.

Later I put the question of whether Duch had been tortured to another former Khmer Rouge, In Sopheap. 'Of course,' he said. Such was the polarisation of political thought between the left and right that brutality had become part of the repression.

In 1970, with the US bombing continuing in the countryside, the situation in Cambodia quickly degenerated. Whilst Sihanouk was abroad, Lon Nol, who had been demoted to marshal, began to stir up anti-Vietnamese sentiment and riots broke out in Phnom Penh. The North Vietnamese embassy was sacked and flags were burned. Soon, 550 local Vietnamese were murdered, their bodies dumped into the Mekong and Tonle Bassac rivers.

Taking advantage of Sihanouk's absence, Lon Nol then overthrew his prince in a coup d'état. He then assumed Cambodia's helm in what was widely believed to have been a CIA-sponsored action. Whatever the truth, the US immediately threw its support behind the new government. Lon Nol expelled the North Vietnamese diplomats and closed their embassy down, declaring war on the Vietnamese and their comrades, the Khmer Rouge. This was then followed by a land invasion by US and South Vietnamese forces inside Cambodia with the same aim of locating and destroying the central command headquarters of the Vietnamese Communists. Lon Nol, despite being the

US's newest ally, first heard of the invasion on television.

For the people on the border, it was announced by explosions and the roar of tanks as they crashed through their villages. With the coup shedding Cambodia's neutrality and a pro-American regime now in Phnom Penh, Cambodia's destruction had begun. Sixty days later, when the US and South Vietnamese troops had withdrawn, 11,000 people were dead. Nixon declared the invasion 'the most successful operation of the war'.

Sihanouk, now in Beijing, then took a decision that was to have profound ramifications for his people. Embracing his former enemies, the Khmer Rouge, he announced the formation of the Front d'Union Nationale du Kampuchea (FUNK). On 23 March 1970 Sihanouk addressed his people on Radio Beijing: 'Brothers and sisters,' he said, 'go to the jungle and join the guerrillas.' At this stage the Khmer Rouge numbered no more than a few thousand and, despite the upheaval in the countryside, were still unable to launch a campaign of their own. (It was to be a further three years before they were able to operate without the support of their powerful ally, the North Vietnamese.) The peasantry in the countryside, although opposed to the repression, were still conservative by nature and reluctant to give their active support to them. Sihanouk provided it. He had given his blessing for his 'children' to rebel. The country rose up. Now there was no stopping them.

On an October morning in 1971, the sun was already high over the airfield, the sugar palms on the other side of the runway quivered and danced in the heat. Sokheang was leaving Cambodia to study in Paris. His mother and father together with two of his siblings had come to see him off. His parents assured him that everything would be all right, that he must go and not worry. At the last minute they said their hurried goodbyes. As he walked out of the door and towards the plane, he didn't look back. He was leaving his family in a country on the brink of total collapse, his village had been incinerated in the inferno and his family left penniless as refugees. They stood and waited as the plane taxied down the runway, shimmering in the heat haze. Silently they watched as the roar of the engines took him away. Shielding their eyes from the bleached sky they watched the plane bank and then turn westward. They stood there until the little speck finally disappeared.

Duch too had left Phnom Penh but in another direction. One of Lon Nol's first actions on seizing power was to announce a general amnesty for hundreds of political prisoners in an attempt to dampen the hostility to his takeover. Duch was one of them. He returned to his family in Stoung and stayed for just two weeks. The province had been devastated by the bombing and was under constant air attack. He then returned to work in Phnom Penh – or so his family thought.

'Then the fighting broke out,' said his sister, and the bridge was destroyed. 'No-one could get in or out.' And that was the last time the family saw Kaing Guek Eav. Five years later he would return as Comrade Duch.

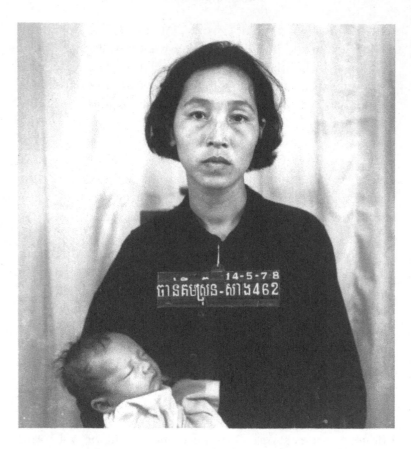

Chan Kim Srun (Saang) and her baby on arrival at S-21 in 1978
(*Courtesy Tuol Sleng Museum*)

PART II

Comrade Duch

CHAPTER 6

A Vision of a Better World

WHEN DUCH LEFT his home in 1970, he disappeared into a new, secret world from which he would not return for more than twenty years. Here in the zones of the Khmer Rouge, he discarded his old identity, assumed a new name and began a new life. He was appointed head of Special Security by his immediate superior, Vorn Vet, and sent to an area at the foot of the Cardamom mountains. There, in the forests of Amleang, he began his new incarnation as a prison commandant.

By May 1972, Lon Nol's US-backed republic was under siege. Apart from a few strips of road linking the provincial capitals, the towns and cities were surrounded. Refugees who had escaped the fighting and bombing camped out in the streets. The towns became little more than garrisons supplied by air lifts.

Far from the front lines, in Amleang, Duch set up his first prison, code-named 'M-13'. A second prison, 'M-99', was also established two years later in the nearby Oral district, closer to the mountains, also under his command.

But it was in M-13 that he spent most of his time.

Amleang was considered a cradle of the revolution, ideal for Duch to begin the task of ridding Khmer Rouge ranks of 'enemies'. It was remote, sparsely populated and far from the prying eyes of the distrusted North Vietnamese. Here he operated with his two deputies, Comrade Chan, whom Duch had been imprisoned with, and Comrade Pon; the same leadership that would later run Tuol Sleng. He ran his camp like a strict abbot of a forest monastery. His subordinates both feared and respected him. Many of them were from the surrounding villages. The area was popu-lated by 'base people', considered by the Khmer Rouge the backbone of their revolution. Many of the staff were related to one another, and many were children.

How many people were killed in M-13 and M-99 will never be known. It is likely that the final death toll for both reached somewhere in the region of 20,000. It could be more. Duch kept a few prisoners alive to work in the service of the prison and several managed to escape. And at least another dozen survived their ordeal. One of them was Ham In.

Sokheang and I travelled from Phnom Penh and found his home not far from Amleang in nearby Kompong Speu province. Sokheang accompanied me on numerous trips to trace Duch's life and with his background in human-rights investigations he proved invaluable. He would help me frame my questions more obliquely; direct questioning could put people on their guard. He knew how to put people at ease and win their trust.

Ham In was lying on a small rattan bed in front of his house when we arrived. The house, little more than a hut, was spotless and shaded by several sugar and coconut palms. He pulled himself up with slow movements that seemed to require an enormous effort. Sitting upright in a crisp white shirt and black fisherman's trousers, he greeted us with a *sompeah* and motioned for us to sit next to him. The whites of his penetrating eyes glowed yellow against his dark skin. His fingers were like the twigs of an apple tree. He had malaria, he told us, a faint smile passing across his handsome face.

Ham In had joined the Khmer Rouge in 1971 as part of a mobile theatre group that toured the area, rallying the troops with patriotic songs and stories. As a musician he played the Khmer violin with his cousin, who was chief of the group. Two years later the group was disbanded, because all healthy young men were now needed at the front. He was then sent with his cousin to 'the Special Zone' that surrounded Phnom Penh, where he joined an artillery unit. One day, in 1973, as he was delivering ammunition, he found four soldiers with AK-47s slung over their shoulders, waiting. They grabbed his hands and tied them behind his back then led him away. 'They told me that I was a spy,' he said.

He was taken with six others, including a cousin and two women. Ham In was sick at the time and couldn't walk fast. 'But,' he said, 'I wasn't afraid because I hadn't done anything wrong.' He began to fear for his life when the soldiers threatened and beat him to hurry him up. Clouded by malaria, he wracked his brain trying to remember what he had done.

After a day and a night they arrived at a riverbank. The soldiers radioed ahead. They sat and waited. Then four armed guards appeared dressed in black, carrying carbines, grenades and AK-47s. The prisoners were handed over to them and they continued their journey. The following morning, just before midday, they arrived at M-13.

The camp was a series of thatch huts surrounded by a fence of bamboo. Duch was there when Ham In and the others were brought in. 'What have I done wrong? Why have I been arrested?' pleaded In. Duch ignored him and walked away. That was the first time that he met him.

Then, without warning, the young guards seized him from behind and tied his hands to a length of rope. They dragged him over to an iron bar and hoisted him up by his hands. His feet were 10cm from the ground. 'It was agony,' he said. 'If you cried they'd hit you with the barrels of their guns.' Most people were suspended for a day, sometimes two. But Ham In was lucky; his ordeal only lasted an hour. He was cut down and tied by his ankle to a post in the open and left there. He lifted his trouser leg and showed me the dark rings around his shins and his wrists. That night the rains came and he sat in the downpour, shivering. From his post he watched as Duch walked around the camp inspecting the prisoners.

Some, like Ham In, were tied to posts, others shackled together in bunkers covered with a roof of leaves. An armed guard sat nearby. There were also individual foxholes. In the larger ones the prisoners, who had been stripped, were linked together by a pole of bamboo.

He never saw Duch give any orders. The guards knew exactly what to do. The prison was well organised and the guards disciplined. Many of them were children of twelve or thirteen, some as young as seven. They were considered more trustworthy than their elders, unpolluted by the old ways. These children had been forcibly separated from their parents and the Organisation became their only family. They became fanatical, blind leaders of the revolution, following every order to the letter, no matter how absurd or brutal. Here in M-13 they were put to deadly effect. The younger Khmer Rouge routinely abused the prisoners with sticks and stones and kicked them as they passed by. When prisoners confessed it was usually the children who did the beating, Ham In said. Occasionally Duch stood nearby, looking on impassively. They gave little food to the prisoners, usually very small amounts of rice porridge, twice a day, but never enough to drink. On his first day they gave him nothing.

'Day and night we heard crying and screams,' Ham In said. There were many prisoners and many forms of torture. They used a mallet to beat people on the shins, on the back, on the throat. Sometimes they would take the resin from a torch and put the flame near and drip it on to the body. The denials of accusations infuriated the guards and they often beat prisoners until they were unconscious. In saw them mix *prahoc*, fish sauce, and detergent in water and force it down prisoners' throats. There was one particular torture called 'the Victory pole' where four people would be tied together, their backs to the pole, facing opposite directions. Then a guard would shoot one in the head covering the others in blood and brains.

At this point Sokheang had to break for a moment. Even with his extensive experience investigating abuse in prisons he found it difficult to listen to Ham In's recollections.

Duch never received any training for his work. Vorn Vet, Duch's superior, had given him some vague instructions on the use of plastic bags over people's heads, but said he wasn't experienced in such matters and told Duch that it was up to him how best to extract confessions. Although a rigorous discipline was in place in M-13, there was no exact science to the torture. It was an experimental school of brutality. Much of the time Duch could be seen inspecting his prison, observing the methods employed by his subordinates.

After more than a month at the prison camp, it was Ham In's turn for interrogation. By now he was petrified. Duch walked over and began by asking him when he was born. 1954, he replied, 'The year of the horse.'

'Oh, so was I,' replied Duch. 'People born in this year were destined to spend time in jail.' He smiled. He told Ham In that if he spied on the other prisoners for him that he would release him. Ham In agreed. It was another two years before Ham In was finally free, only to walk out into the Democratic Kampuchea of Pol Pot.

In all the time Ham In was captive he was never beaten. He was known to many of the guards and this is probably what saved him. They had grown up in the same village not far away and the Khmer Rouge didn't want the locals to turn against them. After all it was in the name of the 'base people' that the revolution was being made. Duch understood this. After three months Ham In was put to work. They took off his handcuffs and sent him to the rice fields for a season. 'That's how I could see what was going on.'

Much of what Ham In learned during his captivity came from overhearing snippets of conversation. Sometimes he was told directly by the guards. He overheard the self-criticism sessions where the guards 'confessed' their flaws in front of the group. The child comrades were ordered to execute two people a day and were often criticised if they failed to meet their quota.

There were five guards at the execution sites. Two guards tied the rope, two took them to the pit, and one carried out the execution. 'One night,' Ham In told me, 'they killed 200 people. They blindfolded them and tied rope around their necks and tightened it and used the bayonet to cut their arteries.' He pointed a stiff finger to his neck. It was hard work, he said. The guards had to stop to rest, eating their meals feet away from their victims' bodies. 'It took two days and one night continuously,' Ham In said.

Duch was always busy, always rushing about, said Ham In. He hardly ever slept. In never saw Duch kill anyone himself. But he did see him beat people. Duch often sent him to fetch his favourite dessert with eggs and sugar. It was made by the wife of Duch's deputy, Comrade Chan.

By April 1975, the camp was dismantled and the area abandoned. Ham In was sent beneath the mountains to work in M-99 with two others. To this day Ham In still has no idea why he was arrested. Under Duch's orders a hundred remaining prisoners at M-13 were then forced to dig their own graves and executed.

Sokheang and I turned off Route 5 and proceeded along a wide rusty laterite road due west toward the Cardamom Mountains. On either side we passed neatly mapped fields ringed with sugar palms and islets of bamboo as far as the eye could see. Beside the road, in between the open stretches, clusters of houses sat in the shade, blankets of white and pink bougainvillea crept along the fences. The cultivated land gradually gave way to wilder terrain of Keluak trees and Lontar palms and eventually we came to the village of Thmar Kep. Sokheang parked the car beside a house under which an old man sat in the shade.

Yes, he said, he remembered Duch. He then offered to take us to the site, further south. We followed him out into the bush, leaving the village behind us.

In silence we walked in Indian file, the old man leading the way, Sokheang after him and me behind. It was a fresh morning in the cool season and the heat had yet to penetrate the breeze. We crossed a number of dried-up streams and clearings, above us a spotless sky of deep blue. The trees were young and straight. Sweat trickled down my brow, soaking my hair. My pulse throbbed in my ears. The old man's pace never faltered; he knew exactly where he was going.

Eventually we came to the meeting of two cart tracks in the stony ground. We sat in the shade of a thicket and drank the water from our bottles as the bamboo groaned and creaked above us. This was Duch's first prison, M-13.

It was an obvious location, among the 'base people' and far from the towns and cities. Save the occasional air attack it was sufficiently behind the lines for the establishment of a prison. It was here that Comrade Duch met a local woman who became his wife. Chhim Sophal, or Rom, had been a dressmaker from a village not far away. She later worked in a hospital in Phnom Penh and bore him four children, one girl and three boys. Unlike Duch, she was from real Khmer peasant stock.

Many cadres married ethnic Khmers from what they called the 'old' or 'base people', especially those, like Duch, who were of mixed parentage. It served to bolster their revolutionary credentials, demonstrating their dedication to the cause, and forged a closer link with the peasants in the area.

Ahead of us was the *chhlik* tree, its large torso surrounded by elephant grass that swayed in the wind. The old man showed me the broken bark from a plane attack from nearly thirty years ago. It was here in 1971 that the French scholar François Bizot was taken with his two Khmer assistants when he was captured by the Khmer Rouge. He was held for three months and interrogated by Comrade Duch. It had been under this tree that Bizot had been held, chained to a post.

The farmer, now with his faded *krama* on his head, told

us that no-one had been allowed to come near here at the time. The whole area had been completely overrun by the Khmer Rouge by 1974.

Back at the village we sat with him under his house in the shade and had lunch. Sokheang said it was quite possible that the people here had been involved in the prison. I looked around. The houses were solid structures of hard wood and roofed with tiles, some thatched. Many of them had survived the war.

In 1973, M-13 had moved to a location further north of the road, known as Trapeang Chrab. It was the second location to which Ham In had been taken. We drove down a cart track through the bamboo. Having parked the car in the shade we walked down to the river's edge and waded through the clear waters. On the other bank we clambered up to some fields where farmers were harvesting their rice. They stopped and stood upright, smiling as we passed. A toddler playing with the stalks took one look at me, froze in terror and then ran to bury his face in his mother's legs. We carried on to the cluster of trees that lined the banks of the river at the end of the golden fields, passing a tall sugar palm that stood bolt upright like a pillar in the middle of a dyke. And then, at the wood's edge, the old man stopped.

Here the prisoners were held in holes in the ground, he told us, shackled together with no shelter from the elements. The large bamboo fence that had surrounded the prison had been three metres high. He pointed out a hollow where the earth had sunk, filled with thin, tall grass. It was a grave. There were several mass graves around us. We squatted down on the edge of one near the riverbank.

During a particularly heavy monsoon downpour the river had burst its banks and flooded the hole where several prisoners had been shackled. They drowned. The Khmer Rouge simply filled it in. Sokheang pointed out that the grass still grew higher in these areas. Passing thickets of large bamboo, I clambered down to the water's edge. It was quiet as the river meandered lazily past; clear waters rippled and flicked light on to the sandy bed. The stippled water spread out before me in a carpet of shade that disappeared with the current into a tunnel of leaves.

Returning I asked how, if this was a secret prison, did the old man know of its existence. 'The pigs found it,' he replied. 'The smell of the bodies was bad. They were eating them.' After that people were too afraid to come near, believing that it was haunted by the spirits of those who had died here. We gazed into the sandy earth below. I imagined the bones of the people still shackled together resting beneath us as we sat at the edge of the sunken hollow.

While Duch was weeding out enemies and perfecting methods of interrogation, in the winter of 1971 Sokheang had arrived in Paris. He enrolled in a postgraduate course in agricultural development at the Institut de Développement Economique et Social at the University of Paris.

The Khmer students in Paris were split between those who supported the US-backed regime in Phnom Penh and those who supported Sihanouk's resistance, the Khmer Rouge. France had not officially recognised Sihanouk's resistance, or FUNK (Front d'Union Nationale du Kampuchea), but had allowed a mission to be set up whilst still maintaining full diplomatic relations with the regime in Phnom Penh. The two groups vied for supporters among the new arrivals. 'The resistance was very kind to us, they helped us as though we were family,' said Sokheang. Several of them were old friends from Cambodia.

The supporters of the resistance realised that Sokheang was sympathetic and did their best to recruit him and his friends. It didn't prove too difficult. 'At that time you couldn't be neutral,' he said. It was here that he met Ong Thong Houeng or Ho, who had arrived in 1965. Ho was now working for the mission of FUNK and Sokheang began to make regular visits. They forged a friendship that was to last more than thirty years.

Sokheang was popular among his contemporaries and his room had become an informal meeting place for students sympathetic to the cause. There they cooked and ate together, debating politics well into the small hours. They would often wake late in the day before trawling the second-hand bookshops of Paris in search of bargains. They were *les révolutionnaires de salon*, bourgeois revolutionaries. 'We were *bons vivants*, we discussed with each other, we went out to Chinese restaurants, which were expensive at that time, we went to the cinema,' he said. During the summer holidays they went to the beach at Mont-Saint-Michel or to Ile d'Eurée on the Mediterranean, they visited the Louvre and the Musée de l'Homme. 'But our minds were always with the struggle against American imperialism.'

They saw themselves as *intellectuels engagés* and believed that they were there to put their minds to practical use. 'We talked about our desire to have a just Cambodia for everyone, for all people to be treated with the same consideration regardless of rank.' They organised meetings, conferences and distributed propaganda, always on the lookout for support for their cause. 'Without declaring it, I had

become a de facto member of FUNK – I was never asked
to sign any paper,' he explained, 'but they always considered me their own.'

Day by day, the situation in Cambodia was worsening.
Through the few letters Sokheang received from his family
and the reports in the papers and on the radio, he knew
security in the capital was degenerating and conditions
were very hard. The corruption had reached mammoth
proportions and the repression had become more heavy-
handed than before. In Phnom Penh student demonstrations against Lon Nol's regime continued. Grenades were
lobbed in public places by supporters of the revolution,
in cinemas and markets, killing and maiming dozens.
Sokheang and his friends viewed the situation with a helpless horror.

One cold January night in 1973, the war came to Paris.
The polarisation of political belief had reached its peak at
the Pavilion du Cambodge, where all the Khmer students
were housed. A supporter of the resistance was denounced
as a spy for the other side and told to leave the group.
He refused to go. Word got around quickly and violence
broke out between supporters of the resistance and
supporters of Lon Nol. Then one student was accidentally
killed and the Pavilion erupted.

Sokheang heard screams and shouts from his room on
the second floor. There he stayed with his friends as the
sounds of fighting echoed down the corridors. It had been
a minority that had been involved in the violence, those
students that were, Sokheang said drily, 'the real fighters,
the real guerrillas'.

Meanwhile, outside in the dark, riot police had
surrounded the grounds. They waited for daybreak before
storming the building. They broke down Sokheang's door

and threw him against the wall, hitting him with a baton. He was then dragged outside with hundreds of others, bundled into a police van and rushed through the sleepy streets of Paris, sirens blaring.

Sokheang never did finish his studies. His application for a second scholarship was turned down. His political affiliations were well known and Lon Nol's embassy in Paris had almost certainly informed Phnom Penh. 'I was afraid to return to Phnom Penh – I was sure I would be in trouble,' he said, blaming government spies. Without a scholarship to support him he was forced to work in a Chinese restaurant washing dishes.

Sokheang pondered his options. China had just opened the door to foreign students. He was becoming increasingly restless. 'I began to dream of returning to Phnom Penh, to be with my family . . . serve the country.' Seeing it as the first step towards returning home, he applied to study in Beijing. On Christmas Eve, 1973, he boarded a plane with twelve other Cambodian students and left for Beijing, where he would spend just over a year.

On arrival in Beijing Sokheang and the others were received by the FUNK or Khmer Rouge embassy staff and sent to the Foreign Language Institute. Sokheang joined the FUNK embassy, working in the department of information and propaganda. All the time he was thinking about his homeland and when he might return.

The decision to return home was for many Khmer students a fatal mistake. Many were taken directly to Tuol Sleng. Later, quite by accident, I came across a photograph of a group of Cambodians in China in the early seventies. There at the back of the group was Sokheang, a Mao cap pulled over his head and a *krama* tucked tightly around his neck. Unlike most formal group portraits, particularly from China, many of them were smiling at the camera. It was clearly cold. There were no leaves on the trees and everyone was wrapped up. When I showed it to him he looked intently at the people that stared back. 'Where did you get this?' he asked. As he looked a smile crept across his face. Then almost as soon as it had appeared, it was gone. He pointed out Keat Chhon, now the Minister of Economics and Finance in the current government.

Out of the thirty-six in the photograph only nine had survived.

To most Khmer Rouge the existence of the Communist Party was still a closely guarded secret. Many believed that they were fighting to restore Sihanouk to his rightful seat of power, something that was reinforced when Sihanouk made a much-publicised visit to the liberated zones.

There was Sihanouk in the photographs, dressed in immaculate Khmer Rouge garb, posing next to the leaders of the movement. It was the first time that people had caught a glimpse of the resistance leaders, all dressed in black with their chequered *krama* and Ho Chi Minh sandals. They treated Sihanouk like a long-lost brother. Several years before, Khieu Samphan a left-wing MP and minister, had been attacked and stripped by Sihanouk's police in the streets of Phnom Penh. It was widely believed that the Prince had had him murdered. Now he was pictured embracing a grinning Khieu Samphan.

Sihanouk saw the Khmer Rouge as a way back to head his country. However, the Khmer Rouge had other plans for him. They knew the value of this propaganda coup and had no intention of placing him in a position of power. What lay behind the smiles and the hugs of these erstwhile enemies was impossible to gauge.

Life in the liberated zones was something of a mystery. Rumours abounded of brutality away from the battlefield, of executions, mass reorganisations and forced marriages. No journalist had survived an encounter with the Khmer Rouge and what went on behind the front lines in the liberated zones was the subject of much fevered speculation.

What little information did trickle out depicted a hard and regimented life, subject to regular attacks from the air. When the Khmer Rouge captured Oudong, the old royal capital, they destroyed what was left of the town, evacuated the population and executed all those associated with the government. The future did not bode well for Cambodia.

Atrocities were commonplace and there were reports of ritualised cannibalism among soldiers of both sides. Some Cambodians believe that to cut out and eat the liver of a dead opponent gives them the strength of the enemy and renders soldiers impervious to harm. They wore protective amulets, magical tattoos and scarves full of Buddha images and charms to protect them against harm. Some were believed to be bullet-proof.

The fighting was heavy. The peasants fought a well equipped, US-backed army with little more than small arms, mortars and artillery. With the photographs of their prince on their side, they were assured of the justice of their cause.

By April 1975 refugees had swollen Phnom Penh's population from just under 600,000 to some two million. The city was being kept alive with a life support of river convoys of aid and food from the Americans as rockets screamed into the suburbs. The Khmer Rouge were now only a few kilometres outside the city.

Him Huy was a young peasant boy of sixteen when he was

forced to 'volunteer' to fight in the Khmer Rouge. Huy was from a small village south-east of the capital and had been recruited for the Special Zone which surrounded Phnom Penh. Like most recruits, he had little understanding of the world beyond his village when he was sent to fight. Although his village was just a two-hour drive from the capital, he had only ever seen cars from a distance and he had no experience of war. 'I was terrified, I had no idea what bullets were,' he said. At the beginning of the 1975 dry season, he took part in the final assault on Phnom Penh.

The troops crossed the Tonle Bati River downstream from the capital and went along the abandoned villages that lined the banks. They were close to the enemy and the bombardment had been heavy. Artillery still rumbled ahead of them as planes dived and circled. They were ordered to dismantle the abandoned houses and retrieve the wood to make trenches. The soil was hard and they spent the whole night digging. There were three people per trench and when the attack began, they rarely saw who they were firing at and fired wildly over their heads.

Young and inexperienced, Huy moved slowly with the others towards the capital, where he joined a reconnaissance unit. They sustained heavy losses and the fighting became so concentrated that within three battles they had lost practically everyone. 'They died one after another,' he said. As one of the few survivors Huy rose through the ranks of his team quickly.

Eventually they arrived on the outskirts of Phnom Penh. The fighting became intense as Lon Nol's troops dug in to hold back the advance of the Khmer Rouge for as long as they could. Eventually they broke through and the remaining government soldiers fled.

Phnom Penh was now totally cut off. The supply convoys

could no longer get through and the airport had been overrun. On 12 April the Americans evacuated their embassy staff by helicopter. Lon Nol fled to Hawaii, abandoning the country he had committed to war. The city was now heaving with refugees cowering from the bombardment and rocket attacks. Food was rapidly becoming scarce and malnutrition and dysentery were widespread. In a desperate attempt to prevent the inevitable, more and more children were handed weapons and sent to fight.

16 April was a day of heavy shelling. There were explosions all over the city as rockets flew overhead. The orange flames of fires licked the thick black smoke that poured into the sky like ink in water. That evening Huy and his men were cautiously making their way through the abandoned streets when they were suddenly attacked from above. They scattered. Grenades were being lobbed at them and there was a hail of bullets from the buildings. Huy saw several of his comrades cut in two by gunfire. He himself was hit in the leg. He managed to crawl under a small house nearby. Early the following morning more Khmer Rouge units came forward and found him lying in a pool of his own blood. They sent him off to a field hospital. 'I only just escaped with my life,' he said.

In April 1975, Sokheang finally had his chance to return home. 'Victory was imminent, but we weren't sure when,' he said. They were warned that the situation was still very unpredictable and dangerous and told to prepare for the worst. This didn't deter him in the least – he was too excited at the prospect of seeing his family to consider the potential dangers. He was to be sent with a Chinese aid convoy for the resistance along with three of his comrades, first by train to the Vietnamese border and then by truck for the remainder of the journey. At the border they were met by a colonel in the North Vietnamese army. They then began the long arduous journey into Laos and down the Ho Chi Minh trail to Cambodia.

There were more than 200 trucks in the convoy. In the forests of Laos it was hot and the roads were dusty. They skirted the edge of ravines and forded rivers. There were Vietnamese soldiers everywhere and occasionally they passed the wreckage of military vehicles. One particularly hot day they stopped for a break in the forest in the early afternoon. Sokheang clambered down with a small radio he had picked up in Beijing and, squatting at the side of the track, listened for the news. He tuned into Khmer Rouge radio and heard the announcement: Phnom Penh had been liberated. It was 17 April 1975.

Five days later, having lumbered over mountain passes and through jungle devastated by B-52's, they arrived at the Cambodian frontier, but it was too late to cross. That night, barely able to contain his excitement, Sokheang found it difficult to sleep. There it was, on the other side of a small river, so tantalisingly close: the homeland he had left four years before.

In April of 1975, Comrade Duch and his men followed on the heels of the revolutionary forces to Phnom Penh. There Duch helped clear the capital of soldiers of the defeated Lon Nol government.

For several months the *Santebal*, or secret police, came under the code name Office 15, with prisons throughout the abandoned capital, from the national police head-quarters south of the new market to Prey Sar prison outside the city to Ta Khmau in the south. At Ta Khmau, Cambodia's only psychiatric hospital was taken over and used as a prison. When the Khmer Rouge advanced on their final push to take Phnom Penh, they burst into the hospital, shooting open the doors and dispersing the patients.

Following the Khmer Rouge victory, Comrade Duch visited his home while on his way to Siem Reap. He arrived in a small Honda car with a few Khmer Rouge bodyguards, all of them teenagers dressed in black carrying AK-47s. He stayed just one night. Word soon spread and there was much excitement among the people when they heard of his arrival. That evening, they gathered around him as he told the assembled neighbours that a new era had dawned and that the future held great promise. 'Soon, we will have schools and hospitals in the cooperative of our commune,' he said. 'It will be easy for us.' He talked of a better life under the Khmer Rouge. They sat and listened attentively. One neighbour and friend of the family had talked with him afterwards and told him that life had been quite hard for them. Duch told him not to worry, that soon the Organisation would provide them with all their needs.

There was nothing that revealed his new role as Pol Pot's chief executioner. And he gave no indication of the horrors that were to come.

CHAPTER 7

Democratic Kampuchea

IN 1975, A new country was born, Democratic Kampuchea, and with it, a new society. The Khmer Rouge were going to return Cambodia to the ancient glories of the lost Khmer empire. Under the guise of a radical communist revolution the construction of a massive irrigation system was to be the first step to a great agrarian society based on rice production.

The Khmer Rouge drove the population hard; they were treated as little more than slaves. In some areas the people were given just five hours rest from labouring in the fields. The work was broken up with three meals of rice gruel that lasted twenty minutes, little more than a few grains of rice in soupy water. In the evenings they would be made to attend political lectures where they were told of the glories of their new revolution.

As Democratic Kampuchea turned the clocks back there were to be no towns, no money, no cars, no religion, no holidays, no schools. In the new society all traces of individuality were to be eradicated. Families were split up, men and women were segregated, the women had to cut short their hair and everyone had to wear black. There was to be no love except love for the Organisation and the nation, and all marriages had to be approved – many were forced. Aside from China, communication with the outside world was severed. The country was plunged into a world of surveillance and fear. Those in any way connected with the old regime were herded into trucks and taken to be executed. The middle classes and the educated from the former regime were singled out together with teachers, students, doctors, engineers, lawyers, professors, bankers, dancers and businessmen. Children were separated from their parents, indoctrinated and taught to spy on their mothers and fathers, reporting back to the cadre with information about what their family had been talking about. Then their parents would disappear.

Cambodia was to be truly independent and self-sufficient. All things foreign were forbidden. In the empty cities, air conditioners, refrigerators, fire engines, ambulances, television sets were all branded 'reactionary' or 'alien' and were gathered from all over Phnom Penh and tossed into ditches or piled up and left to bake in the heat.

It was all part of Pol Pot's vision. With one great leap, a classless society was to arise from the ashes of the old. Cambodia was to become the world's most progressive and radical communist revolution. And the way that this was to be achieved was simple: murder, on a scale never before seen in history. A prison network spread like a cobweb across the country, centred at the headquarters of 'S-21', and at its helm was Comrade Duch.

It had been exactly five years since Duch had been in Phnom Penh. Now in 1975, the grounds of his old *lycée* had been planted with coconut trees and vegetables. The deserted sports field was planted with sugar cane. Down beside the river the temple which he had stayed in as a student no longer echoed with the rhythmic chant of the monks, their quarters abandoned. He wandered about the streets and explored some of the buildings. Now he could go anywhere he wanted. It was quiet. In one building he came across a book entitled *La Torture*, by Alec Mellor, detailing the emergence of torture in modern France. Duch took it with him. The book was later kept in the room used for the interrogation of foreigners at Tuol Sleng.

While Duch walked through the streets of the capital, Sokheang crossed the small river from Laos into his liberated homeland. After a journey by boat down the Mekong they eventually arrived at a new camp, known as B-20, which had been designated as a kind of assembly point and liaison office for returning Khmer Rouge supporters. They had been classified as 'the group of intellectuals'. They were then moved to B-16. All the camps in the area came under the direct supervision of the Communist Party of Kampuchea, producing food, and providing logistical support as well as stockpiling ammunition, salt and *prahok*, or fish paste. Sokheang's group was comprised of students and diplomats as well as ministers of what had been the resistance – the Khmer Rouge's political and diplomatic front. They had returned from Czechoslovakia, France, East Germany, Yugoslavia and North Korea. They were told to take new revolutionary names. Sokheang took the name Comrade Yuth, from *Prayuth*, which means combat.

After several days of whispered speculation about their future they were called to a meeting. Comrade Phum addressed the group. He explained the political situation to them, how Phnom Penh had been taken, the evacuation and what was happening throughout the country. What fate awaited them, however, remained a mystery – they were told nothing. Comrade Phum suggested that they go to the remote province of Preah Vihear. They all agreed.

They had to wait for several days before enough cars could be assembled for the journey. By the time the convoy been arranged, Sokheang was suffering cold sweats and fevers. He had come down with malaria.

They began the journey to Preah Vihear in the afternoon when the heat was at its most unforgiving. The fields were deserted and the road virtually empty as they rumbled slowly through the scorched landscape. He was shocked. 'Everywhere I looked I saw the devastation left by the war,' he said. But he was too sick to take much in. When they got to Kompong Thom at dusk, there wasn't a soul to be seen. Sokheang retired with a raging fever. The following morning they continued north to Preah Vihear province. Eventually they came to the small town of Rovieng, their final destination.

Rovieng had been liberated earlier in the war. It was an area of 'base people' and considered something of a model region. Here Sokheang and his comrades were well received. Soon after, Sokheang had become delirious and had to be hospitalised. He was taken to the zone hospital where he was kept for just over a month, until he had made a complete recovery.

The young nurses were supervised by older, more experienced personnel, 'and the food was better than at the cooperatives,' he said. There was a large stock of western medicine and even traditional massage for patients. It was very different from hospitals in other parts of the country, where staff, most of whom were teenagers, had little or no training. While peasant children carried out operations, real doctors tilled in the fields, desperately trying to conceal their identities.

Molyda Szymusiak, who wrote a book of her experiences at the time, depicted a hospital she was brought to in Battambang province as a dark room full of the dying that reeked of decay and excrement. She described how a swollen corpse was moved from a bamboo bed to make way for her. The day nurse, a child, administered the same injection of an unspecified fluid to all the patients regardless of their complaint. On being given her shot, Molyda immediately felt her heart race and she fell unconscious. The Khmer Rouge doctors had been centrally appointed and displayed a cruel indifference towards the sick. Cures seemed experimental. Patients were bombarded day and night with loud revolutionary music. The smell of death hung in the air like a pall as corpses were buried in shallow graves nearby.

After being discharged from hospital, Sokheang was dispatched with several others to work alongside the 'base people' in the fields. They also made trips to the mountain to look for bamboo and timber. Life was hard, 'but the people were very good with us,' he said. The local people weren't exactly sure who these people in new revolutionary clothing were. And no-one dared ask. They knew by the way they spoke they weren't *tomada* or ordinary. 'We later learned that the people were informed that we were guests of the Organisation,' said Sokheang.

Sokheang made a strong impression on his new hosts. He was more vocal in his support than the others and spoke up during political seminars and in the self-criticism sessions. So forthright and determined was he that he earned the name *Chiv thos*, meaning a new kind of person, a revolutionary of the future.

We had returned to Sokheang's balcony, *le salon* where, with supplies of cigarettes and Thai beer, we talked into the night. 'There are two times in my life that I can remember that I was very, very happy,' he began. 'The first time was when I got my first diploma, my first degree. The second time was when I learned about the victory of April 17. Because I thought that this was a beginning. So what I had dreamt of before could be realised. 'My worst moment during Khmer Rouge time was at the beginning, when I had just arrived.' He had expected to go directly to Phnom Penh to be reunited with his family, believing that they would have a good life together, serving the people and the revolution. But instead of being able to put to use what he had learned abroad, he was put to work as a labourer.

He licked the length of his cigarette and lit up. 'I was *so* upset when I arrived, faced the reality of the revolution,' he said. 'I mean the whole thing was not like I expected when I was Paris or Beijing.

'I realised that our expectations were wrong, completely wrong. I had no idea where my family was.' He slapped his thigh. 'Of course we were prepared to face difficulties. But they sent us to the jungle! This was the first thing that was unacceptable. This wasn't what we were led to believe would happen, at least they have to put us in a safe place with sufficient food with everything, with . . .' he rubbed his thumb and forefinger repeatedly as if reaching for the words, 'the *minimum* necessary.' He only learned of the evacuation of the towns and cities on his trusty radio. 'My heart sank when I heard this.' They were now under the direct control of the Organisation and they knew that they had to be careful. He never dared ask to be reunited with his family. I asked him why not.

'Because we tested the atmosphere . . .' he said. 'The atmosphere in each camp was quiet, like a cemetery. People always worked quietly on the fields.'

Why didn't he feel free to talk since they were so-called 'guests' of the revolution?

'At every step we had to be very, very careful.'

Although they lived a privileged life in comparison to the majority of the population, although not explicit, the warning signs were all around, in the tone of voice, in the absence of any rules or regulations. The atmosphere was tense and intimidating. 'It took me more than a year to come to terms with it and let it go. But I still believed that it couldn't go on like that for ever,' said Sokheang, 'that it would change one day.' But it was too late, the borders were sealed and everyone was being closely watched.

Eight months after his arrival in Cambodia, Sokheang was told to gather his belongings. The Organisation had ordered him to go to Phnom Penh.

Back in Paris others felt the fear too. A year after the Khmer Rouge victory Ho, Sokheang's old friend from his student days in France, was still working at the embassy there. Missing his wife who had already returned, he began to make the necessary arrangements to go back to Cambodia. But he was unsure. 'I couldn't make up my mind at first,' he said one afternoon in Phnom Penh. 'I didn't have any news from her and had many questions in my mind.' Already there were a few refugees in Paris, 'and there were rumours'.

There were about forty people on board the otherwise

empty plane. As it came to a halt on the airstrip he peered through the window. It was deserted. The carcasses of Lon Nol planes lay where they had been destroyed. Two cadres from the Ministry of Foreign Affairs appeared to meet him. 'It was a very cold and oppressive atmosphere,' he said. 'They wore black and immediately I knew there was something wrong.' Their passports were taken from them and thrown in a bin in front of them. Then, he said, 'I felt it was too late.'

Another group who arrived at the airport were taken directly to Tuol Sleng because, declared Ieng Sary, the Khmer Rouge Foreign Minister, they 'had come back from outside the country and thus are separated from the movement'.

Just as the stone faces of the great protector, Jayavarman VII, had looked down upon his subjects, the faceless Organisation monitored the population of Democratic Kampuchea. Through fear and secrecy the Khmer Rouge bound the people in mute obedience. One by one, as they toiled away in the fields, they began to disappear. And some of them were sent to Phnom Penh, the domain of the Higher Organisation, and to Comrade Duch.

CHAPTER 8

The Perfect Institution

I RETURNED TO Tuol Sleng museum. Amputees, victims of landmines, now guarded the entrance to the prison where armed sentries in black had once stood. In place of the Chinese covered trucks that unloaded their cargo of prisoners, buses of tourists now hummed happily away. Holiday-makers were shepherded through the gates by their Cambodian tour guides. The amputees hobbled up on their crutches to greet them with their caps in their hands.

When Duch had been commandant, the prisoners were usually brought in at night, bound at the elbows, ropes joining them together at the neck. The trucks were high off the ground and the prisoners were dragged out, falling hard on the earth below. They were welcomed with screams, kicks and rifle butts that rushed out at them from the darkness.

Now tourists awkwardly passed out money to the assembled beggars. The amputees and motorbike taxis that hovered around the entrance had long given up on me as a regular visitor and cheerfully waved me though.

Soursdei bong, Soksabay Jia te? (Hello brother, how are you?) they would ask. And I would reply in Khmer gibberish, *Saisabok, akun bong bros* (I'm well very, thanks brothers). No matter how many times I said this, they would always crumple under a fit of giggles. It became a kind of ritual between us. I wandered into the main *sala* where tourists looked at their museum brochures and sipped Pepsi.

A *sala* was an open hall with a raised floor, usually located on the edge of the village or in the grounds of the temple, where meetings were held. When the Khmer Rouge were in power, these *salas* were used for political seminars and for self-criticism sessions in which people were forced to confess to imaginary crimes in front of assembled villagers. In 1998, when Pol Pot was denounced by his own people, the event took place in an open hall surrounded by Khmer Rouge villagers.

Here in Tuol Sleng, the *sala* was used as an anteroom where the prisoners were registered. Terrified and disorientated, they had their blindfolds removed. A number was pinned to their chests and they were photographed. They were then stripped to their underclothes and hauled off to the cells. Sometimes Duch would be there, sometimes not.

Over the years, survivors and former members of staff of the prison have been interviewed, and together with the documents found in the prison, a clearer picture of its day-to-day operations has emerged.

Every morning, at 7 a.m., the day began with the raising of the Khmer Rouge flag in the compound of the prison. Almost all of the 300 staff members at the prison lined up to sing the Khmer Rouge national anthem. On occasion Duch was in attendance. It went as follows:

Bright red blood
which covers the towns and plains
Of Kampuchea, our motherland,
Sublime blood of workers and peasants,
Sublime blood of revolutionary men and women
fighters!
The blood changing into unrelenting hatred
And resolute struggle,
On April 17th, under the flag of the revolution,
Free from slavery!

Long live, long live the glorious April 17th!
Glorious victory with greater significance
Than the times of Angkor!

Then they would file out to the canteen near the gate,
passing underneath a sign erected above the entrance that
read, 'Fortify the spirit of the revolution! Be on your guard
against the strategy and tactics of the enemy so as to defend
the country the people and the party.'

After a breakfast of rice porridge, accompanied by revolutionary music played over loudspeakers, they would
disperse to their respective offices and the work would
begin.

At first, S-21 had been headed by In Lon, or Comrade
Nath, a zealous military commander from the elite Division
703. Duch was his deputy. Nath, also a native of Kompong
Thom, was subsequently reassigned to another post and
Duch took over as commandant. By May 1976, all the
prisons in the city had been relocated to the Lycée Tuol
Svay Prey in the southern part of the city. Here, among
the vacant villas of Phnom Penh's wealthier classes, the

imposing buildings of the former *lycée* were requisitioned to become the new headquarters of the Khmer Rouge secret police.

The 'S' in 'S-21' meant *santebal*, an amalgam of two words: *santisuk* meaning security, and *norkorbal* meaning police. It is not clear what the number signified.

Secrecy was central to the control of the population. In order to put into action Pol Pot's plan to move against potential enemies it was essential that no-one knew of the internal dynamics of his operation. Democratic Kampuchea had been divided into 'zones' which replaced the old provincial names and borders. Communes, villages and offices were given code names. The creation of S-21 was central to Pol Pot's plan. Apart from the Higher Organisation, the Khmer Rouge inner party, no-one knew of its existence, since the prison's purpose was for cleansing the ranks of the party itself. The leadership knew that if the location was known, they would have faced a rebellion that they would be unable to suppress.

At the prison itself, units were not permitted to associate with each other and all subordinates who had spouses working elsewhere in the city were sent to work in the prison to avoid any leaks. It was possible that the prisoners, who had been brought from all over the country, never knew that they were in the capital. They arrived at night with blindfolds and that was how they left.

In the cooperatives in the countryside, base people spied on the 'new' and neighbours on each other. No-one could be trusted. The slightest suspicion, based on rumour or innuendo, was enough to have someone taken away. Because of the rigid controls that were placed on the population by the Khmer Rouge and the constant shifting of the rules, people sought other ways to protect themselves. Many vied for position and influence. Revenge was often played out under other pretexts as all the petty jealousies and gossip, so typical of village life, took on a deadly potency. It was as if Cambodia had became one large commune. On occasion, the killing was carried out in public, to set an example. By the time the prisoners had arrived at the gates of S-21, they were both physically and emotionally broken and at the total mercy of their captors.

As a result, there are no stories of heroism from Tuol Sleng, only the desperate acts of those who had lost all hope: the prisoner who set himself alight with kerosene or the one who stabbed himself in the throat with the pen he was writing his confession with. Surrounded by barbed wire and electric fences, completely cut off from the outside world, escape was impossible. S-21 was the Khmer Rouge's best-kept secret. If S-21 didn't exist, then neither did the prisoners – for as soon as they had their picture taken they were as good as dead.

In fact one prisoner did escape from one of the prisons in the city, although it is not clear from where or indeed if he was later caught. There is one reference to the incident in a notebook found at the prison. 'Secrecy was broken,' it read. 'The secrecy we had maintained for the last three to four months has been pierced. If there is no secrecy then there can be no *Santebal*, the term has lost its meaning . . .' This most likely occurred before the prisons were consolidated at Tuol Sleng and might have been the reason for their relocation to the empty school buildings. It is also likely to have contributed to the removal of Comrade Nath, Duch's predecessor, and to Duch's promotion as commandant. Whatever the truth, the new prison had been planned well. S-21 had become a very effective machine where, as the surviving notes between the staff record, 'enemies' were 'processed' before being 'smashed to bits'.

As commandant, Duch set about creating the perfect institution. The prison was set back several streets from Monivong boulevard in an area out of bounds to other Khmer Rouge. The entire area had been sealed off by a large corrugated-iron wall with electrified razor wire running along the top. This time there were to be no escapes and no survivors.

At first the school buildings were used primarily for holding the prisoners. The interrogations were carried out in the deserted houses that surrounded the main compound. In one such house, a field hospital had been set up, close to the main gate. But, when it became apparent that interrogators were sexually abusing female prisoners, Duch converted several rooms within the school building for interrogation purposes. There he could keep an eye on his staff.

Above the individual cells, prisoners were held in the larger classrooms. The prison could accommodate up to 1,500 prisoners at a time and they were kept for anything between several weeks and six months before being executed.

Each balcony had large earthenware pots full of rainwater which prisoners washed with and drank from – when they were permitted. The buildings were covered in a net of barbed wire to prevent prisoners from throwing themselves off the balconies. Behind the main school buildings a workshop had been made in a large open area sealed by a fence of barbed wire. Telephones were installed in the main interrogation rooms and in the office at the entrance. Son Sen, or 'Brother 89', had resurfaced as the Khmer Rouge Minister of National Security and Defence, and it was to him that Duch answered. A regular visitor to the prison, Duch had a direct line to him in his office.

Many senior cadres at the prison had been teachers of Chinese extraction. One senior interrogator, Comrade Pon, had been a maths teacher. The lower ranks were mainly ethnic Khmers from remote areas. Those who had proven their worth were chosen to be interrogators and about half of those who had worked with Duch at M-13 continued to work in Tuol Sleng. The rest were drafted from the army.

Duch knew how to impress his superiors. He had found favour with Son Sen before and it was Son Sen who had appointed him to take over S-21. He was ideal for the job and kept a close eye on the day-to-day running of his prison. He possessed the fastidious mind of a senior bureaucrat, spending much of his time at his office corresponding with the Central Committee, going through confessions, constructing networks of enemies and indexing and signing execution orders. Often he would be seen walking purposefully from one building to the next, chain-smoking as he went. When important prisoners arrived he would supervise and partake in the interrogations, often with his chief interrogator Chan. Sometimes the interrogations continued through the night and into the following morning until what were regarded as the correct answers had been extracted and the formulas fitted.

Many executions took place within the prison perimeters but later, as the numbers increased, the execution site was moved to Choeung Ek, to what had been an old Chinese burial ground south of the capital. It was here, at night, that the majority of prisoners were dispatched. A generator provided the electricity to illuminate the work and Duch went regularly to observe the killing. Tuol Sleng was one of the few places in Democratic Kampuchea that possessed 24-hour electricity. It was illuminated at night by fluorescent strip lighting. The city and the rest of the country remained in darkness.

For the next three years Duch's life revolved around S-21. He lived nearby with his wife Comrade Rom, who worked as a nurse in the hospital further up Monivong Boulevard. They had at least three bodyguards. They lived on the second floor and the first floor was used as a meeting room for receiving high-ranking prisoners before they were taken to the prison. Next door was the meeting hall and behind that, the darkroom where all the photographs of the prisoners were produced. Duch had an assortment of cars, among them an old American Ford jeep, a Chinese jeep and several motorbikes.

The interior was spotless. There was a sofa and later a cot where Duch's daughter slept. There was also a cassette player on which he sometimes played revolutionary songs. On the wall hung a row of framed photographs of Lenin, Stalin, Marx, Engels, Mao and Pol Pot. Above the photographs were two flags side by side. The first was the Communist Party flag with the sickle and hammer and the second was the *tung padevat*, or revolutionary flag of Democratic Kampuchea, with three golden towers of Angkor Wat on a blood-red field.

Of the seven adults who escaped death at Tuol Sleng, only three are still alive. Chum Mey is one of them. Despite the fact that the recollections cause him great distress, he feels compelled to tell his story. He has been interviewed on countless occasions, even agreeing to pose blindfolded in his original cell for a photographer. He did all this in the hopes that one day the world would take notice and arrest those responsible. I wondered if really I had any right to intrude into his painful past yet again.

Chum Mey and I sat in the shadows of a quiet restaurant in Phnom Penh surrounded by potted plants and empty chairs. Outside the traffic roared past. A ceiling fan moved slowly above our heads. Small, white-haired and balding, Chum Mey was dressed in a freshly pressed pea-green shirt with a gold watch hanging loosely from his wrist. His round face wore a brittle expression and an anxiety that he did his best to conceal with a smile.

In 1975, following the crowds from Phnom Penh, Chum Mey and his wife were evacuated north along Route 5. Later he was transferred back to the city to continue work at a garment factory called 'K-9', not far from Tuol Sleng.

At K-9 Chum Mey was assigned to repair trucks, sewing machines, and other electrical equipment in a workshop attached to the garment factory where his wife was sent to work. In October 1978, a meeting was called and Chum Mey was told that the Organisation needed him to work repairing the trucks to be used for troops fighting the Vietnamese. The following morning he reported for duty with his tool kit and clothing. He was told to leave his case behind, that it would be sent for later.

He was then placed in the back of a small three-wheel truck with three soldiers and taken through the deserted streets. They turned a corner and were confronted with a corrugated-iron wall that crossed the road ahead of them. He was hauled out and immediately handcuffed. The soldiers tied his *krama* tightly over his eyes and his world was plunged into darkness. 'I thought that I would surely die,' he said. 'I knew that they would take me to be killed. I called them brothers. I told them: "Please, brothers, tell my wife not to wait for me and take care of my child."' His wife was pregnant at the time with their first child.

No sooner had he spoken than he felt a powerful blow from behind and he fell to the ground. 'Then, with my hands in handcuffs, they grabbed me by my hair.' He was taken inside S-21. They took off the blindfold. He was photographed, measured and stripped to his underwear. He was asked his full name, where he came from, how many brothers and sisters he had, what his parents did and where they lived. 'I didn't dare to look at their faces as I spoke,' he said. He was then hauled off to a cell. The cell was bare except for an old US ammunition case for a toilet. The walls were crudely built and frozen cement oozed from between the cracks. He stood there in shock while they shackled his ankles to a bar. And then they left him.

The conditions of most prisoners varied only in levels of discomfort. Above Chum Mey's cell on the next floor prisoners were held in large rooms. There prisoners were made to lie down in rows on the bare floor, their feet held together by a long iron bar. They were given two spoonfuls of watery rice gruel daily. Permission had to be granted from the guard if a prisoner wanted to change position. They had to ask the guard permission to relieve themselves in the bucket or ammunition box provided. The punishment for defecating or urinating without permission was sixty lashes of a whip. Many of the prisoners were sick and had little control over their bodily functions. Bathing was irregular and short, and disease was rife. Vann Nath, a survivor who was held in one of these rooms, told how the corpses of those who had died during the night wouldn't be taken away for at least ten hours.

There were no mosquito nets and the light which was kept on throughout the night attracted hundreds of insects. When the guard wasn't looking the prisoners tried to grab them and eat them. If the guards saw them they were beaten around the head with a rubber sandal until they spat them out.

Several hours after his arrest, Chum Mey was taken up to Room 04 on the first floor of building A. A typewriter sat on a table. There were bloodstains on the floor. They shackled his feet to a bedstead and the interrogation began.

'How many of you are there who joined the CIA and KGB? Who introduced you to them? Tell us everything, you motherfucker!' the interrogator screamed. Chum Mey pleaded with them, his hands together in a *sompeah*, begging them not to hurt him. He told them he was innocent, and that he'd never even heard of the KGB. They paced around the room. Then one of them rushed at him and beat him. Comrade Seng had sat on his head – a deep insult in Cambodia as the head is considered the most sacred part of the body – and yelled at him, 'If you refuse to confess I will beat you to death, you motherfucker!' On and on it went. Abuse, threats and beatings. He was certain that it was just a matter of time before they killed him. 'I was crying without any tears,' he said. 'I was going to jump from the balcony and kill myself, but I thought that I might only injure myself and become even more miserable if I couldn't die.'

After several hours, they dragged a broken and bleeding Chum Mey back to his cell. He was given watery porridge which he could only sip. It was the end of the rains and the beginning of the cool season and the temperature dropped dramatically at night. Virtually naked, Chum Mey shivered from fear and cold. He thought of the others from his factory who had disappeared and wondered whether they had been brought here. One of them must have implicated him. Whenever he heard footsteps he panicked. 'I was so frightened,' he said, 'I didn't know whether it was my turn or somebody else's.' The prison echoed with the screams of the tormented as beatings continued all through the day and into the night. Sometimes the cries of children could be heard. After midnight when the last batch of prisoners had been sent off Chum Mey, physically exhausted, slept.

The following day, after more beatings, wires were attached to Chum Mey's body and he was electrocuted. He passed out. After he regained consciousness, the beatings continued. By the end, Chum Mey's interrogation had lasted a total of twelve days and twelve nights. As they began to pull out his toenails with a pair of pliers Mey broke down.

At this point in his story, Chum Mey's eyes welled up and he burst into uncontrollable sobs. I asked if he'd rather stop. He shook his head and wiped away the tears.

He couldn't take it anymore, he said. He began admitting to things that he had no comprehension of, telling the interrogators anything they wanted to hear. 'I just gave whatever answers I could think of so that they wouldn't beat me so hard,' he said wiping away the tears. 'It was so painful – they had beaten me so much.'

Chum Mey's confession was neatly typed up and signed in his unsteady hand, his thumbprint next to it. The original document still sits among the mountain of papers at the prison, entitled, 'Chum Mey's Acts of Treason'. In it, his treasonous activities at his factory are listed as breaking sewing needles, wasting too much fabric and allowing the machine belts to burn out.

Normally, when the confession had been approved by Duch and then by Son Sen, Chum Mey would have been sent back to his cell to wait his turn to be taken to the execution ground at Choeung Ek. But it was Chum Mey's skills as a mechanic that saved him. In the upside-down world of Democratic Kampuchea treasonous activities could be put to use serving the regime's most important institution. He was sent back to work in the workshop behind the prison repairing sewing machines and typewriters.

Among the thousands of papers that were found at the prison were lists with the names and dates of executions to be carried out. On one, dated 6 November 1978, was the name Chum Mey. Next to it was an additional note, penned by Duch, 'Keep for a while.'

Chum Mey still bears the scars of his interrogation. One of his fingers was broken and badly bent as he tried to defend himself against the blows. He is plagued by the guilt and the trauma of that time and it comes back to him at times when he least expects it. I asked him how often he thought of S-21.

'Always,' he replied. 'I cannot forget this.'

By the end of his interrogation, Chum Mey had given the names of sixty-four people. He maintains that only ten were real names. Was he worried they would find out that he was lying?

'I just gave any answers I could,' he said. 'But I had implicated some other people.' He looked directly at me. 'That's why I always raise my hands in the air to pray and apologise in case others were arrested.'

Chum Mey saw Duch only once, just before the prison was abandoned. It was early in the morning and Duch was inspecting the workshop. Another prisoner whispered to Chum Mey. 'That's Duch, chief of the prison.' Duch stood there observing them, flanked by his bodyguards. 'I was busy repairing a sewing machine,' said Mey, 'I didn't dare to look at him. I just glanced at him.'

Chum Mey's day of liberation came shortly after 7 January 1979 when the Vietnamese army entered the city. He was taken by some S-21 guards, together with a handful of other prisoners, out of the capital. They made their way out of the city, crossing fields near Prey Sar Prison. There Mey was reunited with his wife (who had been sent to Prey Sar) and his newly born baby. Later their group was intercepted by a group of Vietnamese soldiers and a fire-fight ensued. In the confusion Chum Mey and his wife managed to free themselves of their captors. She wasn't fast enough and she told him to run. Seconds later bullets struck her and the baby down. Chum Mey managed to escape.

He re-married and now has six children, three sons and three daughters and works as the chief mechanic for a company repairing bulldozers and trucks. He is still haunted by the memory of leaving his first wife and child behind. 'My child died, my wife died. Nowadays, I'm in such pain.'

He composed himself and we called for the bill from the staff, who were dozing. Before we parted he turned to me and said, 'Some people say they didn't know and others say they hadn't killed,' he said. 'Nobody has admitted having done anything wrong. I want to have a trial. I want to have proper laws so that the children will learn. Because if there is no trial, the children in the next generation will do the same as the Khmer Rouge did.'

After I left Chum Mey, I went for a long walk through the

streets to the river. There I sat down near a Boddhi tree on the wide promenade. Some people were making offerings of fruit and incense to the spirit house beneath the tree. Behind me was the grey expanse of the Tonle Sap and the Mekong River beyond. It was a scene of rural calm. I watched the couples stroll along the riverside, vendors selling their wares from large round baskets on their heads. The sun was about to set. The spires of the Royal Palace pierced a butterscotch sky and the shadows stretched across the flowerbeds.

In a country as beautiful and beguiling as Cambodia, it is very difficult to begin to conceive of the horrors that people like Chum Mey endured. It seems so at odds with the Cambodia that most people experience; the warmth of the people, their easygoing nature, the intoxicating beauty of the countryside. But to spend à few hours in the company of someone like Chum Mey provides a keyhole, a brief glimpse into the heart of the cataclysm that engulfed this country.

Now that the war was over and the Khmer Rouge were no more, I had begun to indulge myself in believing that all was well in Cambodia. But listening to Chum Mey made me doubt everything again. I wondered how many with blood on their hands had quietly slipped into life beside their former victims. I saw afresh all the things that I had seen when I first arrived in the capital fourteen years ago; the poverty, the decaying buildings, the prostitution, the broken people that begged on the streets and the corrupt police.

CHAPTER 9

The Interrogators' Manual

AMONG THE MESS of papers scattered in the rooms of the prison when the Vietnamese arrived was a small notebook entitled 'The Interrogators' Manual'. It is probably the most chilling document to emerge from the Khmer Rouge period and provides a rare glimpse into the pathology of S-21 and the people who worked there. It contains a list of candid instructions from the mundane to the brutal: from how best to extract confessions, the preparation of confessions to notes about using sharpened pencils and cautioning against the smudging of reports.

The interrogation process was divided into two parts and increased in ferocity over time. To begin with, psychological trickery was encouraged. The interrogators were told to lead prisoners into believing that they would be spared if they told them even the smallest details:

a.   Reassure them by giving them something, some food for instance. Reassure them that the Party would give them back their posts.

If that didn't work the pressure was to be stepped up:

b.   Terrify them, confuse them in clever ways.
Arrange little ploys to make them give up any hope
that they will ever live or ever be able to survive.

Duch understood from his own experience as a prisoner
that the threat or the anticipation of violence, reinforced
by the screams of other prisoners, was often harder to bear
than the violence itself. Often interrogations were deliberately delayed, particularly if the prisoners were likely to
be difficult. It gave them time to reflect, surrounded by the
echoes of screams from the interrogation rooms. It made
it easier to extract confessions when their time came.

One cadre, after being kept at the prison for more than
a week, pleaded with Duch for his life. 'Beloved comrade!'
he wrote. 'No matter how I die, I will be loyal to the Party
to the end . . . Please rescue your younger brother in time.
I would be happy to grow rice with my wife and children
on a cooperative. I don't need an official position . . . please
save me, just let me live.'

'Looking at the problem,' Duch coldly wrote back, 'my
understanding is that you haven't been straight with the
Party. What's your understanding? I ask you to consider
the problem and resolve it. When we agree, we can work
together.' Duch enjoyed playing with the prisoners as a
cat plays with a mouse before killing it. He got a perverse
thrill from the intellectual toying. He was the teacher. He
always won the argument.

Overzealous interrogators were often reprimanded or
even arrested for not getting clear answers during interrogations, as the manual testifies. 'Our experience in the past

has been that our interrogators for the most part tended to fall on the torture side. They emphasised torture over propaganda. This is the wrong way to do it.' It goes on to say that getting a confession demanded a stance of utmost perseverance, but warned against being impatient.

'We must be absolute,' read the manual. 'Only in this way can we work to good effect.' One example laments how one prisoner had not been questioned fully, and torture had gone disastrously wrong:

> Right up to the enemies' deaths, the secrets of the CIA are still inside them in a greater or lesser fashion. The important thing is that the secrets be in them in a lesser fashion. One prisoner, for example, had confessed a good deal, but when he swallowed nails, we had to spend a long time with a medic and good medicine to treat him. The party is poor, and these expenses are difficult to meet.

There was a balance to be struck between interrogation and torture. Interrogators were told that it was the end and not the means that mattered, a distinction that many of these young men had trouble making. Torture had to be methodical and follow a clear line of questioning. 'The purpose of torture is to get responses.'

> It's not something we do for fun. We must hurt them so that they respond quickly. Another purpose is to break them and make them lose their will. It's not something that's done out of individual anger, or for self-satisfaction. So we beat them to make them afraid, but absolutely not to kill them.

Written in a maths exercise book, the manual's forty-two pages were handwritten in red and blue biro and underlined with a ruler. It is a candid and terrifying document born of cold deliberation. Although not written by Duch, it has all the hallmarks of his handiwork. For Duch a good interrogation was slow and patient. It is likely that Son Sen and comrade Chan would have contributed to it. Returning to his role as a teacher, Duch referred to the manual over a microphone in front of his subordinates, instructing them as he used to his pupils. It might have been under his hand in the photograph that I carried in my pocket.

The purpose of these interrogations was to identify and eradicate dissent within the new society and the party itself. As in Mao's Cultural Revolution, the Khmer Rouge believed an obsessive and continuous cleansing of society was essential for producing a pure revolution – enemies were thought to be everywhere.

The first group of tourists walked on ahead as their guide explained the general layout of the prison. Prak Khan and I trailed behind them before stopping outside building B where a frame stood next to two large earthenware water jars. A small illustration next to the frame depicted prisoners being suspended by ropes and dunked in the same pots. Prak Khan told me that neither would have taken place in the open in case the screams were heard outside the prison. He had never seen it himself. All the interrogations had taken place behind closed doors.

Prak Khan knew the operations of the prison intimately because, under Duch, he had worked there as an interrogator. He was a short, dark man with a pinched expression. His hair was closely cut and he walked with a purposeful lilt. He agreed to show me around the prison.

We came to the wall in the last room where the photographs of prisoners who had died during interrogations were displayed. I asked if he could recognise any of them. Tourists passed us by locked in silent horror at the photographs on the wall. We waited until they had filed out. Prak Khan then turned to me with his head bowed pointing to a photograph of an emaciated man on a stretcher, his voice a low murmur. 'This one,' he said. The photograph showed a man on a stretcher. His body bore the marks of torture and his collarbone and ribs were visible under his stretched skin.

He couldn't be sure about the others, he said, as it was a long time ago. As we were talking, another group of tourists wandered into the room, transfixed by the images. A Western tourist stood next to us. I wondered what her reaction would be if she knew that some of the people in the photographs had been tortured by the man now standing next to her. Then I thought of the first time I visited the museum and how I had believed that it was all safely in the past and that the perpetrators of this horror were either dead or somewhere else.

Prak Khan and I drove across the city and over the Tonle Sap River to a small restaurant overlooking the Mekong. We ordered a drink each and Prak Khan began to smoke his way through a packet of Alain Delon cigarettes.

Prak Khan had first been assigned to work in Tuol Sleng as a guard before being promoted to interrogator. He worked in a twelve-man *Angkiem* or 'chewing' unit. The interrogation teams were split into three separate groups, he said. The first group was called *Krom Noyobai* or 'political' unit; the second was known as the *Krom Kdao* or 'hot' unit and the third was called *Krom Angkiem* or 'chewing' unit. The political unit conducted some torture, he said, but very little. The second team was fully involved with torture and, when this team couldn't get the 'correct' answers, they left the prisoners with the 'chewing' unit. 'By "chewing",' he explained, 'it meant chewing the prisoners like a dog chews on a bone.'

In the hours that we talked Prak Khan's blank expression never changed, and his answers were monotone and flat. His posture appeared rigid, as if his entire body had somehow seized up; the only part of him that moved were his eyelids, which blinked slowly, as though he had difficulty keeping them open. I had the impression that I was somehow speaking to an empty shell.

Prak Khan joined the Khmer Rouge as a response to Prince Sihanouk's appeal from Beijing, and began by transporting rice for the troops at the front. It was very hard, he remembered, and the troops had little to eat. They lived on roots, and for much of the time they were starving. He had heard that the Special Zone units were better fed. He then joined an artillery unit. He didn't know why he had been chosen to work in S-21, but believed it was because he was disciplined, honest and obedient. Or as the Khmer Rouge liked to say, he had 'good morals'.

Some of the interrogations had taken place outside the main school buildings in abandoned houses that overlooked the compound. Before, Prak Khan's place of work had been in a small two-storey house with a garden, down a dusty side street not far from the entrance. The building had since gone, a new one had been built in its place and pink bougainvillea flowed over the surviving walls of the garden. On the corner of the street, facing the schoolhouse, was where the field station had been. There, badly wounded prisoners were taken to be patched up before being sent back for further interrogation. At Prak Khan's section, they took the prisoners to be interrogated from the main holding rooms at the prison and returned them at mealtimes.

There were four hours for interrogations in the morning, another four in the afternoon and then another three after dinner, ending at ten at night. Sometimes they went on longer, depending on the importance of the prisoner and the urgency of the case.

Prak Khan began by asking the prisoner what village they came from, what district, when they joined the revolution, what their roles were, how many brothers and sisters were involved in politics. The confession would be written up and then sent to Duch's office. Duch would either return it to Prak Khan with his own instructions or send it on to the Higher Organisation. Then it would come back for further questioning until the satisfactory answers had been obtained. When the network had been established, with names of accomplices, and crimes committed, it was signed by the prisoner, the interrogator and then by Comrade Duch.

Prak Khan regularly attended study sessions conducted by Duch where they were trained in interrogation methods. He followed Duch's instructions to the letter. They had been instructed to play, as he described it, 'political tricks' with the prisoners. He would ask them why they thought they had been arrested. Sometimes they would even forge a confession from one and take it to another prisoner who had refused to talk, telling him that his friend had confessed and implicated him.

The interrogations would become progressively more and more vicious. 'I used an electric wire connected to the power, struck the shackle and the prisoner would fall unconscious,' he said. He listed torture methods that he used:

beatings, cigarette burns, plastic bags, rope, branches, pliers, hammers, axes and whips. 'They screamed when we tortured them, even though they weren't permitted to cry out.'

'The prisoners' backs would be badly bruised and cut after the torture,' he said. 'They couldn't be beaten anymore, and they couldn't wear a shirt because it was so painful.' Gangrene set in and their nails began to rot. He told me about the children of prisoners who had been killed by dropping them from the balconies of S-21. He had witnessed it on several occasions. All he could do, he said, was stand there and watch.

Why children? I asked him.

'Frankly,' he said, 'they were killed to prevent them from being a nuisance.'

Days later, I kept thinking about something Prak Kahn had told me about a young woman prisoner. He told me he had interrogated her, but that he hadn't tortured her. And I wondered why. I decided to see him again, this time with Sokheang at Prak Khan's home in Takeo, south-west of Phnom Penh. I took with me a copy of the woman's confession given to me by the museum archivist.

Prak Khan was waiting opposite a grubby market next to the main road in his small hometown. Plastic bags floated in the tailwind of large trucks that hurtled past, their horns blaring. The road was flanked with the rotting debris from the market. We then drove in Sokheang's car to a secluded spot outside the town.

We sat in a bamboo shelter with a roof of greying thatch. All around us were young teak trees and bamboo. It was a popular spot for picnickers from Phnom Penh but, being a weekday, it was deserted and the other huts were empty.

I asked Prak Khan about the woman he had mentioned.

I brought out her confession and her photograph.

Nai Nan was nineteen years of age when she had been brought through the gates of the prison. The photograph showed a healthy young woman with the simple beauty of a country girl. An apprehensive look in her eyes, her short hair was tucked behind her ears and tied to one side by a hairpin in the regulation Khmer Rouge style. On her collar the number 15 had been attached by a safety pin. Over the five someone had painted a crude four.

I gave it to him.

'Yes,' he said blankly. 'That's her.'

Nai Nan had been a nurse in hospital P-98, situated near Wat Phnom in the centre of the city. She was arrested as a 'hidden element' and brought to the prison in 1976. When she was brought into his interrogation room, he instructed her to sit down on a chair in the middle of the room, facing his desk. Her ankles were shackled. He began asking questions: which organisation did she work for; what was her relationship with the head of her unit; how many people were in her team. 'Some women would confess immediately when I threatened them and slapped the table,' he said. But she pleaded with him, saying that she didn't know anything. After several days of this he asked Comrade Duch and Comrade Chan for advice. They told him to use stronger tactics.

I had been to P-98, the hospital where Nai Nan had worked. Before the Khmer Rouge it was called the Preah Khet Mealea and had been evacuated of all its patients on the day the Khmer Rouge took over the capital. It was then renamed P-98 and served the military units of the Khmer Rouge centre. A basic training was given to female medics, most of whom were illiterate peasant girls. Patients routinely died from incorrect diagnoses. The workers were closely watched and could be arrested for the most minor infractions. One medic was arrested when a power cut destroyed medicine that was stored in a fridge. And, like Nai Nan, he was taken to S-21.

After the Khmer Rouge were ousted, it had been the main military hospital that cared for Vietnamese and Cambodian soldiers. A series of imposing French buildings with high ceilings and dark corridors, it was in a terrible state of disrepair; rubble was scattered around the grounds, wires protruded from the wall sockets, and years of dust and grime coated the floors as rats scampered about the shadows. Amputees clunked their way down the corridors on their new crutches.

There is a photograph taken in a Cambodian hospital, possibly this one, just before the fall of Phnom Penh by the celebrated war photographer Don McCullin. It shows a young double amputee and a woman, presumably his wife, by his side fanning him from the flies and the heat. What struck me about this photograph was that it could have been taken yesterday. There was nothing in the image to date it or place it. I had seen and photographed the same scene all over the country on numerous occasions. Like the thousands of pictures of prisoners in Tuol Sleng, there was a terrible repetition in Cambodia that spanned not just months, but decades.

Like the photographs of prisoners at Tuol Sleng, we cling on to the hope that the people are somehow still alive. Photographs do that; they stave off the inevitable. Until we see a picture of the same person dead, then we keep wondering, hoping against hope against what we *know* must have happened. Perhaps that is why some of the prisoners were photographed after their executions for the Organisation; to cancel out the image of them alive on arrival at the prison.

In reality, at least intellectually, one knows that the young man in McCullin's picture is dead. He was likely to have been a soldier fighting the Khmer Rouge. Most of them were massacred in the first few months. But when I look at McCullin's photograph, they are still there, sitting, waiting, just as they were thirty years ago.

Prak Khan looked at the photograph of Nai Nan and quickly gave it back to me.

What was different about her? I asked.

He looked directly at me. 'I had feelings for her,' he replied.

Prak Khan asked her why she had been arrested. She replied that she didn't know. He stood up and looked at her. He slapped the table and threatened her. He bombarded her with questions, pacing around the room and shouting at her. She was so scared she wet herself. 'I felt very low talking to her,' he said. 'She looked pitiful. She was young and didn't know anything.'

After several hours she confessed and Prak Khan gave her a pen and paper and told her to begin writing her confession. Terrified, she scrawled an indecipherable line in an unsteady hand. He then realised she couldn't read or write. He sat down and began to write it for her. He gave her three options to choose from; she could confess her allegiance to the CIA, the KGB or the Vietnamese. She chose the CIA.

Nai Nan was in a sabotage unit, the confession read, and her superior sent her 'on a mission to shit on the rice and beans next to the toilets in buildings and in houses to ruin the reputation of the command-post hospital because it was a model hospital. My chief then assigned me to a mission to shit in the operating room.'

Did you believe this?

He became quiet and reached for another cigarette.

'I didn't really believe her,' he said. She was gentle and seemed entirely innocent to him. 'Frankly speaking, if I'd been allowed by the Organisation or if I had the power to save her, I would have been willing to marry her.'

Did you tell her about how you felt?

'No, I didn't dare. I just kept it in my heart.'

As a young sixteen-year-old, Prak Khan's mother told him, 'Son, when you go to war, you must determine not to steal anything. You must be honest and not steal some-body's daughter or wife.' 'That was why I didn't dare to touch women,' he said. He had 'good morals and disci-pline', he said and, when faced with Nai Nan, he tried to 'strengthen his spirit'.

In the world of S-21 there were no outlets for any form of expression outside of the interrogation room. Most of the staff of the prison was comprised of young men and teenagers whose sexual impulses had to be controlled lest they should lose 'mastery' over their work, Prak Khan told me. They had to remain 'strong', 'pure' and 'determined', he said. Sex was forbidden and all marriages were arranged by the Organisation. Sex was only permitted between wives and husbands; outside of marriage the punishment for such crimes was death. The regime was obsessed with the notion of purity, and sexual abstinence, as it had been for monks, was part of this new regimen. At least one interrogator had been purged for rape. In S-21, they were expected to lead a life of absolute compliance.

Nai Nan's interrogation lasted a total of three months. By the end, he said she had become thin and drawn. She begged him to ask for forgiveness from the Organisation and to spare her life. But he couldn't do anything. He was part of the machine and couldn't help her without condemning himself. She was an enemy.

'I didn't beat her,' he said. 'I didn't torture her.' Later a friend who had also interviewed Prak Khan told me that he had admitted that he had in fact tortured her.

Four months after her arrest, Nai Nan completed her confession and was taken back to her cell. There she waited to be called again. One night, not long afterwards, she was blindfolded and taken by a guard to the main gate where a large Chinese truck waited. She would have been hauled on to the back along with other prisoners and driven through the streets of Phnom Penh. She may have even noticed the changing sounds as the noise of the engine echoed off the walls of the deserted buildings. After ten or so minutes she would have felt the incline of a bridge. After that the sound of rubber on tarmac was replaced by the grind of sand and the metallic flick of stones as they rumbled along the uneven surface. She may have heard the cicadas hissing in the acacia trees that lined the road. Then the truck would have taken an abrupt turn to the left. After several moments the gears would have ground down to a halt. The engine would have been switched off and the silence of the countryside would have seeped inside the canvas to where she lay, waiting. The truck had arrived at Choeung Ek.

Cambodian soldiers used to believe that death would come to them in the form of a beautiful woman. I was once told that the hamlet of Choeung Ek, situated several kilometres south of Phnom Penh, was known for the beauty of its young women.

Twelve years after Nai Nan had made her last journey, I followed the exact route that her truck would have taken

from Tuol Sleng, my cyclo wobbling in and out of the
potholes as we neared the outskirts of the city. The road
was now lined with recently planted eucalyptus trees as
well as older tamarind and acacia trees. Beside us, the
emerald paddy fields of rice sheaths swept back and forth
in the wind and sugar palms dotted the horizon as far as
the eye could see.

At the turning on the edge of a paddy field was a sign
in Khmer that I couldn't understand – but the crude illustration was graphic enough. Against a flaming red sky as
a backdrop, black-clad Khmer Rouge soldiers clutched
babies by the legs, striking them against trees; victims
kneeled at the edge of graves full of bodies. It seemed
more like a caricature than a graphic depiction of what
had actually taken place there. But perhaps it was so close
to the truth and depicted such horror that my mind automatically placed it in the safe confines of a crass cartoon.
Passing the hamlet of Choeung Ek, we arrived at the gates.

A series of white sign boards at the entrance described
the crimes of the 'Pol Pot – Ieng Sary clique', and included
a plan of the execution ground. A small handwritten leaflet
describing the 'field of death' sat in a box for visitors. A
recently erected *stupa* housed some 8,000 skulls exhumed
from the surrounding graves. The only sign of life was a
lonely cow ambling lazily past the shallow pits.

When Nai Nan arrived, here at Choeung Ek, a team of
eight guards dug the graves. The numbers of prisoners to
be killed on any given night ranged from several dozen
to over 300. They were taken off the truck to a small
wooden hut nearby. They were told not to be afraid, that
they were going to a new home. The generator then started
and the floodlights were switched on, the noise drowning
out the cries of those being killed. One by one they were

taken to the pit. Their names were checked against a list.
They were told to kneel down and then they were clubbed
on the back of the neck with a cart axle. If there were
any unaccounted for, the graves had to be exhumed and
the bodies identified a second time.

Duch would often sit smoking on a mat nearby directing
the guards as they carried out their murderous work. The
stench of death hung heavily in the air, a stench that, in
the words of one of the guards, 'became normal'.

I wandered down the path that snaked its way along
the edge of the pits. There were a few signs placed in
some of the fifty or so graves; 'Mass grave of 166 victims
without heads', 'Mass grave of more than 100 victims, children and women whose majority were naked', and 'Mass
grave of 450 victims'. My cyclo driver showed me a tree
where babies had had their skulls smashed against the
trunk. When the graves had been discovered in 1980,
feeding bottles and tiny sandals had been found among
the rags. Beyond the barbed-wire perimeter were the
shallow indentations of graves yet to be exhumed. Bits of
bone and strands of cloth lay strewn about my feet. When
I looked closer I realised that they were literally coming
out of the ground, each monsoon downpour revealing
more and more.

It was here among the sugar palms and rice paddies
that Nai Nan would have met her end. Like the thousands
before her and the thousands that were to follow, her
emaciated body would have been tossed into one of these
pits.

I walked up to the *stupa*. Row upon row of skulls were
placed carefully on shelves, creating a ladder-like effect as
they rose up into the shadows of the roof. Despite the
sheer enormity of what had taken place here, it left me

strangely cold. I had seen skulls before. Unlike the photographs at the prison, it was difficult to imagine that these were once living beings, stripped of their individuality in the even grin of death. The sun was setting and the reflection cast a red hue on the glass windows; the silhouette of palms revealed the skulls beneath the shadows. The effect was a grotesque picture-postcard image of skulls emerging from a tropical sunset.

CHAPTER 10

A City with No People

FAR FROM THE universe of S-21, on the other side of the city, Sokheang found himself billeted in a building overlooking the river. 'K-7' was a liaison centre and post office which came directly under the control of the Organisation. It took up an entire block of buildings that now includes the Air France office, UNESCO and the favourite haunt of expats on the promenade, the Foreign Correspondents' Club. Sokheang was told to stay there and await instructions. Here messages from all the different administrative centres inside and outside the city were processed. It was also a transit point for cadres going to and from different offices, some known, some unknown – including S-21.

Days went by and nothing happened. Sokheang and his comrades grew restless and decided to venture out into the empty boulevards. The breeze of the cool season swept through the open streets as they climbed inside vacant buildings looking for old books. Sokheang found the atmosphere surreal and unnerving. 'We saw everything scattered, everywhere was in disorder,' he said. 'It was like a

ghost city.' Occasionally, like a reflection, they saw people
in the distance dressed, as they were, in black, wearing
Mao caps; otherwise they were alone. 'We were afraid to
go far from our place, because it was too quiet,' he said.
As they ambled along, he thought of his family and how
he hoped that he would one day be reunited with them.
'It made me very, very sorry and upset.'

   One day Sokheang and his comrades were moved to
another vacant building nearby. While they were cleaning
out an abandoned apartment they knocked down a
wardrobe propped against one of the walls. Behind it they
found tens of thousands of dollars' worth of diamonds
someone had hastily hidden there. The former owner must
have panicked in the last days of the war and stored them
safely away as the black-clad guerrillas strode through the
streets below. They took the diamonds to the head of
K-7, Comrade Ky, and gave them to him to give to the
Organisation, 'for the reconstruction of the country'. They
found other riches, too: they had wandered into a bank
where old Lon Nol banknotes lay strewn about. Sometimes
they came across US dollars lying in the gutter, which they
ignored. 'They were useless to us,' said Sokheang.

   In Khmer Rouge-controlled Cambodia the values of the
old world were turned on their head. Unlike the decadent
ways before, nothing was to be wasted. Old perfume bottles,
Sokheang discovered, could be made into oil lamps. Some
of these lamps could be made out of empty M-16 or AK-
47 magazines that they found lying in the street. They also
looked for cutlery and plates as they too were in short
supply. In the evenings they often walked across the road
and down to the water's edge where they caught fish in
the slow-moving waters of the Tonle Sap River, which they
cooked over fires at night.

Early one morning a messenger arrived telling Sokheang
and his group that they were to go to Wat Ounalom for
a political seminar. This was the pagoda that Duch had
stayed in as a student. It was a five-minute walk from
where K-7 was located. They gathered their things and
wandered up the street to the grey building fashioned in
the Angkorian style.

A grinning Khieu Samphan appeared. 'He was very
friendly, all smiles, he shook hands with everybody and
chatted with some old friends of his,' said Sokheang. Despite
Sokheang's doubts, he felt somewhat reassured by Khieu
Samphan's disarming charisma. Dressed in black with a
krama, as they were, he told them how the war against
US imperialism had been won. After several hours Khieu
Samphan left. That was the only time Sokheang ever saw
him. The rest of the lectures were given by a Comrade
Phum for the ten days that they stayed at the wat.

Sokheang and his comrades were left with a generally
positive view of the revolution. The Khmer Rouge, they
felt, were patriots, he said, and they spoke very eloquently.
The talks seemed to have been designed to allay any fears
that they might have had. 'Even though we didn't agree
with many things, our general perception was that things
were going as planned,' said Sokheang. They were told
that for the revolution to succeed the people had to produce
three tonnes of rice per hectare immediately and industri-
alise the country within thirteen years. 'We felt it wasn't
possible,' said Sokheang. In the countryside people were
literally being worked to death to reach these unrealistic
quotas. The rice was being stored and then sent to unknown
destinations whilst the majority of the people starved.

Every day at the wat, after dinner, they discussed that
day's lectures. Although Sokheang enjoyed the theoretical

lessons he dreaded this time. It was then that the self-criticism sessions began. As in M-13 and S-21, and in communes throughout the country, these sessions were a time for people to assess themselves in front of the others, comparing their performances to revolutionary principles. They had to list their 'strong points' and their 'shortcomings' to each other. They then took it in turns to criticise or praise wherever appropriate with the party line. Finally the chief of the group would make an assessment and later report to the chief of the camp.

Sokheang remembered these meetings well. 'I felt very uncomfortable,' he said. 'It was humiliating to expose myself to the others and let them raise questions and criticise me without limit.' They were permitted to defend themselves, they were told, but they had to accept the criticisms with humility. People's commitments to the revolution were being scrutinised. It was a tightrope, to be handled with care. Under the guise of revolutionary criticism old rivalries could find expression. 'People used this opportunity to raise the old issues and use the sessions for revenge,' he said.

After ten days of political lectures Sokheang and his group were sent back to K-7. Another three weeks went by. Despondency crept back and they grew bored. They were told nothing and given nothing to do. It was then that people began to disappear. Usually a motorbike would materialise.

'Comrade,' they would say, 'please prepare your belongings. The Organisation needs you.' No-one dared ask where they went. When it was time to return to the cooperative in Preah Vihear, ten people out of Sokheang's group of thirty comrades had disappeared.

While Sokheang was kept waiting and guessing what he

would be assigned, Duch was running his prison with a ruthless efficiency.

Nothing in the former schoolhouse took place without Duch's approval. His control was total. If he wasn't on the phone to Son Sen or signing orders, he would inspect the activities of the prison, checking on his staff, often with several bodyguards in tow. The staff never knew when he might appear.

Dressed in black, his green Mao cap pulled over his head and a black-and-white *krama* hung loosely around his neck, in his breast pocket were two pens, the only sign of his rank, which, at the time, was the equivalent of a regimental commander. Under his arm he carried papers in a dossier and concealed beneath his top, in a holster, was his own K-54 pistol.

Duch hurried his way around the prison. The Khmer Rouge produced two different kinds of cigarettes: *Kotab*, which was reserved for senior cadres like Duch, then the unfiltered *Klok* or *Bayon* cigarettes for the lower ranks. *Kotab* were coveted by the staff. Duch never finished his cigarettes. He usually threw them away half-smoked before lighting another. When he had gone, the interrogators and guards picked up the discarded butts to smoke themselves.

Prak Khan rarely saw Duch during the day. It was usually at night that Duch would appear in his interrogation room to observe him at work. Duch would take the day's confessions away from him to read and would later send them back, usually with a note: 'Open the report to see my corrections!' Duch underlined the points he was not satisfied with and instructed the interrogators to question the prisoners still further. When the answers didn't conform to the conspiratorial frameworks that had already been established, or if there wasn't enough detail implicating others,

Duch would return to interrogate the prisoners himself. If the prisoners still gave him the same answers, then he would explode into a rage, kicking and beating them. Most of the time, Prak Khan's team used rods or tree branches to beat the prisoners, but Duch always shocked the prisoner with electrical wires.

Prak Khan was terrified of his commandant. Duch despised what he perceived as laziness or incompetence. If he found fault with the interrogator, or if they couldn't understand what was being demanded of them, Duch would slam his fist on the table and grind his teeth. Prak Khan knew that other interrogators had been arrested for less.

On one occasion, when an interrogator had made a mistake, Duch went to the interrogation room, incensed. Duch grabbed a stick and began to hit him. 'It was very frightening to see,' said one guard. After shouting and threatening the interrogator, Duch bellowed, 'Don't make any mistakes again!' The interrogator was later killed.

Nearly all of Duch's staff were young peasant boys and girls with very little in the way of a formal education. Separated from their families and taken from their homes, they had suffered a gruelling civil war. They then found themselves plucked from obscurity and elevated to work in the regime's most sensitive and important institution. They were perfect fodder for indoctrination.

Looking at the surviving mug shots of the staff one can trace something of the arrogance of youth in their eyes. On my visits to the museum when I leafed through the photographs of the guards, I often tried to imagine them standing in line outside building A with Duch at the front. 'We will be vigilant and determined to successfully guard our enemy!' they cry in robotic unison, their fists pumping the air above their heads. 'Determined! Determined! Determined!'

Having spent so much time looking at S-21's photographs, which are all black and white, I had come to view the Khmer Rouge period in monochrome and the activities of the prison being carried out under a heavy grey sky. In contrast to the golden sunlight that flooded the compound now, it had become impossible to imagine it in any other way.

One black-and-white photograph in the archive showed seven young men from S-21 on top of what looked like a roof of a shophouse. Some have their hands on their hips. One has his sleeve rolled up displaying a watch. Others have their hands in their pockets, their heads tilted back looking with an affected sneer. Only one is smiling. They look like an Asian street gang.

Everything was seen in terms of a constant struggle. There were two revolutionary battlefields: the *Samoraphoum Kraoy* or 'rear battlefield' and the *Samoraphoum Muk* or 'front-line battlefield'. They were the rear. They were told how the entire nation relied on them and that the country expected them to be loyal and move against their enemies with all their might. Here in the confines of the interrogation room their rage was endorsed by the Organisation. They were the last line of defence.

The realm of S-21 was absolute. They were told that these prisoners, including the children, were the 'enemy' and they believed it. They were told that S-21 was 'the right hand of the party', 'the soul of the country', and 'the heart of the nation'. The induction and political lectures given by Duch, Chan and Son Sen were peppered with references to the purity of their cause. They were told to be 'resolute', 'determined' and 'clear' in their undertakings.

The job of S-21, they were told, was to 'uphold the prestige of the nation'.

It was a world of polar opposites and extremes of great clarity, with no room for reflection of any kind. Hardened by the war, moulded by the harsh discipline the Khmer Rouge imposed, and pumped by a righteous rhetoric underscored by fear, the young guards were unstoppable.

Language was essential to the running of the prison. It was used to dehumanise the prisoners in the eyes of the guards and make their brutal work easier. In the communiqués between Duch and the interrogators, the prisoners' names were often prefixed with 'contemptible' or 'wicked' and constantly referred to as 'enemies'. Female prisoners were referred to as female animals, not people. For the most part, the language of the Organisation was abstract and, by extension, so were the prisoners. It was never enough to simply kill the prisoners and the word 'kill' was rarely used in documents. 'Kill' implied a living being. The enemies of Democratic Kampuchea had to be completely erased. More often the word *komtech* was used, meaning to 'smash' or 'destroy'.

Like the process of torture and the gathering of confessions, photography was an integral part of identifying enemies and reducing them in the eyes of the Khmer Rouge. Once prisoners were captured in the frame, they were no longer in possession of their lives. The North American Indians, victims of another genocide, believed that the camera could imprison their souls in photographs. For the prisoners at S-21, once they were photographed they could never be anything but guilty – a kind of trial by camera. They had surrendered the last vestige of their individual identities to the Organisation.

The numbers had replaced their names. These numbers were recycled every twelve hours in a constant rotation, a continuous weeding out of enemies. When Prak Khan came for his prisoners he asked at the guard for 'guilty person number 37, row 12, room 4, building C'. A month later, he could ask for exactly the same digits, but it would be a different prisoner. As in Mao's Cultural Revolution, the work at S-21 was never-ending.

The majority of the photographs of prisoners were taken at the front of the prison in the wooden *sala* at the main entrance. Some were taken in the cells or interrogation rooms. Often a projection screen was erected behind the prisoner or they improvised using a hand-held white sheet. Some prisoners were placed in an old colonial-era photographer's chair used in the past primarily for identification photographs. There was a headrest to keep people steady for long exposures and profile pictures were sometimes taken. The chair still sits in the museum today.

To photograph a person alone, often with a blank backdrop with no context, was further 'proof' of their guilt. There was nothing to relate them to and they weren't part of this world.

As I flicked through the contact sheets at the museum I noticed, almost without exception, that all the photographs of the prisoners were single portraits. Vulnerable and alone, it was as if the act of taking a picture somehow reduced them in size thereby furnishing the idea that they were in the minority.

By contrast, the photographs that survive of the Khmer Rouge identify them as part of a group, like school photographs or members of a team. They all wear Mao caps, they are all in uniform, their *kramas* are arranged around their necks all in the same fashion. The women all have their hair cut in bobs tied with a single hairpin.

Like the Chinese propaganda imagery of the Cultural Revolution, these were deeply political and moralistic images that reflected an idealised vision of the revolution. They project a stark uniformity of purpose and strength in numbers. In Cambodia, it has always been considered foolish to stand apart from the rest and draw attention to oneself. During the time of the Khmer Rouge it could have fatal consequences. As one staff member later told me, 'If we didn't show Duch the proper respect, he might arrest us. He might say we were guilty of being disrespectful.'

Photography for the time of the Khmer Rouge helped reinforce a rigid interpretation of their world. Like a simple mathematical problem, there was only one answer: right or wrong.

In 1944, photographer George Rodger, who had accompanied the allies through Europe during the Second World War, arrived at Belsen concentration camp. As the first photographer there he began taking pictures. After several hours of walking amongst the dead and dying he stopped in his tracks, disgusted. 'My God,' he said, 'what has happened to me?' He had been wandering around arranging piles of corpses into aesthetic compositions in his viewfinder. Shocked by his own behaviour, he resolved never to photograph another war again.

I remember returning from Cambodia in the early nineties after a trip where I had photographed two soldiers who had suffered a particularly gruesome mine accident. One of them, Hearn Boung, was severely wounded and slipped in and out of consciousness. His body was caked in blood and his left calf had been ripped to shreds by the blast. His foot, however, was still miraculously intact, twisted under his thigh. I took pictures as the nurses began to clean him. Hearn Boung fell into shock and I don't think he ever had any idea that I was photographing him. Several days later, after his leg was amputated, he died.

Back in Bangkok, I began the process of editing the images I had taken in Cambodia and placing them in slide mounts. It was only when I looked through my loop at Hearn Boung that I began to feel nauseous. It was as if I was observing the scene for the first time. For days I found it difficult to look at the pictures. I realised that I had viewed him at the time as a series of aesthetic and technical calculations and judgements: the correct exposure that I wanted, the angle, the depth of field.

Later, having photographed countless hospital scenes and operations I realised that the camera acted as a kind of shield allowing me to watch the world through the frame of a television set. Very often, if I found something distressing, my reaction was to photograph it, distance it and then I could move on, unless there was something more practical I could do. Photography became a safety net. The camera had acted as a kind of filter for what I was seeing. Like the prisoners of S-21, people had become mere objects in my viewfinder.

CHAPTER 11

The Photographer

TO BE SURROUNDED by thousands of eyes in an empty room is a profoundly disturbing experience, particularly when you know that all of those staring back at you are dead and may have died in great pain in that very room. It's even more disconcerting when you know that when they look back at you they continue to see their tormentors standing where you now stand. In Cambodia, people say that those who died violently and with their eyes open cannot find peace and are condemned to wander the world of the living for eternity.

Upstairs in the archives there were more pictures, stuffed in a desk. I found one, a head-and-shoulders portrait of a prisoner. To the right of the picture, a man can be partially seen. He was almost certainly a guard, possibly the chief interrogator, Comrade Chan. He is rearranging his *krama* around his neck as he stands on the step of a doorway. His black uniform has merged with the shadows. There is no face. It is lost between frames.

I wanted to shift the frame a little, to move the camera

still further to see who he was talking to, what they looked like and what they were doing. I imagined them in a group, standing around the photographer as they waited for him to take the picture, talking among themselves. I wondered if they could hear screams reverberating around them.

In 2001, I tried to locate the Khmer Rouge photographer who had taken these pictures. Nhem Ein had stayed with the Khmer Rouge almost until the end of the war and I had been warned about him. A Khmer friend told me, 'Old Khmer Rouge cannot turn back – they cannot change.' The same friend also said that I would have to pay for the photographer's time, otherwise he wouldn't talk. 'He's very welcoming but when the interview is over he changes. He wants money – he's very greedy.'

The Khmer Rouge had made Nhem Ein a photographer and, albeit for very different reasons, his portraits of the condemned had made me one too. But unlike other photographers who had influenced me, there was no artistry in his work. It was functional, an extension of the torture, nothing more.

When I first came across the photographs of the prisoners in the *National Geographic*, I was shocked. They were simultaneously compelling and horrifying. As images of faces they seemed so passive and yet there was a violence present, an expectation as well as an accusation. What impressed me most, however, was that they were proof of mass murder collected by the perpetrators.

By the early 1990s, Nhem Ein's negatives at the museum were in danger of being completely destroyed by neglect. The staff in the museum lacked the necessary storage conditions to preserve the archive and mildew, dust and white ants were beginning to take their toll. In 1993, two American photographers, Douglas Niven and Christopher

Riley, realising the documentary importance of the images, began to clean, catalogue and print all the existing negatives. It took them three years.

Niven was the first to discover who Nhem Ein really was. He came across an article in a Khmer newspaper about a defector from the Khmer Rouge headquarters of Anlong Veng who had claimed that Pol Pot was alive and well. The Khmer Rouge had begun to implode and government forces were converging on their jungle base. The defector said that he had been with the Khmer Rouge since 1970 and had trained as a photographer in China. Niven had always suspected the Tuol Sleng photographer had foreign training. 'We'd even thought that a Chinese adviser had helped them get started, as the work they did there was technically very good – good exposures, good processing,' he said. Even fifteen years later, when Niven began printing them, 'the negatives were in remarkable shape.'

Within days Niven had tracked Nhem Ein down. Ein had kept the mug shot he had taken of himself at Tuol Sleng to show to Khmer Rouge as a form of identification and to ensure safe passage through the front lines. Several years later Ein had showed me the same photograph, which he kept laminated in his wallet.

Nhem Ein, was now living in the former Khmer Rouge enclave of Anlong Veng, due north of Siem Reap. He was involved in politics and represented the Royalist Party in the area. I eventually found him visiting Siem Reap on some political business. As my friend had predicted, Nhem Ein asked me for $300 for an hour of his time. Ein's pictures from Tuol Sleng had been reproduced in a book in the United States, and published in the *New York Times*, the *Telegraph Magazine* and countless photography magazines.

They had been exhibited in more than fifteen galleries worldwide. He knew what he was worth. I managed to bargain him down to $50.

Nhem Ein's grin sparkled gold as he grabbed my hand and began speaking in fluent Thai. He was dark, stocky and short and had the burly look of a foreman on a construction site. When the smile faded, it was replaced by a severe look that contrasted with his comically squeaky voice. Later, when I photographed him, he looked intensely into the lens. Only then could I imagine him in his black Khmer Rouge uniform and Mao cap.

Nhem Ein had spent most of his life with the Khmer Rouge. He had been recruited at the age of ten before being thrust into a war which had brutalised him and moulded him into the new kind of Khmer the regime was trying to create. He was a true child of the revolution and it was in that world that he remained. To talk with Ein was to enter the realm of S-21.

Nhem Ein had been a model Khmer Rouge. He was from pure peasant stock, young, ambitious and eager to seek approval from his superiors. 'Those chosen to work in the *Santebal* were all good people,' he said. 'We were like monks in the pagoda. There was no drinking, no prostitution, no gambling, no corruption, no stealing.' As a boy, Ein's father had cautioned him before he left home, 'The rice won't bear grain when it stands tall, but it will if it bows.' Nhem Ein took his father's advice to heart and became an adept survivor.

When Nhem Ein likened S-21's staff to Buddhist monks, he was closer to the Khmer Rouge's origins than he perhaps understood. As young boys, many cadres were taught at pagoda schools. Like the leaders of the Khmer Rouge, Buddha created the monkhood, or *Sangha*, who took vows

of celibacy, poverty, and moral restraint with a conformity
of purpose. By following Buddha's teachings everyone
could attain enlightenment. People under Khmer Rouge
rule were to lead simple rural lives based on equality, self-
sacrifice and a moral regimen of monk-like strictness.
Everything was done for the masses and the nation.
Individual thought was prohibited. Even the Khmer Rouge
practice of killing entire families thought to be tainted by
decadent city living – the new people – was considered
as an act of purification, not dissimilar to Buddhist rites.
'Burn the old grass,' ran the Khmer Rouge adage, 'to let
the new grow through.' When they took power, they
emptied the temples and monasteries, and disrobed the
monks and forced them to work in the fields. Or they
simply killed them: for the Khmer Rouge, monks were
'parasites' who fed off the blood of the people. Pagodas
and schools were turned into pigsties, warehouses and
torture chambers. When I asked a Cambodian friend why,
he replied, 'Because you can't hear the screams.' Pagodas
were often the only village buildings made of brick and
mortar.

Much of what the Khmer Rouge understood was based
on what they saw around them and their thinking was
shaped by the past. Despite their claims to a classless
society, they didn't provide people with an alternative to
the old system; they simply destroyed it and replaced it
with a replica of the same power structures that had existed
before. Their claims that the revolution had no precedent,
that what they were embarking upon had never been done
before in history, were patently untrue.

'The survival and death of the country and nation
depended on Tuol Sleng prison,' said Nhem Ein with an
air of self-importance. 'If there was no Tuol Sleng, the

country and nation would be ruined, because this place was the centre for security. It was the special agency of the country.' I asked him what he meant. 'You are either alive and your heart is beating or you are dead,' he said impatiently. 'Tuol Sleng was the heart of the movement, the heart of the country. If security was not established the situation would become chaotic and the nation would be in trouble,' he said, as though reciting something that had been drummed into him without him understanding what it meant. He sat back looking directly at me, awaiting my reaction. 'It's the only way I know how to explain it. It was the centre, the most important prison.'

After the Khmer Rouge victory in 1975, Nhem Ein worked as a messenger delivering communications, by bicycle, between Monivong hospital in the city centre and Ta Khmao prison on the outskirts. It was a trusted job that earned him respect among the cadre. It was at Monivong hospital that he first met Duch. 'My impression of him was that he looked like a humble person, a reasonable person, but I knew that he was a right-hand man of Pol Pot,' he said. The first meeting was brief, and shortly afterwards Ein was called by the Organisation to go to China. He was sent to Shanghai, along with several hundred Khmer Rouge, where he was trained in photography, printing, film-making, film projection and map-making. It wasn't until he returned to the capital to work at Tuol Sleng that he realised how terrifying his new boss could be. Nhem Ein said that Duch was hot-tempered and irrational, particularly with his staff. 'He became angry without thinking and ignored their reasons,' he said. 'He gave execution orders without hesi- tation.' They lived in constant fear, ruled by the whims of an arbitrary boss. As Ein had said, 'He could accuse me of being an enemy too. And I wasn't even a prisoner.'

Nhem Ein's darkroom and studio were located next to Duch's home, a few minutes' walk from the prison gates. Here he and his assistants worked, sometimes around the clock, producing photographs that were stapled to the confessions and then sent to the Higher Organisation. In the deserted capital, looting for the party was sanctioned. 'We used to get all the chemicals and paper and film from the shops,' he grinned.

Ein learned quickly and became skilled at winning allies among the higher-ranking cadres. It was the way to ensure protection. As well as his work at the prison, he was sometimes ordered to photograph the few foreign visitors to Cambodia, such as Chinese delegations, as well as party meetings and rural construction sites.

'The workers were all equal, like the surface of a board. There was nobody who bowed and saluted you,' said Ein. Even so, Ein became something of a favourite with Duch, who was no doubt impressed by his impeccable revolutionary credentials. 'I was the son of a poor farmer and I'd lived with the Khmer Rouge since 1970. That's why the cadre liked me.' Duch gave Ein a nickname: A Khmao or 'blackie', a reference to his dark peasant's skin. He also called him A Kleum or 'the essence', which also meant, short but very talented. 'He was proud of me,' said Ein. 'And I was also proud of myself.'

As a result Ein was given more freedom than other staff. Unlike others, he could walk around the prison at will and could venture out into the streets of the city.

Nhem Ein both venerated and feared Duch and still refers to him as Ta or 'uncle'. Ein was one of the few who saw him outside the prison, where Duch was relaxed and easygoing. 'But in work he was a perfectionist. Everything had to be perfect,' he said. 'He had many sorts of characters, which varied in different situations. He was a wonderful person. He could be anybody. He could play the role of a giant, a cruel man, a gentle man, a sad man or a miserable man.' He was also an accomplished speaker. During the many seminars and meetings, if Duch saw his staff's concentration wane, he would liven up the talks with jokes and often had them in fits of laughter.

I wondered what the prisoners would have thought, silently listening as the sound of hilarity filtered up to the rooms where they lay waiting.

I looked at the photograph of Duch that I carried around with me. He looked confident and self-possessed at the podium. I later came across another photograph from the archives. In it, S-21 staff and their families were having a meal. The table had been set up in the courtyard of a large villa at night. At the other end is another photographer, one of Ein's assistants, looking through his viewfinder. In between the two photographers, to the side, is a grinning Duch walking confidently behind those seated. At the other end of the table several cadres have their heads turned towards the gate and the darkness beyond. Perhaps another truck had arrived or was departing with its cargo of prisoners.

'He was a clean leader who wasn't corrupt or partisan,' said Ein. The fact that Duch rarely ate separately from his staff impressed him. 'He had good discipline and good morals and didn't betray the masses. He rarely ate at home, because it was an equal society where there were no rich and no poor people. Nor were there people who had more delicious food to eat. If we were to eat spicy, sour soup, everybody would eat the same spicy, sour soup regardless of how high your rank was.'

Ein explained that Duch liked to set an example to his

staff and often referred to his Ho Chi Minh sandals in his speeches or when he wished to make a point. They were the standard footwear of the Khmer Rouge, made of recycled rubber from car tyres, and he had kept them since he joined the revolutionary forces in 1970. They signified how important it was for the revolution to remain true to its idealism and never to forget the origins of the struggle. The last time Ein saw Duch, in the forest in 1979, he was still wearing them.

That Duch had tortured prisoners was certain, but I wondered to what extent he had the power to operate on his own initiative?

'He did nothing without orders,' said Nhem Ein confidently.

Did he ever see Duch beat prisoners? I asked. 'I didn't see him beat the prisoners. No,' he said shaking his head vigorously. I pressed him further still. He became sullen. He resented being contradicted and became evasive, giving monotone one-line answers. 'I just focused on my work as a photographer,' he said, 'he must have beaten people, because he was the chief of the prison.'

I told him that I wanted to know what *he* saw. I began to think that he had been with the Khmer Rouge for so long that he found it difficult to navigate questions directed at what *he* thought and what *he* knew. Before it had been dangerous to confide in others. He had known how to avoid trouble and told those in authority what they had wanted to hear and did exactly as he was ordered. As a result, he was thrown off balance when the questions were aimed at him. He expected to be listened to, not challenged and his answers were often contradictory. Even five years after he left the Khmer Rouge he was still guarded about saying too much. He attempted to lead the conversation elsewhere and talked in vague generalisations – unless really pressed. Then he became angry.

'I didn't see everything!' he snapped. 'There were tens of thousands of prisoners. My duty was as a photographer, I had to take photographs!'

In all the time he worked he didn't see Duch interrogate anyone?

'Only once.'

Nhem Ein abruptly changed the subject and began to tell me of the cameras he had used. He made no attempt to hide his boredom. Later, when I showed him photographs I had found of prisoners who had had their throats cut, asking if he had taken them, he gave a large yawn and replied that he hadn't. He picked up one of my cameras and looked through my portrait lens at me. Unnerved, I tried to continue. He interrupted me and asked how much the camera cost and if I would get him one.

'He beat Sri once,' he said, almost as an afterthought. Sri ran the cookhouse. He had been accused of attempting to poison the staff of the prison. He had found a bottle of what he thought was fish sauce in a house and put some in a large pot of soup. When he found it to be inedible he disposed of the soup in a desperate bid to conceal his mistake but the smell of chemicals betrayed him. It was on the plates when the meal was served. Then there was no soup to eat with the rice, which confirmed his guilt. Sri must have known he wasn't going to get away with it. It was just a matter of time. And sure enough, later that night, the guards came for him.

Sri had been in the interrogation room for an hour before Nhem Ein was sent for. Duch was already there with two other interrogators when he arrived. 'Who told you to do this?' screamed Duch, pointing at Sri's face. 'You wanted to kill all the prison guards to get rid of them!'

He paced around the room with a large rattan stick. Duch then lunged at Sri and beat him with all his might. He was wild with rage. 'He shouted out loud like a giant in a play,' recalled Ein.

'You did this to kill *me*!' Duch yelled. Sri pleaded that it had been an accident. The beatings continued. Later he confessed to being a CIA agent and that he had worked under orders to poison the staff. 'There was no doubt that everyone would have been killed if he had put the poison in the soup,' said Ein. Whether the cook had deliberately done it or not wasn't the point; to destroy food at this time was an act of treason.

When Ein took his photo, Sri had a vacant look in his eyes. 'His body was severely broken,' said Ein. 'He already looked like a corpse.' Ten other members of the kitchen staff were also implicated and interrogated. Among them were two of Nhem Ein's relatives, Chorn and Srun. They were young men who had grown up with Ein, in the same village. Ein remembered Srun as an honest and gentle person. After he took their photographs, they were taken away. 'They said they didn't know anything when they were asked. When the interrogators whipped them harder they too confessed that they were CIA agents.'

I asked him how he felt when he looked at his own relatives through his viewfinder. He thought carefully for a moment. 'I felt sad, scared and confused,' he said. 'I would have died too if I had shown any reaction.'

After Sri and the others had been dealt with, Nhem Ein saw Duch at the canteen. He sat as usual at the table reserved for him with his messenger, Comrade Hor, and the chief interrogator, Comrade Chan. He looked normal, said Ein – as though nothing had happened.

All orders came from the Higher Organisation, explained Nhem Ein. 'Duch only dared to execute prisoners on such orders. But he could make his own decisions about the workers at the prison. He would punish anybody who made mistakes, because during that time the chief of a team of three men had the power to kill his own subordinates.' But, Ein added, he had never seen Duch kill anyone personally.

In the paranoid world of S-21, not even Nhem Ein was immune from the suspicions of his workmates. 'I once got into trouble when I printed a photograph of Pol Pot because it had a black mark on it.' Somebody told Duch, who openly criticised him in a meeting in front of the others. Duch began by congratulating Ein for having done good work in the past. Then he expressed his disappointment in Ein and began to criticise him for becoming complacent and negligent in his duties. Eventually he accused him of being an enemy of the Organisation. 'I was very scared,' said Ein. 'It was a life-and-death situation for me.'

He was then taken away, not to a cell, but to raise livestock for the prison kitchen, outside the city. Meanwhile, Comrade Duch made his own enquiries about Ein. He found out the film was faulty. 'Then, they decided that I was a good person again,' said Ein. Workers at Tuol Sleng were often killed for far lesser crimes.

Nhem Ein didn't just photograph prisoners and foreign delegations. 'Sometimes Duch told me to take photographs of his wife and daughter at their home.' Duch's first child, Ky Siew Kim, was born in 1977. Before long it had turned into a weekly ritual. Ein photographed her in her cot and taking her first steps with her father. 'He would hold her and kiss her and although he was strict he was very good with her.' Duch was a different person at home and posed with his daughter as any proud father might. This wasn't part of Ein's job, but Duch was not to be refused. 'When I took the pictures I was very scared,' he said. Duch framed some, others he put in albums. None of them have survived.

Everyone collects photographs. They are a universal currency of common experience: pictures of babies, school photographs, formal portraits, photographs of weddings and holiday pictures. They define who we are, characterise us and the way we wish to remember and be remembered.

Nowhere is the loss of Cambodia's population under the Khmer Rouge more heavily impressed on the outsider than on the walls of Tuol Sleng. Ein's pictures have become iconic representations of the Cambodian holocaust. The photographic evidence is, on first viewing, a simple and straightforward documentation of mass murder by the killers. There are the mothers with their babies, the young girl with terror in her eyes, the old woman who appears resigned to her fate. But on closer scrutiny, the photographs are the very antithesis of the cut-and-dried confessions, full of ambivalent narratives and subtexts. They depict a world of doubt, of pain and suffering that the words do not.

Death is central to these images and yet, for the most part they depict people who are alive, frozen in time by the fall of the shutter. Their deaths have already taken place, but the people in the pictures continue to live. Looking at Chan Kim Srun and her baby, it is easy to believe she is imploring you to help. It is the illusion of intimacy that is so troubling.

The feeling of helplessness when confronted with the

photographs is almost suffocating. We want to do something, they demand action and yet we know that there is nothing that we can do. They continue to repel, engage, shock, outrage and, worst of all, exclude. The photographs of the dead, like the ones I looked at with Prak Kahn, are grisly, but the dead bear little resemblance to real people. It is the faces of new arrivals that stop us in our tracks. The sheer volume almost dulls the senses. And we stand there helpless in front of these mute faces.

Upstairs in the museum, I found wallets among a pile of discarded Khmer Rouge Mao caps and clothing. In another drawer in the archive I came across several sepia photographs of Khmer Rouge that looked like pictures of comrades and wives, keepsakes with bevelled edges possibly from the wallets. No-one knows who the youthful soldiers are. They are most likely some of the Khmer Rouge from the Eastern Zone, hundreds of whom were purged at Tuol Sleng.

When Ein's pictures were exhibited in the Museum of Modern Art in New York accompanied by a book, I began to wonder whether their meaning had been completely lost, whether what had happened under the Khmer Rouge had been fully understood.

Many of the images from Tuol Sleng were taken in isolation, with a white backdrop, without a context, as though in a void between life and death. More than twenty years after the horror this allowed people to view Ein's pictures simply as portraiture. Viewed in this way the photographs make subjects real to us but at the same time deplete any sense of urgency. In a gallery, they become studies in photography's aesthetic possibilities first, and evidence of mass murder second.

The more explicit images were not among those exhibited in New York such as the photograph of a man whose head had exploded from the impact of a shovel, his blood splattered across the tiled floor. Or a series of pictures of a dying man who tries desperately to escape from the camera, sliding through a pool of his own blood.

The book of mug shots was a sumptuous volume of more than seventy photographs. It was called *The Killing Fields*, borrowing its title from the film, even though all the pictures had been taken in S-21. There were no captions and the two essays at the back were added, it seemed, almost as an afterthought. To view them in this way one feels almost predatory. They looked more like anthropological studies. The victims are presented as the Khmer Rouge saw them: without a name, without family, without an identity or country. By the time Niven and Riley were shown the design it was too late to make any changes. But this didn't dampen publisher Jack Woody's excitement when he first saw the pictures. 'I thought they were the most amazing photographs I'd seen in years,' he said. 'The emotional rapport the viewer has with subjects I hadn't experienced in a long time. I thought to myself, "That's as good as photography gets."'

At the show at MOMA, the photographer was credited as 'unknown', further adding to the mystique surrounding the Khmer Rouge, even though Niven had met Nhem Ein several months before.

It seems disingenuous to me to display these photographs without making clear why it is considered important to show them. There is a danger of it becoming a self-defeating exercise in highbrow voyeurism. One of the reasons there are so few photographs in this book is because of my increasing frustration with photography's limitations. The display of the images becomes a passive act of remembrance, rather than a call for justice. As one visitor wrote

in a visitors' book, 'I don't believe MoMA had the intention to completely objectify these terrible images, but this
mute and "neutral" exhibition does that in the coldest
possible way . . . As a child of Holocaust survivors, I feel
that this kind of behaviour is at best indicative of a smug-
ness and an intellectual laziness – AT WORST IT IS INHU-
MANE.'

Showing the images in this way can also encourage us
to forget what governments do in our name. There was a
direct relationship between the rise of the Khmer Rouge
and the US government. Many people in the pictures had
been accused of being CIA. Kissinger and Nixon had secretly
bombed the country and had sent troops to invade it. The
UN had supported the Khmer Rouge for years and some
of those responsible had lived as diplomats in New York.
These images are all too easily transported into icons of
universal, or 'third world' suffering, disassociated from their
political, historical and social context.

For the majority who lived through the Khmer Rouge,
this is a story without a conclusion. Cambodians still go
to the museum in Phnom Penh today to look through the
pictures and try to find out what happened to lost relatives. On occasion, they find them; the shock of recognition is an end to hope. I wondered what those who had
lost loved ones would feel about images of their husbands,
wives or children being viewed by strangers in art galleries
on another continent. Would Holocaust survivors allow
pictures of Nazi terror to be presented in the same way?

Photographs are a material trace of a past, like a finger-
print or the smear of a hand on a wall. (Some of the negatives from the prison had fingerprints on them.) The pictures
from Tuol Sleng are the last traces of people who have
otherwise vanished. There are few memorials and their

bones remain unidentified. The negative lies at the very heart of eyewitness photography. With the advent of digital photographs the production of negatives is no longer a part of this process. Negatives don't just furnish evidence – they are evidence.

I asked Nhem Ein how he wanted people to react when confronted with his photographs in New York.

'Firstly,' he said, 'they should thank me. Some people sold these images and some made news out of them to make money. For me, when they see that the pictures are nice and clear, they'd admire the photographer's skill.' As he talked he became more animated, his mood changed. 'None have any technical errors. Secondly, they would feel pity and compassion towards the prisoners.' He thought for a moment and then corrected himself. 'Firstly, that they feel pity for the prisoners in the pictures, who are all dead; secondly, they'd say the photographer could take very nice shots.'

I wondered whether Ein's comments were really so different from the photographers of today. There is a need amongst many photojournalists (myself included) to justify what we do. Many imply that they give more than they take and often elevate photography to realms of a higher calling among the ranks of great literature, opera and fine art. Critics drape photographs of starvation in grandiloquent and generalised language and comparisons are made to the works of Goya or to Picasso's *Guernica*. The writer Eduardo Galeano referred to the dying in Sebastião Salgado's photographs of famine as 'a potent magic, a luminous mystery that redeems the human adventure in the world'. The suffering these kinds of pictures often describe is robbed of its impact. As magazines and newspapers become more politically safe and lifestyle-orientated, some of the most important work is often only ever seen in galleries, exposed only to a cultural elite. There they hang cleansed by the antiseptic of the art world.

Such arguments did not concern Nhem Ein. His task was straightforward. Taking photographs was the perfect accompaniment to the bureaucracy, part of a ritual of picture-taking in officialdom. The world of S-21 demanded it. As long as the image appeared clearly on the negative, that was all that mattered.

'Once the prisoners were put in front of the camera lens, nobody ever tried to struggle,' he said. He believed that all the people taken to the prison were guilty. 'Communism,' he said, switching back to his robotic rationale, 'was to abolish the capitalists, the students and the intellectuals. I thought that it was important for society. But some people were good people.'

What about the children? I asked.

'No,' he said quickly, 'for me, I didn't think they were guilty. They were arrested because Duch considered them part of an enemy network that had to be killed. When I saw them though my camera lens, in my heart, I also felt pity, sympathy for them. You'd admit that you were guilty if you were beaten and in pain. They would implicate one after another just like that. These people had not done anything wrong. It's no different from Sri, the cook. He was the only person who was guilty. But he implicated everyone when he was arrested. He implicated the men from my home district. They were just children of poor farmers, but he said they were CIA agents.'

There was nothing he could do, he said. 'A person's hair belongs to their head. Nobody could interfere in the other person's work. You were a medic; you only minded your work. If your work was interrogation, you only minded your interrogation work. In my heart, I felt that it was very unjust. I was like a boy in the pagoda and compassionate towards the victims. I always thought of the old people. I used to put some sugar in a bag of photographs and secretly gave a bottle of sugar to each of the old people. We drank sugar with water to regain our energy.' If this was true, it was a courageous and even reckless thing to do.

Ein had given up photography some time ago and was now hoping to be appointed governor in the former Khmer Rouge stronghold of Anlong Veng. He had left a wife and six children and married another woman. He must have known that he would be called as a witness to any trial and that his photographs would be primary evidence. The thought didn't seem to bother him.

When I gave him the $50, a sheepish grin appeared on his face and he asked for more. I told him that it was all that I had. He pressed me. I gave him an extra five dollars.

CHAPTER 12

The Last Joint Plan

THERE IS ONE other photograph of Duch displayed in the museum. It is a group shot taken by Nhem Ein in Phnom Penh in 1976. Like the wedding photograph in Duch's family home, it is a formal group photo on the steps of a house, possibly Duch's home. Three young children of Duch's staff look somewhat apprehensively at the photographer. To the left stands Comrade Chan, the chief interrogator, who towers above the others. Duch stands behind his wife Rom. She is smiling and looks solid and tough next to her sinewy husband. Duch wears a blank expression, his two pens clearly showing in his pocket.

By 1977, this uniform image of the new society was beginning to crumble and, as the killing reached new heights, internal conflicts, both perceived and real, were eating into the regime. In 1978, comrade Duch had begun to compile and summarise thousands of confessions into a notebook entitled 'The Last Joint Plan'.

He was obsessed with the notion of internal enemies

infiltrating the party to sabotage the revolution. The plan exposed frameworks of conspiracies and plots against the party and described 'percentages of traitors', 'factions', 'sectors', 'subdivisions' and 'summings up'. Saboteurs of the revolution were like 'weevils who bore into wood' and infiltration by the CIA was compared to 'the buffalo who hide themselves to sharpen their horns and come out when the water submerges the reeds'. It described how the Soviets, the Vietnamese and the CIA had attempted to assassinate brothers number one (Pol Pot) and two (Nuon Chea).

For the most part it was an outline of coups against the Organisation. It is a document as arrogant as it was paranoid, fed on the delusions of grandeur that the Organisation had built itself on. The Cambodian revolution, they believed, was the envy of the world. At the end, names of 'traitors' and the dates of 'liquidation' were listed. It was a work of orderly precision and absolute clarity, which Duch would present to the Higher Organisation; 'The Last Joint Plan' was his masterpiece.

The killings stepped up dramatically towards the end as more and more people were brought to Duch. In 1976, just over 2,000 people were taken to S-21. By mid-1978 the number brought to the prison had grown to a staggering 5,765. These were the ones whose records survived. One survivor estimated that among the prisoners were more than 2,000 children. Even pregnant women were not spared.

When Prak Khan had begun work at the prison, relationships with the others from the same division were friendly. They had suffered the same fate during the war and they used to mix informally with one another and chatted freely at mealtimes. Then the purges began.

Nobody knew who would be next as people began to disappear and new cadres replaced the old. People no longer talked as before and colleagues eyed each other with suspicion. Prak Khan did his best to avoid the Organisation's omnipresent gaze from falling upon him. The parameters were in a constant state of flux as arrests were made and victims were replaced by perpetrators. And perpetrators, in turn, became victims.

More and more were arrested from Prak Khan's team. Towards the end of the regime prisoners were constantly being taken to be killed. Eventually the interrogators were ordered to stop their work altogether. Prak Khan was sure that it was just a matter of time before he too was taken. 'We were terrified,' he said. By the end, he was the sole survivor of the original twelve in his team. The rest had been killed.

Duch's former comrades had begun to appear at the gates of S-21 in quick succession. First arrived his former childhood teacher and mentor, Ke Kim Huot. Next came Vorn Vet, who under Pol Pot had risen to Deputy Prime Minister of Economics. Vorn Vet had launched Duch on his career as a commandant as head of M-13. Then came Chhay Kim Hour, who had introduced Duch to the Party.

Ke Kim Huot, who had known Duch since he was a boy, had become a senior cadre in charge of a sector in Pursat province. He allegedly violated the Party's 'absolute proletarian' line by permitting people from the previous regime to continue doing their old jobs. Another of his 'crimes' was failing to fill his quota of rice stocks from his sector. He was transferred to the Foreign Ministry in Phnom Penh. One by one, Ke Kim Huot's comrades, who had also been transferred to the ministry, began to disappear until Ke Kim Huot himself was taken.

He was a stubborn prisoner who refused to give in to Duch's men. After several months in S-21, he still denied being a member of the CIA. In a note to Duch, Ke Kim Huot's interrogators reported that 'on the morning of 21 July 1977, we pummelled him again. This time he reacted verbally that he was no traitor, and that the contemptibles who had implicated him in their responses were all traitors. Healthwise, he was merely weak . . . there were no notable problems. On the evening of 21 July 1977, he was pummelled once more: electric shock and shit. This time he cursed those who were beating him a lot, saying, "Come on you bastards, beat me to death . . ." We fed him three spoonfuls of shit. That night, we hit him with electric shocks yet again, this time with rather higher voltage. When he came out of it he was in a daze, but he was OK. Then he confessed to a certain degree.' They then told Kim Huot that his other colleagues had denounced him. Whether or not Duch was personally involved in his interrogation at any point is unknown. What is certain is that he would have followed Kim Huot's interrogation very closely. After all, he could have implicated Duch himself. 'The Last Joint Plan' listed Ke Kim Huot as part of a CIA underground network charged with overthrowing the revolution.

The paranoia had no limits. After Vorn Vet's execution Duch was ordered by the Higher Organisation to exhume his body and have it photographed as proof – which he did. They knew that Vorn Vet and Duch had been close. By the end of 1978 more than three-quarters of the twenty-two original members of the Central Committee were dead.

'The Last Joint Plan' described how the revolution had

come under 'an assault from outside and a collusion
between the Vietnamese, Soviets, Lao, Thai and US impe-
rialists . . . particularly the Vietnamese expansionists'. By
the end of 1977, Democratic Kampuchea had severed diplomatic relations with Vietnam. The two countries, who had
fought so hard against the US and Lon Nol, were already
embroiled in a full-scale border war.

As early as June 1975 it was reported that fighting had
broken out along the border with Vietnam. Over the next
few years the attacks by Khmer Rouge units into Vietnamese
territory increased in frequency and ferocity. The
Vietnamese counterattacked with equal ferocity as the
Khmer Rouge turned on their former allies with a vengeance.

The Eastern Zone that bordered Vietnam had come
under suspicion and so had their captive populations.
They were dubbed traitors with 'Vietnamese minds in
Khmer bodies' and the area was to be 'swept clean' of
enemies. While Khmer Rouge troops were fighting the
Vietnamese, the purges continued behind the front lines.
Tens of thousands of people were massacred and thousands of Khmer Rouge cadres and civilians fled across
the border to Vietnam. In one area, not far from the
border, Son Sen ordered the killing of more than 100,000
people in six days.

In Phnom Penh, more and more people arrived at the
prison. Many were executed without interrogation – there
wasn't time. The killing had reached dizzying proportions.
As one interrogator asked in a confession, 'If the
Organisation arrests everybody, who will be left to make
a revolution?'

The first commandant of S-21, In Nath, had also been
sent to the prison, this time as a prisoner. His former
deputy, Duch, took him in. Only a couple of pages of

his confession survive. In it he wrote that Son Sen was angry with him because he had delayed purging Division 290 at the border with Vietnam. The date on the second page is Christmas Day 1978, the same day that the Vietnamese launched their invasion. Within two weeks they had reached the outskirts of Phnom Penh. The end was nearing.

Just over a week before the arrival of the Vietnamese army, Duch's wife had given birth to their second child, a son. The timing couldn't have been worse. His wife and children were most likely sent out of the capital to the rendezvous point in Amleang near her home village.

In the weeks before fewer and fewer people were being taken to the increasingly empty prison. 'I hadn't taken a photograph for quite a long time,' said Ein. The staff were instructed to build shelters should aircraft begin strafing the city.

On the morning of 7 January, Nhem Ein went as usual to eat rice porridge at the cooperative. Staff had been on high alert for several days now and the sound of artillery and small arms could be heard. Then F-111 fighter planes belonging to the Vietnamese were seen circling above and the alarm was raised.

An agitated Duch, armed with his pistol, split some of his staff into groups, gave them each a gun and told them to fan out and see what was happening and report back. Prak Khan crept along the dusty streets towards Monivong Boulevard. There he saw several T-55 Soviet-built tanks on the street not far from Duch's house – it was the Vietnamese. They opened fire and he ran for cover, then hurried back to the prison.

Nhem Ein too went over to Monivong Boulevard and

climbed to the top of one of the buildings and peeked through a shuttered window. He watched as the column of armoured personnel carriers and tanks made their way down the street. On that same column sat Ho Van Tay, the photographer who was to discover Tuol Sleng the following day.

'Everyone was running,' said Prak Khan. The remaining prisoners were killed. The staff gathered their weapons and ammunition and Duch split them into groups. They were all to make their own way to Amleang, the assembly point for the Khmer Rouge from the city. They filed out as quickly as possible down the back streets. The Vietnamese and their Khmer allies occupied the main roads, but had yet to secure the smaller ones. Pol Pot and the other members of the central committee had already fled by helicopter towards Sisophon in the west. At about noon a silence descended over the city. The quiet then erupted with gunfire. It was the Vietnamese firing their guns to celebrate their victory. Further out of the city Prak Khan took cover in a sugarcane field. His group lay low and watched as Vietnamese fighter planes strafed Pochentong airfield. There they waited until nightfall.

Chum Mey and the other remaining prisoners had no idea what was going on. He had been in the workshop behind the prison. Like everyone else he had heard the shelling. The women he was working with left for their homes. As he walked towards the main office he saw the prison guards carrying AK-47 rifles and preparing to leave. One of them turned to Chum Mey and said, 'Where are you going, motherfucker? Everybody has already gone.' He was told to go to the reception room. There were three other prisoners sitting inside with about ten guards. They grabbed the prisoners and dragged them into the street. They were taken in a group of about fifty towards the execution grounds of Choeung Ek. Then they cut across through the fields to Prey Sar prison, an annexe of S-21. 'At Prey Sar, we could smell the stink of corpses in the bushes,' said Mey. Then, by chance, Chum Mey was reunited with his wife, who had just given birth to their first child. They were overjoyed. She had been sent to Prey Sar at about the same time that he had been arrested. They all took cover nearby before continuing to walk under the cover of darkness. At dawn they came across Vietnamese troops, who opened fire, and they scattered. His wife told him to run. That was the last time he saw her or his child. They were cut down in a hail of bullets.

Duch was among the last to leave. There was no time to destroy the evidence. Papers, bullets and photographs lay scattered throughout the buildings, exactly the way that Ho Van Tay would find them the following day.

Duch, Nhem Ein and the other remaining staff and prisoners fled north. On Route 3 they encountered Vietnamese troops and in the confusion the group scattered. Some prisoners were able to escape during the ensuing firefight. Later, not far from Amleang, Ein was shot and wounded in the thigh. He was left to recover in a village as his comrades moved on. 'The Vietnamese were everywhere,' he said.

The evacuation of Phnom Penh had begun a week before the city fell. The staff at S-21 were among the very last to leave. Some prisoners from S-21 who had been taken by Duch and his men were killed along the way. The rest were summarily executed in Amleang, beneath the mountains, to the west. Three days later Duch and his men re-grouped not far from the site of Duch's first prison.

CHAPTER 13

Feeding the Guilty

S O FAST WERE the Khmer Rouge to crumble that the
Vietnamese tanks rushed on ahead before their supply
convoys could catch up. Many ran out of fuel just
outside Phnom Penh. Further west, Duch split the remnants
of the *Santebal* into smaller groups. Taking charge of one,
they launched hit-and-run attacks to slow down the
Vietnamese advance and buy time for the rest of the Khmer
Rouge to escape. Duch eventually fled to the Thai border.

Like the others, Prak Khan was sent off to harass the
Vietnamese, but to little effect. The Khmer Rouge were
heavily outnumbered and found themselves being pushed
back further to the mountains and the border with Thailand.
Prak Khan's unit found themselves cut off and isolated.
They decided to head further inland behind the Vietnamese.
'By then the soldiers were very demoralised,' he said.
'There was no hope.' Starving and alone they began to
forage for food in the forests. They had nothing but the
clothes they wore and slept on plastic sheeting on the
ground in the drizzle. Exhausted, and with no support,

Prak Khan gave himself up in Kompong Thom.

With the arrival of the Vietnamese the entire population had taken to the roads in an attempt to return to their shattered homes and villages. Dislocated and traumatised they wandered the entire length of the country in search of surviving family members.

Sokheang and Ho, who had fled Phnom Penh together, decided to split up and take their chances. Sokheang's group managed to free themselves of those in command. They came across abandoned cooperatives where they found food and hungrily ate all they could. On one occasion they saw bodies in the fields near the forest. Eventually Sokheang joined the chain of people who walked along Route 5 and began to make his way west to the Thai border.

Vietnamese trucks and soldiers could be seen among the crowds along the road. Sokheang saw several bodies of Khmer Rouge in the ditch, victims, he was told, of revenge attacks by locals. After three years of brutality a vengeful and angry population had begun to take matters into their own hands. It was the first time that Sokheang understood the scale of the killing. 'When people met each other their first question was, "How many of your family have you lost?" or, "How many survived?"' he said.

Not far away, along the same road, Haing Ngor, who later starred in *The Killing Fields*, watched as a crowd descended on a well-fed man in black after taunting him to say that he was Khmer Rouge. His elbows had been tied behind his back. More and more people struck and cursed him. The Vietnamese soldiers tried to intervene, but were unable to stem the raw hatred for this man. Haing rushed to kick him between the legs as hard as he could. He collapsed in agony. The man was then made to walk a gauntlet of fists and blows, his face bloodied and swollen. A man ran toward him wielding a hatchet and cut him down with one blow. His head was cut off and stuck on a pole with a sign underneath, 'Khmer Rouge – Enemy for ever'.

Sokheang continued by foot towards the western town of Battambang, where he spent the night under a mango tree in the pouring rain. By chance, he met his aunt. They decided to make a bid for the border.

While Sokheang made his way to Thailand, Ho and his family had been stopped by the Vietnamese and told to return to Phnom Penh. Gradually more people came to the city and camped in the empty buildings.

Three days after the fall of Phnom Penh, a new government was proclaimed. The People's Republic of Kampuchea was made up of a number of Khmer Rouge defectors who had escaped the purges to Vietnam.

Ho found a room near Tuol Tum Pong market with his wife and daughter and began to look for work. At the market one morning, he saw women selling fried bananas wrapped in paper with handwriting on it. There had been no paper during the Khmer Rouge. Now, in the semi-derelict city, it was everywhere. Sheets of it blew through the streets. Children had begun to collect it. He picked up one parcel of bananas. He recognised the handwriting – it was the confession of a friend from Paris. When he asked where it had come from a little boy led him down the back streets to Tuol Sleng. He saw the razor wire along the wall and Vietnamese soldiers at the entrance. 'I didn't dare go inside,' he said.

On his way home, Ho bumped into a friend who was now working with a Vietnamese colonel in the former prison. 'My friend told me that there were many confes-

sions of our friends,' recalled Ho. 'They were all dead.' Ho
asked his friend if any, by some slim chance, had survived.
'I tell you,' replied his friend, 'they are all dead.'

The Vietnamese were amassing all the documents for a
trial of Pol Pot and the Khmer Rouge *in absentia*. A few
days later Ho began work in the prison as an archivist,
translating the documents. 'I wanted to find out if anyone
had survived.' Over the course of several months he translated hundreds of pages. There he came across his own
brother's photograph. I asked him how he had felt.

'I was overwhelmed. A *terrible* discovery. Before we
didn't know what had happened to other friends when
they had disappeared,' he said. 'I threw up several times
and I cried . . . I couldn't stop. I felt utterly hopeless. It
was the darkest period of my life.' He cupped his forehead in his hand. 'I felt responsible, I was naïve. I was
angry with myself. I was angry with Pol Pot, but mostly
with Ieng Sary.' Ho had worked under Ieng Sary, the Foreign
Minister. 'He lied directly to us. I hated them for what they
had done. I worked hard to move on.'

After several months working in Tuol Sleng, he made
up his mind. It was time to leave Cambodia.

Under the direction of the Vietnamese colonel, the prison
was reorganised as 'The Tuol Sleng Museum of Genocidal
Crime'. A survivor, who later became the museum's director,
Ung Pech, was sent to Poland and Auschwitz to learn from
its museum. There he saw the photographs of Jewish and
other prisoners displayed next to great piles of shoes and
clothing together with Zyklon B canisters.

Back in Tuol Sleng the archives were translated, organised, copied and filed by Ho and other assistants. The
evidence was arranged for public display and the nega-

tives were shipped to Vietnam for printing. As in Auschwitz, clothes were piled next to instruments of torture. Some of the walls of the single cells had been cleared to hang the mug shots on. Another survivor was commissioned to paint pictures of atrocities, and the map of skulls, which had been taken from the mass graves, was installed. The museum opened to the public in 1980.

Until the Vietnamese arrived in Cambodia few people had heard of Pol Pot. Duch had only seen him once or twice during congresses with hundreds of other cadres. But he knew who 'Brother Number 1' was. The cult of personality, so familiar to the Vietnamese in the form of Ho Chi Minh, had not yet featured in Cambodian communism. There were plans to begin one, hence the portraits and busts of Pol Pot found in the prison by Van Tay. Cambodians had only known the leadership as the Organisation and not who was behind it; most knew nothing beyond their cooperatives. Ironically it was the Vietnamese, one of the sworn enemies of the Khmer Rouge, who personalised the regime. Democratic Kampuchea became 'the Pol Pot time'.

By drawing on the parallels with the Nazi death camps, the Tuol Sleng museum was organised as a deliberate attempt to distance the Vietnamese from their former allies the Khmer Rouge. They wanted to vilify the Khmer Rouge and its leaders still further as part of a propaganda war to justify their invasion. Visitors to the museum were encouraged to think of the Vietnamese as akin to the liberators of Europe's concentration camps.

There was no text narrating progress from room to room. Visitors viewed the museum through a series of images and objects. The intention was to provoke outrage through a primarily sensory experience rather than to enlighten.

The Cold War was at its height and, for many in the West, Tuol Sleng was a propaganda tool for a regime that had seized power through an illegal invasion.

All museums are manipulations. Apart from the map made of skulls created by the Vietnamese, the raw displays were graphic and chilling and, although inaccurate in form, were real in substance. The atrocious nature of the place itself was hard to contrive. The fact that visitors were being manipulated and that the information on display was there to serve a political purpose seemed to pale in comparison when faced with such overwhelming viciousness.

On the other side of the Thai border thousands of ragged and starving refugees were emerging from a medieval nightmare. Every day more people succumbed to disease and starvation and every day still more arrived. It seemed as though Cambodia was emptying itself of people.

On the border, the Thai military were on a heightened state of alert. Just across the frontier were 200,000 Vietnamese troops, one of the world's largest and most experienced standing armies, and one with the full backing of the Soviet Union. Thailand's army, by comparison, had a strength a little over 160,000. The American 'domino-theory' of Soviet expansionism seemed to have been fulfilled and now the feared Vietnamese could be seen across the Poipet bridge at the border. To complicate matters further, the Thai army was faced with a massive refugee influx from Cambodia that included Khmer Rouge soldiers. The Khmer Rouge had been closely allied with the Thai communist insurgency and had raided Thai villages, massacring their inhabitants just as they had done on the Vietnamese border. Now here they were, with civilians in tow, begging for help.

At first, unsure of what to do with these people, the

Thai military panicked. In one incident, they drove more than 40,000 refugees at gunpoint over a cliff at the border and into minefields below in the largest forced repatriation since the Second World War. Hundreds, possibly thousands, perished.

Among the sick and the dying was the Khmer Rouge Foreign Minister, Ieng Sary. He had arrived at the border barefoot and was met on the Thai side by Chinese diplomats, with clean clothes and a new pair of shoes. In January 1979, exactly a week after the liberation of Phnom Penh, a top-secret meeting was held at Utapao air base in Thailand. China announced they would cease support for the Thai Communist Party if Thailand would give the Khmer Rouge safe haven and provide logistical support for their war against the Vietnamese. Thailand then announced its 'open-door policy' of allowing the refugees sanctuary on Thai soil. A few days later a shipment of arms and ammunition arrived from China for the Khmer Rouge. Cambodia was to become the battleground for the containment of 'Soviet expansionism', and a war of attrition had begun that would continue for another nineteen years.

Within months, one of the largest humanitarian relief efforts in history began. The sleepy Thai border town of Aranyaprathet was transformed almost overnight, as the tragedy at the border offered opportunities for a wide array of individuals and organisations, including aid workers, missionaries, black marketeers, smugglers, prostitutes, academics, soldiers, activists, Thai, Chinese and American intelligence officers, journalists, Thai entrepreneurs – and of course photographers.

Cambodia, or more accurately the Cambodian border, had become something of a *cause célèbre*. Many of those journalists who had covered Vietnam had relocated to Bangkok and were now on the story. Few went to Phnom Penh – it was easier to jump in a car and drive from Bangkok than to enter the country to see where the majority of the population was. And Sakeo became the stop for many members of the press. *Time* magazine ran a cover story, 'Death Watch in Cambodia', reported entirely from the border. Many photographs from the time showed mothers cradling their babies in the classic Madonna-and-child pose. It was as if the photograph of Chan Kim Srun from Tuol Sleng that had troubled me so much as a teenager had re-emerged on the border as another icon of Cambodian suffering.

The response in the West to these images was unprecedented. John Pilger and David Munro's powerful film *Year Zero* helped raise millions in the UK. One of the few organisations who went inside the country was Oxfam, who mounted an appeal in the UK. Money poured in. The children's TV programme, *Blue Peter*, raised a staggering £3,500,000 through Oxfam shops alone.

The Thai military told the United Nations High Commissioner for Refugees (UNHCR) that they were moving 90,000 people from the border to a new location and instructed them to make the necessary arrangements. This new camp was to be outside Sakeo some sixty kilometres *inside* Thailand. What was less known was that the refugees were mostly Khmer Rouge soldiers and their families. The movement was now on the verge of total collapse. The plan to resuscitate the Khmer Rouge was put into effect and the creation of the Sakeo camp was central to that plan.

Conditions at Sakeo were appalling. The site had been ill-chosen and it flooded in the monsoon downpour. People were packed in tents in the mud, surrounded by large drainage ditches. Every day scores of people died from disease and malnutrition.

The camp was under the control of the Thai military and the UNHCR, with various relief organisations providing assistance.

The Vietnam-era singer Joan Baez visited Sakeo. President Jimmy Carter, who had described the Khmer Rouge as 'the world's worst violators of human rights', sent his wife to visit the refugees. Roselyn Carter arrived with her entourage while the Khmer Rouge looked on. Photographers and cameramen jostled with Thai military escorts to get a better shot of the First Lady. A photo opportunity was dutifully produced in the form of the First Lady cradling a dying child. And then she, along with the press, was gone.

But while these shocking and dramatic scenes of thousands of starving refugees spurred people to help, they also created a misleading impression of what was really going on. Sakeo camp was not, as it may have appeared, a place of refuge – it was a place of control.

The Khmer Rouge kept a close eye on the population and the foreigners who worked there. There were reports of abuses of refugees by the leaders. One aid worker saw the Khmer Rouge push a man into a barrel and light a fire underneath. Another aid worker had to be transferred after a death threat. The man in charge was a Khmer Rouge commander named Phak Lim who was responsible for the purges in Battambang and Pursat. Accompanied by several bodyguards he swaggered around the camp with a megaphone, ordering those that disobeyed the Organisation to be beaten, tied up and left in the open or buried up to their necks.

The reality was not lost on everyone. As two aid workers,

Linda Brown and Roger Mason, pointed out, 'The Vietnamese had succeeded in isolating and weakening the Khmer Rouge into military impotence. The relief organisations were now resuscitating them.' And much of this aid was coming from those with a vested interest in bringing the Khmer Rouge back to life. 'The US government, which funded the bulk of the relief operation,' wrote Brown and Mason, 'insisted that the Khmer Rouge be fed.' With the relief effort being used to cloak the real intentions of the superpowers, the stage was set for the next chapter of the Cambodian tragedy as the Thai military, the US and China revived the Khmer Rouge.

The refugee population of Sakeo was trapped. The Khmer Rouge wanted to move the refugees back to the border and began to circulate forms to declare that they were returning to Cambodia voluntarily. Despite the protestations of some aid workers, the Khmer Rouge circulated warnings to the civilians of the camp. One of them went:

Those who go back first will sleep on cots.
Those who go back second will sleep on mats.
Those who go back third will sleep in the mud.
And those who go back last will sleep under the ground.

After the Khmer Rouge collapse in 1979, Cambodia lay in ruins. A third of the population was dead. Of 550 doctors, only forty-eight had survived; out of 11,000 university students, 450 were found; and out of 106,000 secondary-school students, only 5,300 survived. The country had no existing infrastructure to speak of. In Kompong Thom, Duch's home province, only two schools out of 180 remained standing and roughly two-thirds of the temples had been destroyed. Mass graves were being discovered in every province.

It is generally acknowledged that during the 1,364 days of Khmer Rouge rule, two million people died as a result of their policies, approximately 1,466 people a day. By percentage of population, the Cambodian holocaust remains the worst to have occurred anywhere in the world, eclipsing the numbers killed in Nazi-occupied Europe and the Rwandan genocide put together. In that sense, the Khmer Rouge remain the most effective mass murderers in modern history.

The UN declared the Vietnamese invasion illegal and voted once again to have the Khmer Rouge occupy the Cambodian seat as the legitimate representatives of the Cambodian people. A resolution was then approved by the UN General Assembly which strongly appealed to all member states and humanitarian organisations 'to render, on an urgent and non-discriminatory basis, humanitarian relief to the civilian population of Kampuchea'. Since the UN recognised the Khmer Rouge as the legitimate representatives of Cambodia, this didn't mean much on paper. It meant even less on the ground.

The US placed an embargo which pushed Cambodia still further into the Soviet camp, in turn justifying Washington and Beijing's support of the border and the Khmer Rouge. As a result, Cambodia was denied UN development aid. It was also banned from the Asian Development Bank, the IMF, the World Bank and denied assistance from the World Health Organisation. Apart from convoys from Vietnam and the Soviet Union, and aid from a handful of western agencies in Phnom Penh, throughout the 1980s the people of Cambodia were completely isolated. And for every dollar that went inside the country, $160 went to the border, to the Khmer Rouge and to their allies. On their Khmer-language programme, the Voice of America urged Cambodians to come to the border and to 'freedom'. By 1980, there were more than a million refugees scattered along the frontier.

Behind the scenes of refugee camps, an extensive and complex network of depots, logistical facilities and camps were established in the jungle that covered much of the ill-defined frontier. Large Thai military convoys rumbled from the coast, sometimes during the day, mostly at night. Artillery, tanks, ammunition and weapons from both China and the West were delivered and shipped off to secret locations inside Cambodia. This became known as 'the hidden border', a secret world out of reach of the aid organisations and the UN. One aid worker had been caught behind a convoy of these Thai trucks one night. For a split second the canvas tarpaulin of the truck in front flapped open and there, caught in his headlights, were Khmer Rouge troops tightly packed inside. An estimated 500 tonnes of military supplies were being shipped every month. The Khmer Rouge were soon to emerge as the most powerful fighting force on the border.

At this time there were reports that one camp along the forested frontier was being run by a Khmer Rouge cadre called Comrade Duch. He had apparently been given the name 'the butcher' because of his murderous reputation.

Eventually Sokheang and his relatives managed to cross the minefields and the border into Khao-I-Dang camp in Thailand. There they registered with the UNHCR for repatriation to Australia.

According to Sokheang, many Khmer Rouge responsible for killings did slip through the net. 'I remembered one person who had been the chief of a cooperative living next door to me in the camp,' he said. 'He was accepted by the US without checks on his background.' More than 230,000 were relocated to the US, Europe, Australia, Canada and elsewhere. Among the refugees were Khmer Rouge from Sakeo, perhaps even some of Duch's killers from S-21.

In Khao-I-Dang camp, Khmer Rouge representatives tried to convince Sokheang to return and help in the fight against the Vietnamese. After eight months of waiting he and his relatives were sent to an internment camp not far from Bangkok. Before his interview with the Australian embassy personnel Sokheang was already having doubts. 'I told them all my true history, that I was in Paris, I participated, I went to Bejing, I came to Cambodia by the Ho Chi Minh trail,' he said. 'I told them this intentionally so that they would fail me,' he smiled. 'But at the end of the interview,' and much to Sokheang's disappointment, 'they said, "OK, good, no problem".'

After several months of waiting for his application to be processed Sokheang made the decision to go back to the Khmer Rouge. He was then spirited away to a house in Bangkok where five other Khmer Rouge waited for him. There he was told how the Khmer Rouge were going to announce some cosmetic changes for international consumption, but really they were going to pursue the same policies. Several days later, Sokheang was taken to a secret camp inside Thailand twelve kilometres from the Cambodian frontier and back to the domain of the Khmer Rouge.

The camps where Sokheang was sent were collectively called 'Thor – 100' ('The New House' and 'The Old House') and sat at the base of an imposing mountain. He was later transferred to a logistics-and-supplies depot just up the road. Here stockpiles for the front were kept. Every month Thai military trucks delivered more supplies from China. There were a few visitors, mostly Chinese and Thai, among them the Thai army commander-in-chief General Chavalit Yongchaiyuth, who later went on to become the Thai Prime Minister. It was a small island of Khmer Rouge-controlled Cambodia enclosed by barbed wire. Sokheang was given no work and no assignments; there was nothing for him and his comrades to do. Time crawled by. He was a prisoner of the revolution once again.

Yet despite his confinement, Sokheang knew that he fared better than most of the people on the border – he and his comrades had security.

Later back in Phnom Penh, sitting outside as we always did in the cool evenings, we talked of the various twists and turns his life had taken. Much of the time, political events had directly shaped Sokheang's life and left him with few choices. But he did make one clear choice: to rejoin the Khmer Rouge who had killed so many, including three of his brothers. Why?

There was a pause as he stared out into the night. 'This is a difficult question to answer,' he sighed. 'Firstly, I was single. I also believed that the Khmer Rouge would change.'

Did he *really* believe that they could? I asked.

'It wasn't question of whether we believed or not, it was a question of how to participate in the struggle against the Vietnamese invasion,' he said. 'I couldn't support the presence of Vietnamese troops on Cambodia territory. I wanted to liberate my country *even* though I learned of the Khmer Rouge atrocities. But the invasion and occupation of Cambodia, I felt, was more pressing. There was a risk that my country, my nation and my people could disappear from the world.'

This hostility towards the Vietnamese and the fear that Cambodia would one day be overrun by either Vietnam or Thailand was ages old. There is a popular story widely believed to be true. During one of the many wars some Vietnamese soldiers captured three Khmer prisoners, buried them up to their necks and built a fire between their heads, placing a cooking stove on top.

As a minority, the Vietnamese had always been in Cambodia, mostly as fisher folk on the Great Lake. Unlike the Chinese, who assimilated easily, often intermarrying, the Vietnamese stayed apart from mainstream Khmer society, to the point, Sokheang told me, where Khmers weren't welcomed into Vietnamese villages. Culturally, linguistically, racially, they had always remained as outsiders in Cambodia and suspicion ran deep. But still, this didn't explain his return to the Khmer Rouge. This was all abstract, I argued, and it went against the fact of the deaths of his brothers.

'I was quite sure that the Khmer Rouge had changed,' he said pausing to swill his glass of beer. 'More or less, at least about the killing of people – the innocent especially.' I looked doubtful. 'I'm not a "Vietnaphobe",' he said defensively, 'but this is fact. Our history has taught us not to forget this. During the Vietnamese time, the regime was also communist or socialist and people's lives were hard. Not like the Pol Pot time, but hard. Many rights were denied, everything was closely controlled.'

Although this was true, it was a far cry from the regimented and institutionalised brutality of the Khmer Rouge. However unpleasant the new regime and the occupation, the truth was that the invasion had halted a genocide. It was highly possible that the killing would have come round to Sokheang. Some of his friends had been taken to Duch. He later discovered that his name had been mentioned in at least three of his comrades' confessions from the prison.

Whenever we talked of his decision to return, the answers were often the same. I couldn't understand how such an experienced human-rights worker with a passion for uncovering the truth could argue this. It went against everything that Sokheang believed in. I began to question whether I had understood him at all. I had known Sokheang for several years now. He was a proud and stubborn man and despite all he had been through, still fiercely idealistic. This traditional antipathy towards the Vietnamese, I realised, produced its own internal logic. It enabled Sokheang and others to sideline and in some cases ignore what had happened under Pol Pot. It seemed Sokheang had thrown in his lot with the Khmer Rouge, and needed a way to rationalise that decision.

'I understand my decision was questionable,' he said folding his arms. 'I wanted the problem to be solved by Cambodians, not the Vietnamese. If there was a multinational force, I would have fully supported that.' Again I told him that not many people would understand him. By now the evening light had shrunk to the fluorescent light of our balcony. 'This was the biggest mistake that I made,' he said softly, leaning back, his arms still folded.

There was a loud metallic clunk as a large cicada flew into the fluorescent strip above Sokheang. It fell at our feet and buzzed frantically on its back, unable to get up. He gazed at the layer of insects in the pool of light, lost in thought. 'I also thought the war wouldn't last as long as it did,' he murmured.

Did he ever consider trying to escape? I asked.

'No, not at that time,' he replied.

Why not?

He looked up. 'Totalitarianism traps people,' he said quietly, an almost pleading expression on his face. 'The perception is there.' Here camp life was little more than extension of life in the country when it was Democratic Kampuchea. 'I believed that I would be able to return and be reunited with my family and my fiancée. If she was still waiting for me.'

Before Sokheang had gone to Paris he had fallen in love with a young woman who was a distant relative. No-one had known of their affair but they planned to marry when he returned from his studies. Then when Sokheang had met his aunt before heading for the border she told him that this young woman was nearby. Thinking Sokheang wasn't going to return, she had married someone else. Sokheang was devastated. 'It was such a shock for me, but I kept my thoughts to myself.' When they met she wept openly, then secretly proposed that they escape to the border together. But he believed it was too late and quietly left with his aunt and cousins.

In 1982, it was announced that three factions on the border would join to form a coalition. The Coalition Government of Democratic Kampuchea was comprised of Royalists, remnants of Lon Nol's republic, and the Khmer Rouge, with Sihanouk as head. It provided the necessary respectability to the Khmer Rouge, the ultimate beneficiaries of such support. These erstwhile enemies were united by one common goal: to roll back the Vietnamese invasion and oust their client regime in Phnom Penh.

After this coalition was formed Sokheang realised he was trapped and abandoned any hope of being reunited with his fiancée. In the same year, he married Van Heng, who had been a porter for Khmer Rouge troops and one of

Ieng Sary's cooks. The wedding, as was customary with the Khmer Rouge, was a sombre affair. After some speeches, they were given instant noodles and some soft drinks. And that was it.

CHAPTER 14

My Enemy's Enemy Is My Friend

THE VIETNAMESE INVASION had saved Duch. Before the collapse of the Khmer Rouge the issue of weeding out spies had been taken over by the need to fight the Vietnamese. Without their intervention it is almost certain that Duch too would have been killed. He had ensured that all references to him in the confessions had been erased before they were sent to the Higher Organisation. But more prisoners kept coming; and more confessions produced more names, which in turn meant more arrests and more killing.

When Duch arrived at the border he disappeared into the murky world of secret camps that made up 'the hidden border'. Details of his whereabouts remain sketchy. It is believed that he went to the forests of Samlaut, which was still a Khmer Rouge zone, under the direct control of Pol Pot. Here he was reunited with his family in Nuon Chea's headquarters, known as camp 404. He was demoted by Nuon Chea, apparently because of his failure to destroy the documents at Tuol Sleng, then offered a job in logistics.

Duch didn't get along with Nuon Chea. In fact Nuon

Chea had reproached him on at least two occasions whilst he worked in S-21. 'Brother Number 2' wasn't liked by many of the cadres. Whilst Pol Pot had always been charismatic and revered, Nuon Chea was aloof and arrogant. The fact that most of the archive had fallen into the hands of the Vietnamese reflected badly on Brother Number 2, and badly on Duch. As a result Duch was relieved of his duties.

While Duch's position had been an extremely important one, it was also extremely precarious. He could be a liability – he had a lot of incriminating information, which only strengthened the case for eliminating him. It seems a wonder that he wasn't killed. I later found out that he taught Son Sen's children in one of the camps. Duch also became close friends with Khieu Samphan's wife. He was still close to the leadership. He must have had the protection of someone in the party, most likely his former boss, Son Sen.

Here on the border Duch learned to speak Thai. He also taught himself English and apparently worked on producing school textbooks. In 1983, he had an accident with an AK-47 that he was cleaning and blew his finger off. If he had returned to teaching as some said or, if he had no duties at all, what was he doing with an assault rifle, I wondered?

When Duch went to Son Sen's camp he would have had to traverse the length of the border. The only way to do that would have been through the safety of Thailand. He would have gone through countless checkpoints and past the town of Aranyaprathet up over the Dangrek mountains and on to Ubon near the Lao border, courtesy of the Thai military.

Here, in this zone of impunity, the Khmer Rouge leadership led a life of privilege. They could come and go as they pleased. They had houses in the coastal town of Bang Saen and near the provincial town of Trat. Their bases along the border were protected by Thai soldiers and

artillery, many of them safe and out of reach of the
Vietnamese. They were escorted through the VIP channel
at Bangkok International Airport and accorded all the
formality and benefits that other foreign VIPs and diplomats enjoyed. When Ta Mok, the Khmer Rouge commander
known as 'the butcher', lost his leg to a mine in the early
1980s, he was reportedly evacuated to Bangkok, where he
was treated in St Louis Hospital. Ieng Sary's daughter studied
in Thailand's prestigious Thammasat University before going
on to City College in New York, where her father was a
UN diplomat. Every month they visited the nearby Thai
resort city of Pattaya escorted in unmarked cars with black-
tinted windows.

   Based alongside the relief agencies in the Thai border
town of Aranyaprathet, Unit 838 had been set up by the
Thai military specifically to look after the needs of the
Khmer Rouge coalition. From shipments of arms to intelligence and strategic planning and support, this secret unit
coordinated the Cambodian war effort against the
Vietnamese and the regime in Phnom Penh. When Khmer
Rouge forces were pushed out at one point on the border
the Thais would pick them up, close the roads and move
them to another more secure part of the border. Being close
to the leadership, Duch would have been taken to these
various camps by Unit 838. Some of the relief agencies may
have been waved down by Thai soldiers as his convoy was
rushed through the checkpoints before being permitted to
continue on to their work assisting the refugees.

While Duch had Thai military protection, life for the majority
on the border was as precarious as ever. The Thai-
Cambodian border was defined by what the Thais called
a strategic canal. A deep ditch, the width of two squash

courts and about five metres deep, ran the entire length of the frontier to prevent Vietnamese tanks from gaining easy access to Thai territory.

On Christmas Morning 1984, a young Jesuit, Bob Maat, began another day's work in Nong Samet, a camp controlled by the non-communist resistance in the coalition. When he arrived he was faced with the sight of some 60,000 terrified people huddled in the ditch as the sound of shells thundered across the skies. The Vietnamese had launched a major attack.

Maat watched a woman help her sick husband with one arm and carry their two-year-old daughter with the other, their bag of essentials slung over her shoulder. The husband told his wife to leave him at the side of the road and carry on without him. The shells were landing closer. Crying, she refused to abandon him. People searched frantically among the crowds for their children and loved ones lost in the panic.

At the ditch the Thai soldiers were everywhere. The shells were getting closer and closer. Large clouds of smoke drifted over the refugees' heads. The camp was now burning and large flames leaped into the sky. A number of handicapped were seated together in the ditch; some in their wheelchairs, some with crutches. The trauma made some pregnant women go into labour. Maat, who had been trained as a physician's assistant, helped deliver a baby boy among the crowds in the ditch. The shells were so close now that he could feel the percussion against his face as they landed. There were over twenty births in that ditch that morning. And more than 10,000 shells fell on the camp.

After the attack, new refugee camps were established along the frontier in what became a permanent humanitarian emergency as the political stalemate continued. The United Nations Border Relief Operation was set up to coordinate the relief agencies working in the camps and, apart from Khao-I-Dang, all of them were ruled by these coalition forces. There were two controlled by Lon Nol's old army, the KPNLF, one under the Royalists and a total of five under the Khmer Rouge. The camp populations provided a pool of recruits for these armies. The majority of the Khmer Rouge camps were virtually out of bounds to UN and other NGO staff, and access was severely limited. For the Thai military, the camps provided a perfect strategic buffer against the Vietnamese. They were also a great source of revenue, particularly from the humanitarian relief programme.

In order to appease the more squeamish of their supporters, the Khmer Rouge mounted a propaganda offensive claiming that they had changed. Site 8, the largest and most accessible of the Khmer Rouge camps, was referred to by UN and aid workers, as 'the showcase camp'. Here, against a backdrop of dramatic limestone cliffs, 30,000 people lived in huts neatly laid out on a bed of red laterite. Here the Khmer Rouge demonstrated how they had now embraced liberal capitalism. This was the façade which Duch and others hid behind. It wasn't particularly sophisticated, but it had the desired effect.

In contrast to the other Khmer Rouge camps, visitors to Site 8 would be mobbed by throngs of smiling children selling trinkets and souvenirs. With the correct papers journalists were permitted to walk through the gates manned by the Thai military to wander at will. One photographer described how you knew that you were in a Khmer Rouge camp by the bright colours people wore. They had replaced their black uniformity with garish colours of varying hue. Here people smiled and could approach foreigners and talk apparently freely. There was a bustling black market where anything from talcum powder to Coca-Cola could be bought

– proof of newly found capitalist credentials. There was also a human-rights office (a judicial system had been set up with the help of the UN) and even a Buddhist temple. There was a growing swell of opinion among some diplomats, journalists and aid workers that the Khmer Rouge were softening. Many who worked on the border described these camps as better managed and less corrupt than the non-communist ones. One diplomat said that the Khmer Rouge provided the refugees with security and care. Some wishful thinkers began to believe that a more 'reasonable' generation of leaders was gaining a foothold. As one former British ambassador wrote, 'Exposure to Western and local Thai influences is beginning to have its effect.' While it may have made the jobs of the UN and the NGOs easier, not everyone regarded this discipline as a positive attribute.

Where were these observers getting their information from? Since there were no new reports of mass murder many were wilfully lulled into believing that the Khmer Rouge had indeed reformed.

Come nightfall, when relief agencies had left the camp for the safety of Aranyaprathet, the fear that had paralysed people in the past swooped over the camps and descended once again.

In moves eerily reminiscent of the mass deportations of Khmer Rouge rule, thousands of people disappeared from these camps literally overnight. In 1985, 5,000 people were moved by the Khmer Rouge from Site 8 and across the Thai border into Cambodia. The following year, more than 1,500 people were taken to Natrao, Ta Mok's camp. Many more were used to porter ammunition.

In fact little had changed. As Norah Niland, a researcher from Trinity College Dublin wrote, 'The idea of openly "disobeying" Khmer Rouge camp administrators was too frightening a prospect for any refugee to contemplate.' By most accounts the structure and behaviour of the Khmer Rouge in the camps had changed little since the seventies. Reports of disappearances, interrogations, public beatings and summary executions were commonplace as they exerted their control over their captive populations. The same Khmer Rouge leadership remained in control. And it was the same leadership that had presided over S-21.

One of the camps Duch did spend time in was located to the south, just inside Thailand.

Borai was virtually cut off from outsiders. Just as before, the Khmer Rouge kept the population tightly controlled and in fear. Here in the jungle of the border 4,000 men, women and children lived in makeshift houses surrounded by malarial forest.

Duch taught English and maths at the school and was paid in food and clothing by the UN. Since most of the Khmer Rouge leaders at Borai didn't speak English, it is believed that he became one of the main liaison persons for the outside world with the UN and the few NGOs who supplied the camp.

Despite all the diplomatic and practical support the Khmer Rouge were given, they still treated outsiders with a barely concealed hostility. Like all the camps the UN supplied, this was supposed to be a civilian camp. The UN had repeatedly asked that the troops from the factions drop their weapons at the satellite camps nearby before entering the civilian ones. The request was met with a cursory agreement, but it was a losing battle. On occasion, with the enlisted support of Thai soldiers who guarded the camp, aid workers would arrange searches for weapons. In one particular house where the inhabitants were all blind, an aid worker talked to one old man then lifted his eyes to the roof above. There, hanging from the rafters, were an assortment of AK-47s, rocket-propelled grenades and other small arms.

In other camps controlled by the allies of the Khmer Rouge, the people didn't fare much better. Site 2 was the largest camp under the remnants of Lon Nol's army. With a population of 152,000 people it was one of the most densely populated areas in the world. Fenced on one side by bamboo and barbed wire and by landmines on the other, it was Cambodia's second-largest city after Phnom Penh and it was in Thailand.

As before it was the Americans who provided support to the guerrillas. They were paying $24 million annually in assistance to these factions, the logic being that they provided a counterbalance to the Khmer Rouge, something Washington assiduously promoted. But the label 'non-communist' conveniently disguised the fact that they were also non-democratic. With this aid they could keep their civilian populations under control and violence became a way of life and Site 2 descended into lawlessness.

Ordinary refugees trapped in these camps had little say in the matter; their lives were governed by varying degrees of brutality, the Khmer Rouge being the worst perpetrators.

The non-communist camps were more open to the aid workers. There they were permitted to work and were able to provide comprehensive health care, nutrition, sanitation, food and a wide variety of educational and social services. What these camps could not do, however, was give people what they sought most: safety and hope.

Not far beneath the smiles of the refugees was a mood of hopeless despair. With the political deadlock, the continuing war and insecurity and little chance of resettlement abroad, the listlessness of camp life was becoming a cause for serious concern. Depression had set in and the social fabric of whatever was left after the Khmer Rouge, the war and the bombing, was beginning to unravel.

Incidents of domestic abuse and rape were on the increase. As one aid worker, referring to a spate of murders in Site 2, reported, 'It's not just a cut here or there. They're stabbed multiple times, twenty to thirty times. People are axing, knifing, throwing grenades, and hitting each other in record numbers.'

Stephane Rousseau, who worked as an UNBRO security officer at Site 2, recalled hearing about a possible murder of a woman outside the camp. He went to investigate with another colleague. They walked for about two kilometres through the wild brush before they came across tufts of hair and pools of blood on the ground. They followed the trail. 'You knew that the person must have really fought for their life,' Rousseau said.

They arrived at a clearing where the soil had recently been disturbed. A group of men with tools began to dig. After a few minutes they uncovered the body of a naked woman of about thirty years of age. 'She had been really atrociously mutilated,' said Rousseau. 'She had been axed everywhere, in the head and on the arm and on the leg,' he said. Her brother, who had come with them, agreed they should cremate her body on the spot.

The woman was well known in the camp; she had been deaf and mute. A lover was thought to have murdered her. He had seen her with another man and in a fit of rage had killed her.

'And I remember thinking of her last few minutes,' Rousseau said. 'It was horrible to that think that this woman couldn't even scream for help.'

*   *   *

In June 1986 Duch, on the orders of Son Sen, was sent to China to teach as a Khmer-language expert at Beijing's Foreign Language Institute. It was at the height of the conflict against the Vietnamese and the Chinese were supplying the Khmer Rouge with all the weaponry and training they needed. Most likely, Duch taught Chinese intelligence personnel and advisers before they left for the border. The Chinese at first didn't know who he was. When they found out that he had been head of Tuol Sleng, they didn't review his contract and cancelled his visa. He returned to the border a year later. If he had taught intelligence personnel it was possible that he was still connected to the *Santebal*.

On his return, however, Duch changed his name to Hang Pin and went to work in Camp 505, just inside the Cambodian border. This was Pol Pot's secretariat, where he worked as a senior bureaucrat.

Looking over the border now, it's hard to imagine that such momentous events ever took place here. Much of the terrain is flat and featureless scrubland. The brick model of Angkor Wat at the entrance of Khao-I-Dang is now overgrown with weeds. Apart from the regimented gridwork pattern of the sections of the camps, there is virtually no trace that they ever existed. Their populations are now scattered all over Cambodia and across the globe. Tens, perhaps hundreds, of thousands of people died crossing this invisible frontier. Thousands more died in the camps. Many were also born there, into a no-man's-land between Thailand and Cambodia. Here China, the Soviet Union and the West played politics with the lives of countless, expendable Cambodians in a front line of the Cold War.

On a hill just south of Aranyaprathet, on the Thai side

of the border, two ancient brick *Prasats*, or sanctuary towers, sit among the trees on the summit. It is the only hill for miles around. In early 1992, I sat here listening to a tropical storm as it growled above the hills in the distance. Below me, through the trees, the sound of children's laughter and music came from across the border in Cambodia.

At the foot of the hill, accompanied by a Thai friend who worked in one of the refugee camps, I followed a network of tarmacked roads that disappeared into an unkempt landscape of bamboo. I followed the music and laughter to the end of one road until it petered out into a path that disappeared into the wild brush of the border.

We came to a clearing of several fallow paddy fields. Up ahead I could see TV aerials and a radio antenna. The music and laughter were becoming more distinct. A rickety bridge made of planks of wood stood over a small river. On the other side were several houses built from the wood of Chinese ammunition cases. It was a Khmer Rouge village. We crossed over.

Several people turned to watch me as I walked into the village. The children who were sitting on the dark earthen floor stopped playing and stared at me. I greeted a man sitting on the doorstep of his house; he looked right through me as though I were a ghost. All the men were wearing the Chinese green of the Khmer Rouge which had become standard issue since they were ousted by the Vietnamese. After several minutes I was summoned to the largest house beside the river.

The village was part of a Khmer Rouge enclave that ran down much of the border to the Gulf of Thailand. We were welcomed by a smiling cadre in a freshly pressed Chinese uniform. After shaking us warmly by the hand he invited us to sit down at the table on his veranda. Above him was a calendar with a photograph of Khmer Rouge troops walking along a paddy dyke towards a horizon of sugar palms. We were given hot tea and we chatted for some moments before he asked us the purpose of our unannounced visit. I told him we wanted to visit 'liberated Cambodia'. He asked what country I came from so I said I was British. I knew that the British would have been known by the Khmer Rouge.

He smiled and said that since we didn't have permission to be here we should leave. Next time we would have to go through the 'appropriate channels' in Bangkok, he told us. He then took us to the bridge that marked the border and, warning us of the mines, told us to keep to the path. Before I crossed, he shook me by the hand and thanked me for Britain's support for the struggle to liberate his country.

It was well known that the US and other governments were supporting this coalition, but the true extent of the involvement wasn't revealed until the end of the eighties. When Prime Minister Margaret Thatcher was questioned about British support for the Khmer Rouge-led coalition on BBC television she replied, 'Some of the Khmer Rouge of course were very different. I think that there are probably two parts to the Khmer Rouge: those who supported Pol Pot and then there is a much, much more reasonable group with the Khmer Rouge.'

It was revealed in the *Daily Telegraph* and in TV reports by John Pilger that the SAS had been training members of the non-communist forces in the Khmer Rouge coalition. These claims were vigorously denied by the Conservative Government at the time. However, in 1991, in a written parliamentary answer, the government admitted that the SAS had indeed provided training to the Khmer Rouge's allies since 1983. It was then revealed that the SAS had trained Pol Pot's guerrillas directly. A Human Rights Watch report, written by former British serviceman Rae McGrath, revealed that the SAS had taught the non-communist factions how to set up booby traps, attack airports, blow up bridges and railway lines, and lay minefields. 'The very things,' McGrath told Pilger, 'that we call terrorism.'

Over the years I had met many Cambodian soldiers who had been trained by the Thais, the Malaysians, the Americans and the British. None of them had been Khmer Rouge, but members of the non-communist forces. I continued to ask former Khmer Rouge in different parts of the country. Yet still, more than ten years after these reports, no-one had talked to a former Khmer Rouge who had attended these trainings.

Then I had a meeting with another former Khmer Rouge in a village south of Battambang. I asked him if he had ever received training by foreigners. He replied that he had.

He was a small, dark man in his late forties who had spent all his life with the Khmer Rouge. He was visiting from another part of the country and appeared unused to talking with a foreigner. It was like talking to a shy teenager.

In late 1986, he had received a direct order from Ta Mok, 'the butcher', to attend a series of training courses. The courses lasted for a period of six months and, as it was too dangerous for them to take place on Cambodian soil, they were held at a secret base ten kilometres inside Thai territory in Sisaket province.

The camp covered an area of some five square kilometres with forest on one side and Thai fruit orchards on the other. It was supplied by the Thai military. There were several warehouses where food, ammunition and other supplies were stored.

He said that he was among a group of twelve other Khmer Rouge divisional commanders. In total there were five different workshops and five British instructors, but only one trained his group. His instructor was called 'Mr Gary'.

'How did you know they were British?' I asked.

'Because they told us.'

He didn't recognise their insignia but they all wore 'light grey' berets. 'They were very well equipped,' he said. They were all officers. There was also a general who was in charge who carried a walking cane.

They were taught tactical guerrilla fighting, arms training, weapons technology, including booby traps, and sabotage. He was also trained in mines technology and strategy. He said that, despite having extensive experience, he didn't know much, but what he learned was, 'very useful'.

Outside of the training they had no informal contact with the British, but often saw them eating and drinking tea with Ta Mok. 'They were friendly with him.' The British also accompanied them on long-range reconnaissance patrols deep inside the country. One time they even went as far as the forests that surround the temples of Angkor. They never took part in the fighting and acted only in an advisory role. They helped in the planning and debriefed the guerrillas afterwards.

To date, the British government has never admitted to the training of the Khmer Rouge. Nor has it explained why the SAS, at the expense of the British taxpayer, was sent to train these groups in the first place.

The Vietnamese knew they could never win. The world was changing and the Cold War was coming to an end.

In 1989 Soviet troops left Afghanistan, the Berlin Wall came down and Communist rule ended in Poland, Hungary, Czechoslovakia and East Germany. The crippling effects of the US embargo and the war in Cambodia were proving too costly for the Vietnamese to sustain their 'irreversible' occupation without Soviet support. By 1989, save a few advisers, all ground troops had left. As soon as the last Vietnamese soldiers crossed back into Vietnam, the Khmer Rouge and their allies swept over the border and attacked government forces. In less than two months, the strategically important town of Pailin had fallen to the Khmer Rouge with, it was rumoured, Thai support. The Khmer Rouge had then begun to advance up Route 10 towards Battambang, Cambodia's second-largest city. The same was reported all over the country, in Kompong Speu, Kompong Thom as well as Siem Reap and Beantey Meanchey. Khmer Rouge activity was reported less than two hours from the capital and a curfew was imposed.

By May 1990, alarmed by Khmer Rouge gains and an upsurge in fighting in Cambodia, the public outcry prompted both Ireland and Sweden to withdraw their support for the coalition seat at the UN. Mounting domestic pressure was put on western governments to prevent a return of the Khmer Rouge.

In Phnom Penh a curfew was imposed. People would stop me in the street and ask me anxiously whether the Khmer Rouge would return. In my previous visits I had assured them confidently that the world wouldn't allow it. Now with the Khmer Rouge just over an hour from the capital, I wasn't so sure.

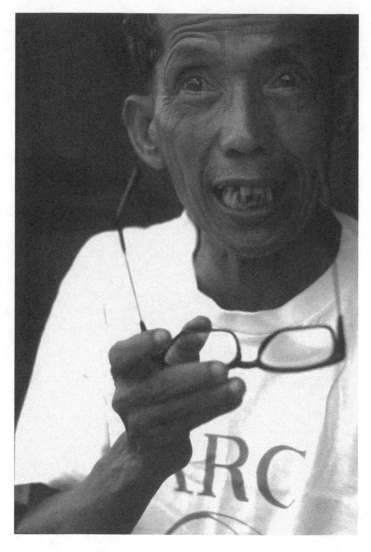

Comrade Duch confesses to mass murder, Ta Sanh, Samlaut 1999
(*Photograph by Nic Dunlop*)

PART III

Hang Pin

CHAPTER 15

The Return of the Khmer Rouge

IN OCTOBER 1991, while Duch was still in Borai refugee camp, an agreement was reached in Paris that paved the way for the largest, most ambitious peacekeeping mission in UN history. At a cost of $2 billion, 22,000 troops and UN personnel were charged with creating 'a politically neutral environment' in the lead-up to 'free and fair elections' and an end to the war.

A ceasefire was announced and Cambodian sovereignty enshrined in a transitional government headed by Prince Sihanouk in Phnom Penh. Here representatives from all sides in the war were to sit in the run-up to elections. The Royalist Party, headed by Sihanouk's son Rannariddh, the Kampuchean People's National Liberation Front, the Phnom Penh regime, headed by Hun Sen, and the Khmer Rouge. After more than twenty years of bombing, civil war, mass murder, invasion and occupation at last, it seemed, there was hope.

Shortly after the Paris agreement Duch returned to Cambodia. He moved with his wife and four children to a small isolated village called Phkoam, not far from the Thai border. The area was under Khmer Rouge control, but was far from secure. Nevertheless, he bought some land, built a house and began teaching in the local school.

Phkoam was a small island of greenery surrounded by empty paddy fields at the foot of a small hill. It was an old and busy village of tightly packed houses shaded by coconut palms and banana trees. Duch built the family a house on the dusty road that bisected the village which led to the school.

They were a popular family and kind to their neighbours. Soi Sang, a woman in her mid-fifties who lived opposite, remembered Duch as quiet and somewhat withdrawn. Rom, Duch's wife, was very talkative and liked to gossip. By the standard of the village, the family was quite well off and owned three paddy fields, a motorbike and several cows. They also had a small medicine stall. Duch often shared meat with Soi Sang's family and gave medicine on credit. Sometimes Duch lent money interest-free, often for up to a month. He was very polite, said another villager.

Duch was one of the best teachers in the school and often gave extra lessons for free. But he was known among his students for his fierce temper. 'When he got angry he was very frightening,' said Khean Kheach, one of his former pupils. Duch's eldest son, Ky Siew Pheng, who had been born a few days before the fall of Phnom Penh, was a tearaway. He gambled, stole motorbikes from other villages and regularly got into trouble. As punishment, Duch drew a circle in the dirt and, tying Pheng up, ordered him to stand in the centre, forbidding him from stepping out of the circle. If he moved Duch would hit him with a stick and threaten him, 'If you do this again, I will whip you till you die. If this were the Pol Pot time, I would recommend to the Organisation that you be taken away.'

Not all of his own children were treated with the same degree of severity. Duch spent a great deal of time with his youngest son, Thai An, partly because he reminded Duch of his own grandfather and partly because Thai An worked hard at his studies. Thai An was the favourite and Duch took him everywhere. When Duch went to work at school, he let him play outside the classroom while he taught mathematics and physics. Duch was patient when it came to homework, and although he pushed his children to study hard, he was always ready to explain problems, encouraging them to ask if they didn't understand. I asked Thai An which subjects he found difficult. 'Mathematics and physics,' he replied with a knowing smile.

'One time he bought a ball and played soccer with us,' said Thai An, 'but he was a terrible player. He preferred us to use our minds.'

After their homework and Duch's favourite dinner of *Samlor Pror Hoeur*, a fish soup with vegetables, he would often tell the children stories before bedtime. Around an oil lamp they would listen as he told them old folk tales, some of them from the *Gatiloke*. 'He was a good story-teller,' said Thai An. He would put on performances for the more humorous tales, pulling faces and mimicking voices of ogres. He had more control over the children than their mother did. As the softer of the two, Rom's commands fell on deaf ears. Thai An couldn't remember much about his mother, he said. 'I was very young when she was killed.'

At the same time as Duch returned to Cambodia I arrived in Phnom Penh to find an air of frenzied optimism. I was there to witness the triumphant return of Prince Sihanouk after more than thirteen years in exile, an event that, for older Cambodians, augured peace. The US-led embargo had been lifted and people were talking excitedly about the arrival of the UN peacekeepers and the end of the war. I set out to record the peace process from the viewpoint of the poor in the countryside. It would give me the opportunity to learn more in communities where the Khmer Rouge had come from and to see if the war really was over.

Phnom Penh was booming. Shops were bursting on to the streets with consumer goods. Garish cloth appeared in the markets alongside televisions, videos, motorbikes, ghetto blasters and other western goods. Cambodians were embracing the wonders of the free market that had been denied them for so long. On virtually every side road I would see new hotels, restaurants and dance halls as expatriate Cambodians returned from adopted countries armed with dollars and eager to invest. New Japanese cars appeared on the streets and construction sites emerged in dilapidated parts of the city. The Australians installed a telephone system and I remember making my first telephone call to London from the Central Post Office.

Rents soared in expectation of the army of aid workers and UN personnel. Prices were soon on a par with central London. Old houses were requisitioned and squatters evicted. I was told by a member of a major aid agency that their Cambodian landlord in Phnom Penh had been approached by a UN official who promised to double the rent if he evicted them. They were already paying about US $2,200 per month.

The recently opened Cambodiana Hotel became the haven for the expatriate community. A seventies monstrosity on the Bassac River, its construction had been halted when the Khmer Rouge encircled the city in 1975. It had provided temporary refuge for hundreds of families fleeing the fighting in the countryside, camping in squalor in the unfinished rooms. Now the Cambodiana had been rebuilt by a foreign company touting it as Cambodia's first (and only) luxury hotel.

Walking into the hotel's gaudy lobby one night, I was gripped by a gust of arctic air conditioning. The glass doors were flanked by Cambodian guards in ill-fitting uniforms who smiled and bowed. The bar was awash with expats and a Filipino band crooned 'Let it Be' and 'Hotel California'. Aid workers, journalists, diplomats, UN soldiers, photographers, Cambodian officials and other camp followers crowded around the bar for happy-hour drinks served by enthusiastic Cambodians eager to please.

Sitting beside the Cambodiana Hotel's swimming pool, I would gaze across the silver water of the Bassac River to the tree-lined bank in the distance and imagine an oriental paradise a million miles away. When my eyes became accustomed to the darkness I could make out shapes just beyond the hotel's razor-wire perimeter. Here lived impoverished families forced off their land or unable to find mine-free fields on which to farm. Drawn to Phnom Penh in search of work they were now squatting at the water's edge. From their shacks of dirty plastic and stolen wood they would look up at the beaming light of the pool and hear laughter and the clinking of glasses.

The massive influx of aid money and aid agencies changed Phnom Penh's appearance overnight. For many of these expats life was good. Along with a clean conscience and a righteous determination, they could afford many privileges in a place as poor as Cambodia. Often they received a daily allowance, plus a housing allowance, their tax-free salaries being paid directly into bank accounts back home. Among aid workers there was a feeling, never made explicit, that as long as you lived just below the UN in terms of comfort and expense then that was all right. Most were paid in US dollars of course and never needed to touch their salaries as their living expenses and children's education were catered for. Cambodia had two currencies. One for the foreigners, US dollars, and another for Cambodians, the riel.

The foreigners occupied large villas, some of which were old colonial buildings. Included in the package would be air conditioning, a maid, and a guard. Sometimes even satellite TV could be justified in a hardship posting such as Cambodia. Crime became a big problem. Often the guard would keep an AK-47 stored away and his employer would turn a blind eye. Unlike the Cambodian family next door, they would have a generator should the electricity fail, a regular occurrence. Such was the demand for electricity, one of the most common items to be stolen from a *barang*, or foreign household, would be a generator. They were hardly luxury items and their disappearance was more a statement of the country's desperate condition than a lawless act of greed. Before I left Cambodia, I would see hospital operations performed without electricity, surgeons working in near darkness.

UN transport planes growled away on the other side of Pochentong airfield, delivering the incredible tonnage of equipment that the UN troops and civilian personnel demanded. Old Soviet helicopters were requisitioned much to the delight of the Russian pilots who were stranded after the end of the Cold War. They were now receiving their salaries in American dollars, and could often be seen spending this newfound wealth on ever-greater quantities of vodka, before climbing unsteadily into the cockpit on UN missions.

On the other side of the airfield several unmarked helicopters sat in the heat. They were Jolly Green Giants belonging to the US military. The last time they had been seen in the skies of Cambodia had been on 12 April 1975, the day the Americans had evacuated their embassy and left the country to the approaching Khmer Rouge. Now, nearly twenty years later, they were back, not to help Cambodia, but to retrieve the bones of a handful of US servicemen who had been killed in the war before 1975.

Soldiers and police from as far away as Cameroon, Germany, Ghana and Fiji arrived and set up bases in different parts of the country. In this vast logistical exercise UNTAC was faced with operating in a country with almost no infrastructure. Cambodia's legendary appalling roads were little more than cratered tracks. Outside the capital the telephone system was non-existent. When an aid-worker friend in Battambang spoke with his headquarters in Phnom Penh, he had to use the old Soviet military radio belonging to the Cambodian army. It could take up to twenty minutes to make a connection. A total of $92 million was set aside for air-conditioned LandCruisers for the UN. The biggest sponsor of the peace plan was the Japanese Government and the vehicles purchased for the operation came from Toyota. By comparison, just $20 million was allocated for the repair and construction of roads and bridges. Much of the mission's money went right back into pockets of donor countries.

The influx of so much money and the relaxation that capitalism brought exacerbated Cambodia's endemic corruption beyond all proportion. While trained surgeons had to feed families on a monthly salary of $12, some UN personnel were getting living allowances of $135 a day. There was a mad rush to supply the foreigners with every possible comfort and foreign businessmen took advantage of Cambodia's inability to provide what Cambodia sorely lacked. 'Exploitation is the name of the game here,' one expatriate remarked. 'Cambodia is the discount store in the region. Cheap girls, cheap labour. Take your pick. If you were a businessman without scruples, you'd do quite well here. This kind of place appeals to the worst kind of cowboys, and they are eating Cambodia for breakfast.'

The blue berets of UN troops could be seen bobbing above the crowds in the markets, their oversized trucks parked outside brothels. UN officials in LandCruisers sped around, flags fluttering. They held meetings to discuss what they hoped would be the country's transition overnight from a one-party state to a multi-party democracy, from a country at war to a country at peace.

With the UN's arrival came unprecedented freedom of expression. A plethora of political parties appeared in the run-up to elections, including the Khmer Citizen Party, the Khmer Nation Party, the Khmer Angkor Party and the Buddhist Liberal Democratic Party, one party's offices displayed the slogan 'Communism is Evil', a quote from former US president Ronald Reagan. Nearly all of them had logos that sported the towered profile of Angkor Wat. Newspapers sprang up and a number of indigenous NGOs emerged, including several human-rights organisations. However, for many Cambodians out in the countryside, the closest they came to this flurry of activity was the sight of these white LandCruisers as they sped past in clouds of red dust.

The heady effects of this injection of money were largely restricted to Phnom Penh and the provincial capitals where most foreign workers were based. In the countryside nothing much had changed and the ceasefire was not holding. The Khmer Rouge had launched attacks on twenty-five villages near Kompong Thom, sending 11,000 people fleeing for their lives.

The wild beauty of the countryside and the long evening shadows concealed hidden dangers. Dusk was the time when the Khmer Rouge would reappear. Fifteen years after they were ousted from power, the Khmer Rouge had left an indelible mark on the population here. When several hundred Buddhist monks and lay people traversed the province on a peace walk, they blessed local people by pouring water on their heads saying, *Santepheap* ('Peace'). Many replied with the Khmer Rouge cry, *Romdos!* ('Liberation!').

In the midst of all this Tuol Sleng remained still and empty. Few UN officials visited the museum to pay their respects and those that did visited in a private capacity. It was as if they saw it as a curiosity from another age. Few in the hallowed halls of the UN mission's headquarters in Phnom Penh or aid-agency offices talked of it and all that it represented. It was considered irrelevant, even impolite to talk about. They ignored it precisely because it lay right at the very heart of the problem.

The rooms at Tuol Sleng remained the same, but the contents had moved and some items had disappeared altogether. The wooden building in the centre had been the office where photographs had been taken of incoming prisoners. Now it was once again the administrative centre, where guides sat in the shade waiting for visitors to pay a fluctuating entrance fee (before it had been a voluntary donation). The office had been turned into a gift shop selling *kramas*, Coke, pirate copies of *The Killing Fields*, and money which the Khmer Rouge had printed but never issued.

Tuol Sleng was becoming an essential stop for the increasing number of visitors on their way to the temples of Angkor. Later it would be advertised in guide books and maps as part of all tour-company itineraries. There is probably no country in the world that advertises its dark history like Cambodia. Like much else in Phnom Penh, genocide had become a commercial enterprise.

Later, tour buses would make a day out of visiting the horrors of 'the Pol Pot time'. Tourists would be picked up from their hotel in the morning and taken to the museum. Afterwards they could have lunch at a restaurant looking over the museum, housed next to what had once been a field station for prisoners between torture sessions. And then go out of town to the killing ground of Choeung Ek before returning to a buffet dinner on the riverfront.

While Sihanouk arrived with much pomp and ceremony, another ally quietly returned to the capital. Son Sen, Duch's former superior and commander of the Khmer Rouge forces, who had made regular visits to Tuol Sleng, moved into a building next to where I was staying. There he remained, protected by guards of the Phnom Penh regime.

Khieu Samphan arrived to join him. What had at first been an organised mob soon turned into one angry with the Khmer Rouge. A crowd attacked the building where he was staying. Khieu Samphan received a blow to the head before being bundled into an armoured personnel carrier and spirited back to the airport and then to Bangkok.

Afterwards, the Khmer Rouge received guarantees from the UN and the government in Phnom Penh for their safety.

Khieu Samphan returned to take his position at the table of the Supreme National Council as an equal partner in the country his organisation had almost destroyed. The sanitising of the past had begun. All official references to mass murder and genocide were dropped and reduced to the phrase, 'the policies and practices of the recent past'. The Australian Foreign Minister and one of the architects of the plan, Gareth Evans, confidently asserted that the 'genocide issue and all the emotion associated with that had now been resolved'. Khmer Rouge guerrillas were elevated to the status of an organised army with the respectable-sounding title of the National Army of Democratic Kampuchea. The Cambodian government army was reduced to the Cambodian People's Armed Forces, which sounded more like a ragbag militia. The UN spokesperson, Eric Falt, did his best to avoid using the term 'Khmer Rouge' in press briefings, instead calling them 'The Party of Democratic Kampuchea', as the UN position in all this was to be one of great neutrality. Any sceptics were met with looks of incredulity followed by outright hostility, from threats of press passes being withdrawn and permission to travel on UN helicopters revoked, to being barred from interviews and press conferences.

With all the talk of national reconciliation and the effective whitewash of the Khmer Rouge's bloody past, it was now safe for them to come back.

While Duch was settling into his new home, Sokheang was permitted to leave the Khmer Rouge. He arranged to be met in Sisophon by his youngest brother Ly. Sokheang had asked an old friend to accompany Ly, since Sokheang couldn't remember what his brother looked like. Ly had last seen Sokheang at Pochentong airport twenty-one years before. After the 1975 fall of Phnom Penh, the family were sent to work in Kompong Cham where their three brothers had been killed. The surviving family – the parents, Ly and his three sisters – had no idea Sokheang was living in the same province and had assumed he was safely in France. It was not until 1982 that the family received word that Sokheang had returned to Cambodia and began to suspect that he was with the Khmer Rouge.

Then one day, a photograph of Sokheang with his new wife arrived in the post. I asked Ly how his family reacted.

'We were . . .' He paused to choose his words carefully. 'We were happy and at the same time shocked,' he said finally.

After Sokheang's departure, their father had fallen into a deep depression which lasted several months, and at one point he became suicidal. Everything he had owned and had worked hard for had been destroyed. The country was in ruins and his eldest son had left for France.

Traditionally in Chinese-Khmer families, the eldest son is, after the father, the guardian of the family and its name. As the eldest, Sokheang was expected to take over the family's affairs and provide for his ageing parents in later life. Parental approval of a son's future wife was also important. Sokheang had lost contact with tradition and had broken an unwritten rule: he had married a stranger.

It was 'difficult' to understand his brother's decision to join the Khmer Rouge, said Ly. He couldn't relate to his brother's political activism; he blamed communism and the Khmer Rouge. 'He knows that politics in Cambodia is completely different from politics in other countries,' he said. 'Politics in Cambodia is the politics of revenge.'

Haing Ngor once described the Cambodian belief in *Kum*, or karma, as a concept of revenge. It was, he wrote, 'the infection that grows on our national soul'. Acts carried out during a lifetime or from a previous life dictate a person's position in the next. In Cambodia, *Kum* was the kind of revenge that tended to be out of proportion to the original crime. The anger that feeds it can remain hidden for years, so well concealed that the victim can even maintain friendly relations with the person who wronged him. Then one day, the victim will turn to kill that person. He gave an example of police who steal chickens from a peasant and then later the peasant launches a surprise attack on the garrison. This is *Kum*. 'We can smile,' Sihanouk had once said of his own people, 'but we can also kill.'

For Ly, the gap in years and the effects of long separation and different experiences was all too evident. Ly had stayed with the family during the war and through the Khmer Rouge period. He had been with his parents when his brothers had been taken away to their deaths and had stayed with them during the Vietnamese occupation. As a doctor in a front-line province he saw the results of this idealism and what it was doing to ordinary people. He had no experience of the political world and the side of the war that had shaped the thinking of his brother in the 1960s and later in Paris. Sokheang was the eldest and Ly the youngest. They hardly knew each other.

CHAPTER 16

'Policies and Practices of the Recent Past'

O N THE FIRST anniversary of the signing of the Paris agreement, the UN organised a parade in front of the Royal Palace. On the lawn, overlooking the river, I watched as UN soldiers swept the area for land-mines before the fanfare commenced. All the contingents were represented. The peacekeepers stood to attention in freshly pressed uniforms, guns gleaming in the mid-morning heat. A large UN flag held by an American guard flowed above the crowd. Citing security concerns, the entire area had been sealed off and ordinary Cambodians were kept away, while the UN celebrated the peace as the world's cameras looked on.

A crowd of dignitaries that included diplomats and other UN personnel had been invited to watch. After the speeches, the soldiers were inspected by Prince Sihanouk and Lt.-Col. Sanderson, the UN force commander, together with the head of the UN mission, Yasushi Akashi. The VIPs sat there, quietly cooking, sweat stains gradually spreading across their suits. A zealous Ghanaian band master presented himself and, to the tune of 'Onward Christian Soldiers', they marched, saluted and marched again despite the fact that Cambodia was Buddhist. Moments later a series of UN helicopters and planes rumbled low over Phnom Penh's rooftops and paratroopers glided down and landed among the troops, UN flags rippling beneath their feet.

I scanned the crowd of VIPs. There was Hun Sen, the Prime Minister of the Phnom Penh regime, the British ambassador, the US ambassador, the heads of the various UN agencies and an assortment of diplomats and dignitaries. And there, among them all, in a gleaming cream suit, a white-haired Cambodian sat smiling and clapping just as he had done the world over. It was Khieu Samphan of the Khmer Rouge.

This was the same Khieu Samphan who had watched the exodus from Phnom Penh and later taken over as head of state. Since the fall of the Khmer Rouge, he had spent much time flying around the world, smiling and waving, treated with the courtesy and privilege accorded all international diplomats. He had visited Sihanouk in France, where they enjoyed fine French cuisine, presenting the world and the Khmer Rouge paymasters with an image of the acceptable face of the Khmer Rouge. However, on several occasions since the fall of his regime, Khieu Samphan had been confronted by the barbarous record of the regime. When Cambodia scholar Stephen Heder confronted him about the killings he replied, 'There was no mistake.' All those who had been 'smashed' had been 'enemies', he said. But he did concede that perhaps one old man had been falsely accused.

Son Sen was nowhere to be seen. As Duch's former boss and one of the Khmer Rouge leaders known to be directly associated with the killings, perhaps his presence would have muddied that most cherished UN virtue: impartiality. Curious Cambodians, trying to get a glimpse of all this, were held back by Indonesian soldiers and UN police.

As part of the Paris agreement, seventy per cent of each faction's army, including the government forces, were to disarm. Out of approximately 200,000 soldiers expected to hand over their weapons, a mere 12,000 had shown up. The Khmer Rouge had refused altogether.

Because of the delay in the UN's deployment, the Khmer Rouge had greatly extended their zones of influence, hidden arms and moved troops to penetrate deeper and deeper into Cambodian territory. Even before the first UN soldier had set foot in the country there had been clashes. Out in the countryside there was shelling in Kompong Thom and Kompong Cham and Kompong Chhnang, in Banteay Meanchay, Siem Reap and Battambang provinces. Stoung, Duch's hometown, was subjected to a nightlong barrage by Khmer Rouge artillery. At first, the fighting was far from the urban centres, but just sharp and fast enough to keep people from feeling too secure. The normality was deceptive. This unpredictable violence could break out anywhere, at any time. Gradually, as it became clear the UN would not react, the violence escalated.

Less than a year later, and in spite of the presence of thousands of peacekeepers, the ceasefire began to completely disintegrate. Such was the scale of the fighting that the front stretched several kilometres along the western part of the country.

It could have been a scene plucked from the Middle Ages. Sitting on the edge of the slope I watched as children ran into the murky water that stretched out as far as the scrub-jungle on the other side. Women, indifferent to the children's splashing and peals of laughter, scrubbed away at their piles of laundry. Further on, two bullock carts filled with slender poles of recently felled timber were ambling their way through the shallows of the lake.

But this wasn't a lake. It was a dam built by the Khmer Rouge at the cost of thousands of people's lives as they toiled day and night in the fierce tropical heat. I imagined lines of regimented workers in black transporting loads of earth by hand under the flapping blood-red flags of Democratic Kampuchea. All over the country at that time hundreds of irrigation projects had been initiated, sometimes with no discernible purpose. Uneducated cadres, who had perhaps been courageous fighters during the war, had been rewarded with position and rank and given charge of these work sites. In some cases, with the arrogance of latter-day Canutes, there were even attempts to get water to flow uphill. Very often engineers would be working as manual labourers on the same sites that the untutored cadres had designed as they tried desperately to conceal their identities in case they should be found out and taken away. In the revolutionary world of the Khmer Rouge, ignorance was a virtue, and knowledge a threat.

The dam had long since been abandoned. It was now so overgrown that it seemed natural until one looked at the straight shoreline and contrasted it with the other side. Further along the road that ran along the top of the dyke there were concrete sluice gates from which young teenage boys jumped and twirled through the air, hitting the water in white explosions.

Above all the screams of the children and the noise from a ghetto blaster, the sound of heavy thunder echoed across the water. It was a constant rumble that sometimes grew in its intensity, like waves crashing on a shore. But it was

the dry season and there was no storm. It was the sound
of one of the fiercest offensives by the government on
Khmer Rouge positions since the peace had begun nearly
a year before.

The UN had begun to repatriate the refugees from their
camps in Thailand in large fleets of buses. 'When there is
peace in Cambodia,' read one poster in an office I saw,
'UNHCR will return you back to your homes in safety and
with dignity.' These convoys were colourful affairs with
inevitable UN logos plastered on the sides; perfect news-
photo material ensuring the international public could be
given the reassuring line that at last something was being
done for the refugees of the border.

While the repatriation grabbed the headlines, there were
already more than 200,000 refugees inside the country.
These refugees, or 'internally displaced persons' in NGO-
speak, had been there for several years and were not
considered a story. The refugees from the border received
vastly preferential treatment both in materials and the attention of the UN's publicity machine.

Many of those from the border ended up joining the
internal refugees and I spent much time taking pictures in
these encampments. The ubiquitous plastic sheeting given
to them was all around and the stencils of the aid organisations were everywhere. Nothing seemed to escape the
branding of the aid world. With pressure from donor governments, the aim of the UNHCR's repatriation was clear: to
get the border refugees back in time for the election. The
plight of these internal refugees wasn't as fashionable, nor
was it as lucrative. With the refugees back the UN in Phnom
Penh could claim their success. For the many who ended
up in these camps all the UN had done was shift the

border. One refugee told an aid worker he was happy to be back, 'Because at least here we can run from the fighting.'

The Khmer Rouge had stepped up their campaign of terror, particularly against the Vietnamese. The attacks became more frequent and more vicious. In one hour-long orgy of terror, the Khmer Rouge attacked a village, dashed the head of a week-old baby, split open the head of a seven-year-old girl, disembowelled a man and executed five others.

They refused to disarm, repeatedly refused UN access to their zones of control and stopped the head of the UN mission going beyond their checkpoints. They opened fire on helicopters and kidnapped UN soldiers. In response Akashi, the UN mission head, threatened to report the Khmer Rouge to the UN security council, and the UN military commander sent what he called 'a very strong' letter to the Khmer Rouge, saying that the attacks would have serious consequences for the guerrillas. Eager to play down the threat posed by this degeneration, the UN pushed on with the plan, hoping the situation would improve. One UN official declared that, although the resolution of the situation depended on the Khmer Rouge, 'things were going quite well'.

Things, however, were not going well and the resolve of the UN was put to the test once again.

In March 1993, on the Tonle Sap lake near Siem Reap the single worst massacre of the UN period occurred. The attack had been expected for a month and the UN had been informed. The local police had fled and the villagers, disarmed by the UN, were virtually defenceless. The people were ethnic Vietnamese fishermen who had lived on the lake for generations. When the Khmer Rouge attack eventually came, thirty-three men, women and children were murdered and a further twenty-four wounded. A UN naval observer stationed nearby said that the Bangladeshi troops were not in a position to do anything since they were there to protect him and his men.

As a result of this massacre and an unwillingness to move against the Khmer Rouge, 400 Vietnamese families fled down the Mekong to seek refuge in Vietnam. The UN provided the flotilla with an escort. UN chief Yasushi Akashi called on the Khmer Rouge to halt, as he put it, 'the hideous practice of ethnic cleansing'. The use of the word 'genocide' would have obliged the UN to act and protect the people and arrest those responsible. Instead, Akashi believed in 'patient diplomacy' and in doing things 'the Asian way' – by gentle persuasion, as if Asians adhered to a different set of UN principles. As the days went by, and the attacks continued, it was clear that this approach wasn't working.

Many UN soldiers I talked to were frustrated by the bureaucratic nature of their body. It was a language they found difficult to comprehend, with its talk of 'implementation', 'peacekeeping' and – instead of 'genocide' – 'the policies and practices of the recent past'. Faced with so much provocation, it was humiliating for soldiers to be bound by the red tape of non-intervention. On several occasions I was mistakenly identified as a UN official and accosted by angry Cambodian troops who complained to me that the UN were doing nothing to stop the Khmer Rouge.

Not everyone in the UN believed the Khmer Rouge deserved a second chance. Nearly a year before this massacre, the deputy commander of UNTAC, General Loridon, was removed from the mission. Frustrated by the lack of will to respond to the Khmer Rouge belligerence, he left disgusted. 'Here was our chance to deal with the

Khmer Rouge,' he lamented. 'One may lose 200 men – and that could include myself – but the Khmer Rouge problem would be solved for good.'

As the Khmer Rouge continued to harass, intimidate and kill, crime reached new levels. It became increasingly dangerous to travel through the streets of Phnom Penh at night. On several occasions the capital was the scene of firefights. Owning a motorbike, especially the coveted Honda 'Dream', was a liability. Owners were shot by thieves, who sold the bikes to cross-border traders. Theft from offices of NGOs and the UN itself was becoming commonplace. The UN LandCruisers, at a cost of US $35,000 each, were being stolen at a rate of three to four a day. One LandCruiser made its way into the hands of Ta Mok, the Khmer Rouge commander known as 'the butcher'.

'This all makes me sick,' one UN bureaucrat told the *Phnom Penh Post*. 'We write reports, security does an investigation, maybe they even find the driver who copied the keys, and then – nothing.'

By now, the UN-sponsored elections – which the Khmer Rouge had vowed to disrupt – were less than two months away.

Just before the election, I found myself in a minefield near Siem Reap, not far from the fabled temples of Angkor. I stood there in the baking heat, shivering with fever, watching as Cambodian soldiers were trained to clear minefields, supervised by UN soldiers. I made my excuses and headed to the nearest hospital, which was run by the Indian army contingent. I just wanted some medicine but the doctor in charge insisted that I stay. The UN had requisitioned a building that had been used for party meetings in another age. The paint was peeling, patches of the ceiling had begun to collapse and doors were hanging on hinges. Sparing no expense, the UN had organised the delivery of air-conditioned cubicles for their offices outside and the car park was lined with rows of pristine white LandCruisers.

Within an hour I was in the hospital, dressed in a pair of blue-and-white-striped pyjamas. I was shown a bed in the cool dark interior of what had been the building's main meeting hall. I remember how comforting the clean sheets felt against my skin as I slipped down into the warmth of my fever. Grateful for the privileges that my UN press pass entitled me to, and at the insistence of the doctor, I ended up staying there for several days. Every morning I awakened to toast with a thick layer of jam and a cup of milky sweet Indian tea served by smiling Indian soldiers.

The following day I awoke to the roar of helicopter rotors. I tottered over and opened the door, and was temporarily blinded by a cloud of white dust. A UN helicopter had arrived and two Indian soldiers, bent over with a stretcher, ran to where the helicopter was landing. I could see them lift out a wounded man, a drip held above their heads. They then trotted past me and into the makeshift operating theatre that looked a little like a giant air-conditioned balloon. As they passed me I guessed that he was in his late forties and, judging by his injuries, the victim of a landmine.

I discharged myself from the hospital and went to visit Siem Reap provincial hospital to photograph the wounded. There I saw the bloody consequences of the reports I had been hearing. Entire families sat nursing their wounded in the corridors. Many were victims of mines. Others had been shot or peppered with shrapnel.

I came across a farmer lying motionless on a mat. His bullock cart had driven over a mine, forcing shrapnel into his feet and legs. I began taking photographs. Then he moved, the wound opened up and began to haemorrhage, thick, dark blood spreading across the mat. I stood there and watched helplessly as a doctor took charge and stuck his finger in the hole of the old man's foot to stem the flow. I had to leave.

There was something different about Siem Reap. The road seemed unusually busy. And there was this intermittent pounding. When I reached the market, scores of heavily armed Cambodian soldiers suddenly appeared. A UN Land-Rover sped past me and screeched to a halt. Pakistani UN troops wearing oversized flak jackets and carrying AK-47 automatic rifles jumped down and fanned out among the stalls. I asked a tense-looking Pakistani officer what was going on. The Cambodian soldiers had just been paid for the first time in months, he told me, and had gone to the market to buy gold, where they were told that the Cambodian riel had devalued. One of them had shot and killed a money dealer.

The thudding I had heard earlier had been growing louder and closer. Hundreds of people had clambered up on to buildings around the market, all looking in the opposite direction. I climbed up to see what was going on, and at last saw the source of the sound; large plumes of smoke appeared in the distance followed by a thud; it was shelling less than two kilometres away.

Credible rumours were now circulating that the Khmer Rouge were about to attack Siem Reap. If they wanted to discredit the UN, Siem Reap – the town next to the ancient centre of the Khmer empire and the metaphorical heart of the nation – was the ideal target.

Concerned about being cut off by the fighting, I decided to leave for Battambang, Cambodia's second city and a place that had become my temporary home. Getting there by car was difficult. Bandits made it dangerous to travel after nightfall, although ironically this had not been the case before the UN arrived. Now, together with the Khmer Rouge, Cambodian soldiers, were resorting to random violence. Demobbed as part of the Paris agreement, many had been sent home, often without pay and, with little hope of finding new jobs, many turned to banditry to feed their families. I went to Siem Reap's deserted airport and hitched a ride in a UN helicopter to Battambang. That night in Battambang, I sat chatting with a friend on a veranda. It felt good to be somewhere I knew and felt safe in, far from the paranoia of Siem Reap. Then a couple of shots rang out. It was common enough to hear gunfire at night and so we paid no attention. Then the sky lit up with bursts of tracer fire and the thunderous racket of AK-47s. We rushed to turn off the lights and threw ourselves on the floor. I could see tracer zip past the house of an aid worker I knew. After about ten minutes it died down and the sound of the night crickets returned.

The assault on Siem Reap came a week later. Three hundred Khmer Rouge launched a pre-dawn attack from three directions and came into town, firing their weapons. Within four hours the attack was over. Two civilians, four Khmer Rouge and one Cambodian soldier were dead. The Khmer Rouge had made no attempt to occupy the town. The message had been sent: the UN were no longer in control and the Khmer Rouge could do what they wanted.

Then the Khmer Rouge began to target the UN directly. Bulgarian UN soldiers, who had been friendly with the local Khmer Rouge, invited them to join them for dinner. After the meal and without warning the Khmer Rouge shot and killed the three Bulgarians in cold blood.

But the violence was not restricted to the Khmer Rouge. The Phnom Penh government of Hun Sen and his Cambodian People's Party began their campaign of intimidation against other parties. To be a party representative was becoming a dangerous occupation. Grenade attacks on party offices became more frequent and harassment increased. People were beaten, shot, assassinated and generally terrorised. Voter intimidation was widespread. It seemed light years away from the 'politically neutral environment' that the UN had promised. The UN mission was being held hostage by both the Khmer Rouge and the Phnom Penh regime of Hun Sen.

A month before polling began the Khmer Rouge withdrew completely from the process, closing their offices in Phnom Penh and returning to their zones of control. The peace had now become war.

Between 23 and 28 May 1993, in spite of the violence, the election went ahead as planned. In defiance of the men with guns, a staggering ninety-six per cent of registered voters cast their ballots. The Royalist Party, led by Sihanouk's son Prince Ranariddh, won a clear victory over the Phnom Penh government of Hun Sen. Hun Sen then forced his way into an uneasy power-sharing alliance, with Rannariddh as 'First Prime Minister' and Hun Sen as 'Second Prime Minister'. Sihanouk was restored as a constitutional monarch. The UN then announced its mission a success and began to withdraw its peacekeepers.

The UN had deliberately kept the goals and language of their mission vague. With a lack of political will they were powerless to do anything. The whole experience, despite the positive by-products of the beginnings of a local civil society, the repatriation and a new government, was little more than an expensive public-relations exercise to enable China to extract itself from the Khmer Rouge. If the plan didn't work, then the Security Council and the powers behind it could turn around and blame Cambodians for their inherent inability to live in peace. What was supposed to have been a test case for Cambodia was a test case for the sincerity of the international community – the people had voted for the party that they believed would bring a peace that the UN had failed to deliver.

CHAPTER 17

Salvation

IT BEGAN TO dawn on me that perhaps I hadn't been the first to identify Duch. The more I talked with people in and around Phkoam village, the more I realised was being concealed. People gave confusing and occasionally conflicting accounts and I could sense an anxiety present. Although the people were friendly they continued to be wary of outsiders and some requested anonymity. I brought Sokheang with me. He understood the concerns of the people I spoke with and was able to put their fears to rest.

With the UN gone, Cambodia was left to deal with the Khmer Rouge alone, and the war continued. In 1994, the new government outlawed the Khmer Rouge. As part of a strategy to break the guerrilla movement, amnesties were given to the growing number of soldiers who defected to the government side. In some cases they were rewarded with promotions within the ranks of the army.

The area that Duch had moved to had always been one of the more lawless, where different guerrilla groups could

appear at any moment, including the Khmer Rouge. Some
commanders were little more than warlords, who forged
new allegiances with other commanders several times. The
Khmer Rouge too had their internal conflicts.

Duch wasn't the only former Khmer Rouge in the area.
When the US-backed KPNLF, remnants of Nol Lon's army,
joined with the government they mounted mopping-up
operations, intimidating, and in some cases killing, former
Khmer Rouge. Duch had been harassed and robbed on at
least one occasion and, no longer feeling secure, sought
protection from a KPNLF commander who was also head
of education in the area. He was issued with a pass and
granted permission to continue teaching at the school. But
the harassment didn't stop completely.

While Duch taught at the village, he also began teaching
in Svay Chek college, an hour from Phkoam. Among his
teaching colleagues, although respected, he was considered something of an eccentric and, despite his popularity,
he never really fitted in. He was strict, thorough, devoted
to his work and always punctual. As a cadre before, he
understood the need to set an example and everything was
done by the book.

Sometime in 1994, several teachers from the province
attended training sessions in Phnom Penh. After their meetings in the capital one of them decided to visit Tuol Sleng
to see if he could find out more about the fate of his
brother-in-law who had gone missing in 1975.

Accompanied by several others he wandered the corridors and searched the faces on the walls. Then one of
them saw the group portrait and a small man at the back
sandwiched between two taller men. He then turned to
see Duch's portrait on another wall.

'Is that him, is that Hang Pin?!' he asked his colleagues.

They stood looking at the photograph of their fellow teacher above them in the empty room. They couldn't believe that the modest, softly spoken man they had known all these years had been the commandant of such a place. 'We were frightened,' he said.

They left the museum in silence. After much worried debate they all agreed to keep quiet. They feared for their families. They also believed that Duch wanted to change – Duch had often said he never wanted to go back to the Khmer Rouge so they convinced themselves that it was pointless to confront him.

Then one night in November 1995, bandits attacked Duch's home. Duch and his family were forced at gunpoint to lie face down on the ground and told not to move. The armed men demanded gold and money. The youngest child, Thai An, began to cry. His mother pleaded with them that they didn't have any. They didn't believe her and stabbed her to death with a bayonet. They then bayoneted Duch twice in the back, stole what they could and fled into the night. Duch was taken to the Khmer American Friendship hospital in nearby Thmar Pouk, where he was operated on by a doctor from Médecins Sans Frontières. After four days, Duch discharged himself.

Was it an assassination attempt or just another act of random lawlessness? It is impossible to be certain. One teacher said Duch believed the Khmer Rouge wanted him dead. Duch had asked him for help because of the security situation. Another villager said there was a rumour he was still with the Khmer Rouge and was a supply-and-logistics officer for the area. A third teacher heard he changed his name many times.

Having returned to Phkoam, Duch sold all his possessions and secured a transfer to the Svay Chek college, where he moved with his children to teach full-time. Duch may have been trying to cut his ties from the Khmer Rouge and remain in the village as a teacher but it was possible he still had connections with them. Nuon Chea, Brother Number 2, had offered him a job in logistics after his arrival at the border. Perhaps he knew he could never really leave. Working as logistics officer might have been the price to pay for a degree of independence. Whichever way he turned he needed the Organisation.

But perhaps the attack really was just theft. What is clear, however, is that he no longer had a protector, implying that he had indeed left the Khmer Rouge. But would its leadership have trusted him to keep quiet?

Since the UN withdrawal, the war between the new government and the Khmer Rouge continued. When Chinese support for the guerrillas dried up, the Khmer Rouge turned to cross-border trade, dealing in gems and wood to finance their war effort and reaped huge profits from Thai businessmen and members of the Thai military.

It was then that I realised how I had boxed myself into a profession and a story that had little currency anymore. Every year I returned to the UK with my pictures and tried to interest magazines and newspapers. 'Cambodia,' I was told, 'has been done.' The world had moved on.

In 1994, government forces overran the Khmer Rouge headquarters of Pailin, but after several days were pushed back up Route 10 in a major counter-offensive. Forty thousand refugees had fled to the outskirts of Battambang, pursued by the ominous boom of artillery. Government troops, overloaded with spoils after their orgy of looting in Pailin, retreated in disarray. Now the front line was

less than fifteen kilometres from Battambang city. By
night, dead government soldiers were smuggled into
Battambang and secretly cremated at a temple to conceal
their losses. Foreign aid workers urgently discussed the
security situation. A curfew was imposed and food prices
rose by twenty per cent. Then shells landed on the
outskirts, and two convoys of foreign aid workers fled
the city. The refugees from this latest round of fighting
were allocated land on which to camp just outside
Battambang. I went to photograph the encampment for
Oxfam.

As the sun set behind Phnom Sampeou, we turned off
the road and into several large fields surrounded by trees.
The smoke from cooking fires hovered above the shacks
and tents. People milled about and small children shivered
and shrieked under the water pump of a nearby well as
their mothers filled their buckets. I approached the camp
with a sense of foreboding. I knew the area where the
refugees had come from and people had come to recognise me. As I climbed down from the LandCruiser and
wandered over I heard someone cry out my name.
Suddenly, I felt a tight pair of little arms wrap themselves
around my thighs and looked down to see Channy, her
large smiling eyes peering up at me. I looked up to see
her mother standing nearby.

Two years before, I had stayed in Bangkok with the
Jesuits. Having virtually no money, I was glad of the offer
of a free bed and wasn't particularly fussed about comfort.
The Jesuits' offices were in a large compound of three buildings where I spent much of my time with Burmese student
refugees who had left their homeland after the bloody crackdown in 1988. One day a young girl and her mother arrived
from Site 2 refugee camp on the Thai-Cambodian border.

The mother, Srey, had been brought down to Bangkok by the Jesuits to be fitted with special prosthetic arms. Her husband had been shot dead in front of her by gunmen in the camp. When she went to cradle him they shot her twice in each wrist. She tried to conceal her stumps by wearing a *krama* as a shawl and was entirely dependent on her daughter, Channy, who spoon-fed her at mealtimes. Channy, a pretty nine-year-old, spent much of the day in the compound's swimming pool. She had lived all her life in refugee camps and it was the first time she had ever seen one. One afternoon I took them to the cinema. The film was violent and noisy, but they seemed to enjoy themselves. A few days later they were taken back to the netherworld of camp life and that was the last I saw of them.

Until now. Here they lived in a semi-open shack surrounded by rice stalks of brilliant green. It was bare except for a rattan bed and a few cooking pots. The walls were made of palm leaves, but had large holes and provided little privacy. Srey had remarried and I was introduced to her new husband. We sat talking for a while. When it was time to leave they followed me to the car, Channy holding my hand, my cameras dangling on either side of me.

Now that the UN had brought peace to Cambodia the public, I was told, didn't want the UN version complicated by the reality on the ground. The pages of publications were being filled with lifestyle and celebrity images and there was little space or desire to have another depressing report from a small country, far from home. Meeting Channy and her mother and taking pictures of yet another refugee camp I began to question whether photography had any purpose. Most of the time, my pictures ended up in a drawer, never seeing the light of day.

*   *   *

Shortly after his wife's murder, Duch began to attend prayer meetings in Battambang. The meetings were held by an evangelical Khmer-American pastor now living in the United States called Christopher Lapel. Lapel had studied in the Pacific Christian College, a non-denominational university in California, and made regular trips back to Cambodia as a representative of the Golden West Cambodian Christian Church based in Los Angeles. He remembered Duch well. 'Sad, hopeless, empty, he used to sit at the back of the meetings,' he told me.

Duch's friend took the pastor aside and told him a little about Duch's situation. It was the same friend who had taken him to hospital after the attack. At the end of the meeting, Duch approached Lapel, asking more specific questions about the Bible. They sat together at lunch. Lapel asked him what had happened and he told him about his wife and the attack.

'My life ... I've never had peace in my life,' he said. He was guarded and withdrawn. 'He was careful about saying too much,' said Lapel. Duch then turned to the pastor, and said, 'I have sinned, *really* sinned, a big sin. I don't think that my brothers and sisters can forgive me.' He wanted to change, he went on, become a new person. 'Don't worry,' Lapel told him. 'Everyone has sinned.' The pastor said that he too could be forgiven.

Duch changed. 'He became a totally different person, he called me *Kru* [teacher] Christopher,' said Lapel. He became more animated and excited. 'The word of God hit him very hard,' said Lapel. He had moved from the rear of the congregation to the front row, hanging on every word, taking copious notes from Lapel's sermons. Of all the people Lapel had met, 'he took the best notes, he was amazing, very neat'.

Eventually, he approached Lapel again and asked the pastor to baptise him.

Lapel led a group down to the Sangke River, which runs through Battambang. There, Duch was baptised in the river, his sins washed away with the silt that flowed from Khmer Rouge ruby mines in the mountains. Duch later attended training sessions conducted by Lapel and eventually became a lay pastor.

'I'm glad that I gave my life to the Lord,' he told Lapel. 'I feel confident, I feel peace, I feel love – I want you to teach me more.'

Duch never mentioned his past and Lapel never asked. Although quiet and reserved, Lapel remembered him as a friendly and gentle man. 'Not just with me,' said Lapel, 'but with everyone.'

After the training Duch returned to Svay Chek and marched his sons and only daughter off to be baptised. When he returned to school, he even tried to convert his students. With the same zeal as he had once embraced communism, leading young recruits to join the Khmer Rouge, Duch set about spreading a new faith. On his return to Svay Chek he reportedly converted fourteen families.

The small town of Svay Chek was centred around an open area flanked by concrete shop houses. It was midday and the sun was at its strongest. The college where Duch had taught was a group of one-storey classrooms on a flat area of burnt grass, a flagpole in the centre. I walked through the gates to the office where a group of teachers was sitting in neatly pressed white shirts, clutching folders. They greeted me and invited me inside. The director, Hun Smean, sat me down beside his desk and they all crowded around.

Smean told me that after his baptism Duch returned to

teaching with new vigour. Duch was so persistent about spreading the gospel that some staff resented his enthusiasm. He spoke about God constantly and even had plans to build a church. Every Sunday he would go to church in Sisophon.

He only once mentioned the Pol Pot time. Smean and the other teachers were discussing the Khmer Rouge when he interrupted them. 'If you don't know about the Khmer Rouge then you shouldn't say anything,' he snapped. Sometimes Duch would slip into Khmer Rouge language, referring to a colleague as Comrade, but Smean didn't think it important. He knew Duch was well educated. Duch told them he had studied in China and that he was very close friends with Khieu Samphan's wife. Whether he had told them this as a subtle warning for protection or if he was showing off, none of them could say.

When I asked Smean if he had any photographs of his former colleague, he rustled around in some messy desk drawers. After a few moments he produced the registry book where all the staff put their names and photographs. I found Duch's spidery signature but the space for his photograph was blank. Smean said he had never given one. 'He was very shy about having his photograph taken,' he said. 'He was running from his past.'

One time Duch went to collect his salary from the education office in Sisophon, where the Minister of Education was making an official visit. The minister who had approved his appointment as Hang Pin had been a student at Kompong Thom Lycée with Duch and Sokheang. 'I can't stay here,' said Duch and he fled before the minister laid eyes on him.

Eventually, word got to the provincial educational department and Duch was summoned to a meeting with one of the staff. The official, who requested anonymity, told Duch that he had been identified from the photograph in the museum. After several denials, he gave in. The official suggested that he give himself up and tell the authorities that he was following orders when he had been the commandant. Duch pleaded for his secret to remain concealed. The official asked him if anyone could offer him protection. Duch replied that there were people in Samlaut he knew. He was then offered the job of Director of Education in Samlaut, which he accepted immediately.

At the education offices in Sisophon I was given copies of his biography and a curriculum vitae he had written in his own hand. He gave his birthplace as Acha Leak village in Kompong Thom. It mentioned nothing of his imprisonment under Sihanouk. 'From 1970 until 1992,' he wrote, 'working with the Khmer Rouge, responsible for teaching, helping write school textbooks, assigned as a Khmer-language expert at the Beijing University of Foreign Languages.' Further below he had written that both parents were deceased. There was no mention of his sisters.

One worker at the office then handed me a small postage-stamp-sized envelope. Inside was a photograph of Duch from his application. His hair was tightly brushed back and the deep blue backdrop dwarfed him. His white shirt was immaculate and crisp and fitted him as though it were made of cardboard. A diminutive Duch looked intently at the camera, frozen as though his life depended on it. The picture showed a man on his best behaviour, careful to appear unremarkable.

In Samlaut Duch was reunited with his youngest sister and her family. In August 1996 Ieng Sary, the former Khmer Rouge Foreign Minister, split from the Khmer Rouge leadership and defected to the government, bringing most of the

Western Zones over to the government side. It was a major
blow to Pol Pot and the guerrilla movement. Ieng Sary's
area of control centred in the gem-mining town of Pailin,
which remained a great source of revenue for the guerrillas. It was to remain a neutral autonomous zone in
exchange for an amnesty and a cessation of hostilities.

At this time, tension between the two co-Prime Ministers
was mounting. As they vied for support among Khmer
Rouge defectors, disagreements had become increasingly
pronounced. It wasn't long before Hun Sen took the initiative and mounted a violent coup to oust Rannaridh. In
Phnom Penh, tanks moved on troops loyal to the Prince
and the airport was closed. Fighting erupted in different
parts of the country. Some Khmer Rouge declared their
support for the Prince and others sided with Hun Sen. Ieng
Sary and his enclave remained neutral, watching from the
sidelines.

When the fighting broke out Duch, his sister and their
families fled to the safety of Thailand. They found themselves in a camp that had been set up just inside Thailand
called Ban Ma Muang. It was here in the camp that Duch
put his new faith into action, this time as a humanitarian.

CHAPTER 18

The Humanitarian

THE FIGHTING HAD sent more than 60,000 refugees fleeing into Thailand. In one camp I visited on the northern border, I passed a Khmer Rouge soldier in the cramped market and greeted him with a broad smile. He glared back at me. On sale were stacks of Khmer Rouge uniforms and Mao caps, next to soap and clothing donated by the relief agencies. Ban Ma Muang, the camp that Duch had fled to, was populated by Khmer Rouge from Samlaut. It was here, once again, that Duch put his skills as a leader into practice.

As an aid worker, Tess Prombuth had worked with Cambodians for almost twenty years. She had arrived on the border just after the Khmer Rouge were driven from power by the Vietnamese. In 1998, just after Hun Sen's coup, she worked briefly with the American Refugee Committee (ARC) in Ban Ma Muang camp, helping to set up a community health programme. The border camp, which housed a population of 12,000, was located beneath ragged green mountains and was run by the United Nations High Commissioner for Refugees.

Before Prombuth began work, she searched among the refugees for an assistant. One ARC doctor suggested a former teacher who spoke French, English and Thai. It was Duch. As Hang Pin, he seemed the logical choice to be Community Health Supervisor. He received a small stipend and a UN food allowance.

Duch's youngest sister, Hang Kim Hoeung, also began working with ARC. She had trained as a midwife under the Khmer Rouge and had worked in the same hospital as Duch's wife. After the Vietnamese invasion she too had fled to the Thai border. There she worked as a nurse with a Thai Catholic relief agency in Borai camp while her brother taught in the school.

In Ban Ma Muang, it was important to work as quickly as possible since the rains were coming, and with them, the risk of diseases from water-born parasites and malaria. Working closely with the various leaders, Prombuth and Duch began to train teams of community health workers. Much time was spent explaining to the people the importance of sanitation and effective irrigation. At the end of each month, Prombuth and Duch sat down together to assess the progress before setting themselves new objectives for the following month. The camp hospital was run by ARC. Duch also coordinated different departments, following up on discharged patients. He worked hard, often staying up late into the night reading medical books.

Prombuth and Duch got along well. Every morning when she arrived in the camp Duch greeted her with a 'Lord!'. In the camp all the refugees knew and respected him, she said. He listened intently to people's difficulties, and often came up with his own solutions to problems. When he wasn't working with Prombuth directly, he acted as a translator for a Senegalese doctor. They often talked about matters of faith since the doctor was also a Baptist (unlike Prombuth, who was a Catholic).

When the fighting subsided and some normality returned to the country, the UNHCR had made plans to return the refugees. 'So now I'm going back to Cambodia,' Duch said, mentioning his eldest sister and the rest of the family in Kompong Thom. Prombuth thanked him for all his hard work. According to an ARC official, Duch had been instrumental in stemming a typhoid outbreak in the camp, saving countless lives in the process. 'Oh thank you,' he beamed. He told her how happy he was to have worked with her and that he had learned a lot. Before she left, she gave him a prayer book. Then he said, 'When I go back I really don't know what will happen with my life.' She suggested, with his experience and educational background, that perhaps he could find work with the Christian aid agency World Vision.

'Yes,' he replied, 'I will try.'

Years later when I met Prombuth in Battambang, where she was working for another aid agency, I asked if she had any photographs of Duch. She only had one. There were more, she said, but the American Refugee Committee probably had them. The picture showed an ARC meeting inside a makeshift tent in the camp. Duch is sitting with his back to the camera on a plastic garden chair that swallowed his small frame. He is wearing glasses and, from his demeanour, I could tell that he was immersed in the mass of papers on the table. The others around seemed distracted by something out of frame. Duch seemed not to pay any attention.

In late 1998, Duch returned to Cambodia with the other refugees. Fighting continued in the forested north. At Anlong

Veng the last of the Khmer Rouge battled for their survival. Meanwhile, the news reached Phnom Penh that Son Sen, Duch's former boss, had been executed with his wife and ten members of his family, including children. A truck had been used to crush the bodies after they were killed. The order had been given by Pol Pot, who was promptly placed under house arrest by Ta Mok, 'the butcher', who assumed control. Pol Pot was then put on trial by 'the People's Tribunal of Anlong Veng'. Journalist Nate Thayer and two cameramen were invited to witness. It was the first time the elusive leader had been seen for twenty years. The Khmer Rouge had begun to implode.

By June 1998, Anlong Veng had come over to the government and I went to witness the remnants of Pol Pot's army at a reintegration ceremony at their jungle headquarters.

Early in the morning we sat in the shade of the car near the runway of Phnom Penh's airbase. Ahead was an aged Russian MI-26 transport helicopter; large enough to play badminton in its belly. Just looking at it filled me with dread. These old Soviet helicopters had a reputation for being less than reliable.

Now that the Khmer Rouge had declared their allegiance to the government the press were invited, along with an assortment of officials, diplomats and soldiers, to attend the official reintegration ceremony of the remainder of their guerrillas. More cars of journalists arrived armed with invitations embossed with the Cambodian royal coat of arms. Then a friend told me that Reuters in Bangkok had said that Ta Mok, the renegade Khmer Rouge leader, was planning to attack the ceremony we were going to witness.

Eventually the Russian pilots arrived. At first we watched those with invitations queue up in an orderly fashion as the rotors began to swing and strain, eventually reaching an even pitch as the great prehistoric insect came to life. As the last of the invited crowd climbed the steps into its bowels there was a frenzied scramble of elbows and jabs to get inside. I found myself being carried by pressing bodies into the darkness. Suddenly there was a jerk and we all lurched backward as it thudded into the sky.

Inside we stood in the heat and noise, awaiting our final destination, unable to talk in the din of the engines. The officials were given plastic garden chairs to sit on. I found a space on the floor and sat with the barrel of a soldier's AK-47 pointing at my buttocks. Next to me was Ieng Vuth, the son of the former Khmer Rouge Foreign Minister, Ieng Sary. Like the Khmer Rouge we were going to see now, he had defected with his father several years before. After forty minutes we were in sight of the Thai border and Anlong Veng. Through the scratched bubble window I could see the Dangrek mountain range. The helicopter then swerved and banked and I caught a glimpse of pristine forest below. Then we began a circular motion and I sat back down as the helicopter descended in the usual corkscrew fashion. Eventually the door was opened and we all scrambled out into the light.

It was like stepping into a forgotten world. Anlong Veng was a collection of wooden houses spread out over an area of semi-denuded forest. There was only one concrete building, beside a reservoir of dead trees that pierced the blue waters like a bed of nails. The photographers and cameramen fanned out to take pictures of Khmer Rouge soldiers who stood nearby, many of them amputees. Ahead was a Chinese battle tank, its turret gun pointing towards the forest. Looking on with evident disdain were members of a Médecins Sans Frontières team who had arrived days before.

Further ahead Khmer Rouge soldiers had lined up under some trees. They looked tough and undernourished in their ill-fitting uniforms; swirls of creases swamped their wiry frames. Some of them were well into their fifties, some were mere boys. Their families looked on. Many of the children were thin, with distended bellies and yellow streaks in their matted hair.

Then Tea Banh, the Cambodian Minister of Defence, appeared with an entourage of bodyguards and a garland of jasmine around his neck. He could have flown in from Hawaii. With his buck-toothed grin, his unkempt hair and well-fed appearance, he was clearly enjoying himself, aware of his position and the power he commanded. After more than twenty years of fighting the Khmer Rouge the minister had now come to preside over their defeat.

Tea Banh wandered past the lines of guerrillas, hounded by cameras, giving a *sompeah* to nobody in particular, before climbing up to the hastily erected stage. A band blared out Khmer music at stadium volume. Then the speeches began.

Anlong Veng's villagers sat behind the guerrillas and watched all the proceedings with the same concentration that one might watch aliens. Few had seen foreigners before and now the place was crawling with them. They were a reserved people, a peasant army who had been cut off from the outside world for years. Brutalised by an authoritarian regime, they had spent much of their lives being shelled and attacked in the forests. Now they were on parade for the outside world. 'For them,' one Khmer journalist said to me, '"Year Zero" has only just ended.'

The Khmer Rouge soldiers stood with impassive faces, resigned to the tedious formality of the occasion. The scene reminded me of photographs of Khmer Rouge political meetings, which were emblematic of their regimented lives. They would speak, applaud the Organisation and shout a slogan. Everybody would be required to punch the air in unison three times and shout, 'Long live the Cambodian Revolution!'

After the speeches, three Khmer Rouge commanders joined the Defence Minister on the podium and grinned sheepishly at their new overlord. He gave them their new government uniforms and off they went to change. They returned to their rows as before, this time as members of a different army. The rest of the troops did the same. I followed them and watched an old Khmer Rouge soldier discard his worn Ho Chi Minh sandals and struggle with the laces of his new boots. Judging by the way he was tying them it was the first time he had ever worn boots. Some of them had been barefoot.

I pulled out my photograph of Duch as a cadre and began asking in halting Khmer if anyone had seen him. No-one had. They seemed amused at my request. Then the ceremony was over and we were trucked back to the waiting helicopter.

The helicopter dangled there as if unsure what to do next. It then swerved and jolted. It seemed the pilot was having problems getting enough power. Then, with a jerk it moved with all its might. I looked out of the window as a tree-top passed alarmingly close. We were airborne.

When we arrived at Siem Reap I wandered over to the Russian pilot and asked him apprehensively if everything was alright before we carried on to Phnom Penh. 'In Anlong Veng,' he cheerfully replied in thick accented English, 'we had a little problem.' The helicopter had been unable to get off the ground because of the sheer weight of ex-Khmer Rouge soldiers who, taking advantage of their new status as government troops, had clambered aboard. Here at Siem Reap they poured out and ran off across the runway towards the town. 'Now,' said the pilot, 'no problem.'

Six months later, December 1998 saw the surrender of Khieu Samphan and Nuon Chea – Brother Number 2. They were flown to Phnom Penh to meet Hun Sen, the Prime Minister. At a press conference they were asked if they felt any remorse for the killing when they had been in power. 'Yes – sorry, sorry, sorry, I am very sorry,' replied a smiling Khieu Samphan. 'Actually, we're very sorry,' added Nuon Chea, 'not just for the lives of the people, but also for the lives of animals that suffered in the war.' They then called on the world to 'let bygones be bygones'. Hun Sen called on people to 'dig a hole and bury the past'.

Later, Khieu Samphan was welcomed with embraces from the former UN Secretary-General, Boutros Boutros-Ghali. He was visiting Phnom Penh to promote French as a language and took time to praise Hun Sen for his policy of 'national reconciliation'. He then announced that the mass murder by the Khmer Rouge was an internal affair of a sovereign state and should not be the subject of 'interference' by outsiders. Cambodians must find their own route to resolving their rights issues, he said.

In a country plagued by an almost total lack of justice and continued political violence, Boutros Boutros-Ghali's comments represented the lowest point of impunity. As if all Cambodians needed was a brief apology.

A year later, in a low-key ceremony at the cliff-edge temple of Preah Vihear, the last of the Khmer Rouge formally surrendered to the government. It was the end of an insurgency that had begun on the slopes of Samlaut more than thirty years before. Now, nearly three million lives later, the country was finally at peace. Three months later, the last of the Khmer Rouge leaders, Ta Mok, was arrested and placed in prison in Phnom Penh. He had refused to surrender.

Khieu Samphan and Nuon Chea were then sent on a state-sponsored tour of the country they had almost destroyed. They visited Angkor Wat as well as the seaside resort of Kompong Som, escorted by bodyguards and police travelling in convoys of LandCruisers.

At about the same time as I was handing out Duch's picture in Anlong Veng, Duch returned with the other refugees from the border. They were taken through the city of Battambang and from there down Route 10 towards Samlaut. It was to be one of his last journeys as Hang Pin.

There was still fighting in Samlaut and so Duch camped off Route 10. Along with 2,000 other refugees, he set up camp in the village of Andao Hep in Rattanak Mondul or 'the Place of the Gems'. It was here that he worked closely with World Vision, the Christian relief organisation assisting the refugees.

Chreng Darren of World Vision was introduced to Duch and his sister at a meeting of village leaders. Because of his experience with ARC on the border, Duch was able to help with World Vision's health volunteers in immunising women and the younger children. If someone needed further treatment, Duch would help organise transport for them to the local clinic. He soon proved himself the most able of the volunteers.

Darren liked him immediately. He thought Duch pleasant, polite, respectful, very qualified and genuinely popular with the people. One time Darren visited Duch's family shelter, which was much like the others apart from the neat files of documents and reports from the camp. They were organised day-by-day, week-by-week. Duch had proudly shown Darren his Bible and his training certificates to become a lay pastor, and he talked of wanting to join World Vision. When Darren asked who had baptised him Duch replied, 'Oh, a very good man,' and produced a picture of himself with Pastor Lapel. To Darren he was one of the most capable among the refugees; a natural leader who 'showed a lot of initiative'.

Duch hitched rides with World Vision back to Battambang, where he attended meetings at the education offices. He still collected his salary from Sisophon and visited his mother and sister, who now lived in Siem Reap.

In the early 1990s, Andao Hep village, where Duch and the refugees had made their temporary home, was what my friends and I used to call a 'grey area'. I spent much time in the area taking pictures. Andao Hep was located down a dark tunnelled track of mango, palm and *hoki* trees, close to the military zone that severed the district in two. To the west was the Khmer Rouge zone, to the east was government-controlled territory and Andao Hep was caught in the middle.

Then, to walk through the village, I found it hard to imagine this as a front line. I had always thought of a front line as a network of carefully dug bunkers with razor wire, packed with soldiers. In reality, it was somebody's home or a field or a school. Children played games and pigs rummaged in the mud. Women sat outside making thatching from grass they had retrieved from the minefields nearby. Crude spirit houses with incense guarded their tiny shacks.

Many of the people from the district were known, with some derision by the lowland people, as *Khmer Khmao* or 'black Khmer'; real peasants. They had been so cut off from the outside world that when cars first appeared in the district they had cut grass to feed them. The loyalties of the people here were at best murky. Although under nominal government control, many families of Khmer Rouge fighters lived there. Often, at night, Khmer Rouge soldiers would leave their weapons behind, cross the river and climb the banks and come into the villages to visit their relatives.

Five years after the end of the war I once again journeyed down Route 10 and followed Duch's route on the back of an aged Honda motorbike. It bounced and swerved along the road, past a cluster of sugar palms that stood like sentinels in the middle of the plains. They marked the closest point the Khmer Rouge ever got to taking Battambang. The sky began to spit rain and I could smell the wet earth as I turned off the road and carried on down the track to Andao Hep.

I asked if anyone recognised the man in the photograph, or if they had ever heard of Hang Pin. They shook their heads. I stopped to talk to a man in a wheelchair. He had lost both his legs in a mine accident as a Khmer Rouge soldier in Samlaut. He said he didn't know Hang Pin either. I then passed the photograph to him. There was a flicker of recognition in his eyes before he passed it back, shaking his head. Further along, I spoke to another man, also a former Khmer Rouge soldier. He told me he didn't know Hang Pin. When he saw the picture he said, 'Oh, Grandpa Duch!' He had never talked with Duch directly, he said, because Duch was of a higher rank.

I returned down Route 10. Beyond it, had been the military zone, a rough strip of abandoned scrub jungle covered in mines. Rattanak Mondul had been on the front line for years. Both Khmer Rouge and government soldiers had swept up and down Route 10, leaving fresh crops of land-mines behind them. As a result, there were about half a million mines concealed in its dark soils, making it one the most heavily mined areas in the world.

The Cambodian conflict may be the first war that has claimed more lives and limbs to landmines than any other weapon. One estimate put the number of mines awaiting victims in Cambodia at ten million; more than one for every man, woman and child.

It was from the agony of minefields in places like Rattanak Mondul that one of the most extraordinary grassroots move-ments of recent times emerged. In 1992, the International Campaign to Ban Landmines was launched, bringing together 350 aid organisations to place a total ban on anti-personnel landmines. It quickly gathered momentum. Today, the Campaign includes more than 1,100 organisa-tions in sixty countries worldwide which continue to press to have these weapons outlawed. In 1997, the Campaign was awarded the Nobel Peace Prize.

Cambodia galvanished people's resolve to act together and, more importantly, to speak out. And it was paying off. Many of these organisations helped people affected by these hidden killers. Mine-clearance teams have destroyed millions of the weapons all over the world, enabling refugees to return home and farmers to plant their crops once again. In an area I had spent much time photo-graphing, the concrete results of this campaign lay all around as the untamed grass of mined land had given way to fertile fields that spread out on either side of the road.

For many years the abandoned town of Treng had been the last stop on Route 10 before the Khmer Rouge zone. Before, in the early 1990s, it had been completely deserted apart from old Soviet-built tanks and a few impoverished soldiers with their families. The area had been laced with mines and the fallow fields were being devoured by the encroaching jungle. Above the trees the shattered roof of the temple could be seen. During the Khmer Rouge time, it had been used as a prison and execution site. When the Khmer Rouge swept into the area in the wake of the Vietnamese withdrawal, they collected all the bones and burnt them. Here the road divided. Ahead was the Khmer Rouge gem-mining town of Pailin and to the left, Samlaut.

Now Treng was a small town of packed shops, restaurants and stalls. Behind, the fields were once again cultivated and the jungle had retreated from the road.

Further south was Samlaut, which had exploded into violence in 1967, signalling the beginning of the Khmer Rouge armed struggle. It was also the last place to give up the fight. The leaders here were still deeply suspicious of outsiders and it came under the control of Sou Sameth, a veteran Khmer Rouge military commander, who had been deeply involved in the killings and regularly sent people to S-21.

In early 1999, I was commissioned again to photograph mine-clearance teams in Cambodia. After the assignment I had a day free. The organisation I was with had a meeting with the Khmer Rouge in Samlaut and I asked if I could accompany them. Early in the morning we travelled out in convoy down Route 10 and beyond Treng to our final destination, the hamlet of Ta Sanh. It was just a few months before Duch returned down the same road to the protection of Sou Samet.

CHAPTER 19

The Confession

A S I STOOD before Comrade Duch, I did my best to avoid singling him out from the others. It was hard to believe this small, disarming man in front of me had been the commandant of Tuol Sleng.

Introducing himself as Hang Pin, he told me that he had originally come from Phnom Penh and had been a maths teacher. Recently, he said, he had been working in a refugee camp on the Thai border.

Although the fighting had just ended, the Khmer Rouge still controlled the area and I had no idea if Duch wielded any influence. I had no intention of confronting him there and then. In the two hours I spent at the district offices, I managed surreptitiously to take a photograph of him before he disappeared. On the way out, I asked people if Hang Pin lived nearby. He did.

Back in my home in Bangkok, I printed up the photograph in my darkroom. It was back-lit, but clear enough. Emerging from the developer was Duch in his ARC T-shirt, a coy grin on his face. Behind him was a Khmer Rouge

soldier who looked directly at the camera. I compared it
to the creased picture that I had carried in my pocket for
so long. There was no doubt in my mind. His hairline,
although greying, remained the same and his stretched lips
revealed identical teeth.

Not long after, I returned to Samlaut, this time to garner
more information, establish where Duch lived and, if
possible, film him.

Arriving back in the district with a friend, I stopped for
a drink near the district offices where I had first seen Duch.
A truck full of former Khmer Rouge soldiers pulled up next
to us. Then I saw Duch in a pair of shorts, barking orders
while straining to carry a large jerrycan in his hands. He
turned and recognised me, and smiled. He seemed pleased
to see me and shook me by the hand. I asked him if he
would accompany me to interview some of the returning
refugees up the road. He agreed.

We walked to a newly built house and sat underneath to talk with a man in his late thirties. He too was
a teacher and had come from the same refugee camp
as Duch. I began asking him about conditions in the
district, the problem of mines and land availability. Duch
interpreted. I had now switched on my small video
camera.

After some time I began to direct the questions towards
the Khmer Rouge and the current political situation and
placed the small camera on my knee. Duch explained that
the war in Samlaut was the longest. I asked the teacher
about the much vaunted trial of the Khmer Rouge, now
that Ta Mok was in prison. The teacher said he was just
a teacher and didn't know about such things. As he talked,
I watched Duch. He seemed distracted and gazed off into
the distance. I then asked Duch if he felt that Ta Mok

should be tried. He turned to me, a little startled.

'I'm not interested in him,' he replied dismissively. 'I'm interested in three things: schools for the children, my stomach and God.' A large expectant grin spread across his face. 'I want to tell everyone about the gospel, I want to have a church here.' He looked intently at me, awaiting my reaction.

'I learned to be a Christian when I was a student in school. I studied philosophy, Buddhism and I studied Islam and I compared them all. I had a difficult life and decided to give my life to Christ.' We continued talking but Duch clammed up when I tried to get him to reveal more of his background. I switched off the camera.

As we shook hands, I told Duch I would return soon. As my truck pulled away, I turned to wave to Duch, but he had already vanished. Large storm clouds were beginning to gather and gusts of red dust swept across the road ahead of us. The truck pulled out and on to the road towards the forest ahead. I hoped that the rain would let us leave since the road was almost impassable in some parts. A single downpour could wash away the track in seconds, leaving us stranded.

As we turned the corner the driver jabbed his thumb over his shoulder. 'Duch,' he said. 'A very bad man.'

Back in Bangkok I called the *Far Eastern Economic Review* with my story. I also called Nate Thayer, the last western journalist to have interviewed Pol Pot before his death. The editors at the *Review* wanted me to go back and give Duch the opportunity to defend himself. Nate asked me if he could come along. Reluctant to return to Samlaut alone, and fearful of the possible repercussions when confronting Duch, I agreed.

*   *   *

Ta Sanh, Samlaut, April 1999: Nate and I got out of the
car and, as casually as possible, sat down at a stall next
to Duch's home. The shop was a half-built shack covered
with the standard blue plastic sheeting given to refugees.
At the next table, a group of soldiers in Khmer Rouge
uniforms sat drinking whisky. They told us that they had
served under Sam Bith, a Khmer Rouge commander who
had executed three foreign backpackers a few years earlier.
They looked as though they had been with the Khmer
Rouge all their lives. When they had satisfied their curiosity
they returned to talking among themselves.

Then I heard Duch's voice. Walking behind the shack,
I found him perched on the side of his new house, chatting with a Khmer Rouge soldier. Giving me a toothy grin
of recognition, Duch stood up, shook my hand and asked
after my health. Behind, his pregnant niece lay on a mat
in the shade, a drip attached to her arm. I waved Nate
over, and introduced him to Duch. We then settled down
and began asking him general questions about life in the
district.

Duch seemed happy to talk. He told us of his conversion to Christianity and showed us the two laminated certificates that he had received after attending the seminars held
by Pastor Lapel. The certificates applauded his 'personal
leadership development, teambuilding and deepening
commitment to Jesus Christ'. 'I am a son of God,' he told
Nate with a grin.

He went on to tell us of his life in Phkoam and the
attack in which his wife had been killed. Matter-of-factly
he told us what had happened, lifting his shirt to show us
the scars. Beads of sweat trickled down my back and my
camera became slippery in my hands. I looked around to
see if anyone was watching. As far as I could see, we were

alone. He told us about the accident with the AK-47 that had blown his finger off. After the attack he returned here to Samlaut where, he said, 'I am safe.' As head of education in the district he was now working to re-establish Samlaut's education system. He was planning to build several schools and, one day, on the plot of land next to where we were sitting, a church. He appeared eager to tell us what he thought we would like to hear. 'I want the ARC to come and help with disease, to coordinate health-care here,' he said.

Then Nate said, 'I believe that you also worked with the security services during the Khmer Rouge period?' Duch appeared startled and avoided our eyes. He replied that he worked with the Ministry of Education, translating children's textbooks. Again Nate put the question to him. He shifted. He said he had been a simple teacher before 1979. He looked unsettled and his eyes darted about. He was aware we were watching him. My heart was pounding in my chest. I began to think that he wouldn't be drawn.

I suggested to Duch that, if he wanted, he could write a letter to Dr Emmanuel of ARC, whom Duch had known in Ban Ma Muang refugee camp, and I would deliver it. Duch and the doctor had been close. That way, I would have a sample of his handwriting if he refused to talk and I could verify it with the notations from the confessions. He agreed, happy to change the subject. I pulled out a page from a notebook and, putting on his glasses, he went over to a bench to write. When he had finished the short letter he then glanced at Nate's business card. A concentrated expression appeared on his face; and he turned slowly to me, looking directly into my eyes. 'I believe, Nic, that your friend has interviewed Monsieur Ta Mok and Monsieur Pol Pot?'

'Yes,' I replied. 'That's right.'

There was a long pause. He sat back down, the letter in his hand, and exhaled deeply. 'It is God's will that you are here,' he said. 'Now my future is in God's hands.'

For the first time, Kaing Guek Eav, alias Comrade Duch, began to speak about his role in one of the bloodiest revolutions of the twentieth century.

'I have done very bad things before in my life,' he began, his voice almost inaudible. 'Now it is time for *les représailles* of my actions.' *Les représailles*: the consequences. At first haltingly, but with what seemed like a growing resignation at the real purpose of our visit, the former commandant of S-21 began his own confession.

'The first half of my life I'll remember for ever,' he said. 'Then I thought God was very bad, that only bad men prayed to God. My unique fault is that I didn't serve God, I served men, I served communism.' Assured of his audience, his eyes never met ours and we listened in silence. Later, when I looked at the photographs that I had taken of him, I realised he had never once looked into the lens. 'I feel very sorry about the killings and the past – I wanted to be a good communist; I did not take any pleasure in my work, All the confessions of the prisoners – I worried, is that true or not?'

We presented him with copies of confessions from the prison with annotations scrawled across them. He placed his glasses back on and leafed through, studying them intently. He ran his finger over a handwritten sentence that read, 'Use the hot method. Even if it kills him, it is OK.'

'That is my handwriting, and this handwriting is Nuon Chea's and this one Son Sen's,' he said pointing to more annotations in the margins.

He spoke directly, casually even, as though this confession were a continuation of our preliminary chat. It occurred to me that Duch had been expecting this, that the occasion had been rehearsed. I glanced around to see who might be watching and listening. The soldiers were still at their table, unaware.

Until appointed to head the *Santebal*, Duch was later to tell the authorities, he had never killed anybody. He was reluctant to take the position as commandant. He believed that his close friend Chhay Kim Hour was better qualified and more deserving. However, once you were given an order by the Organisation, he said, you couldn't refuse. Then the party began its course of obsessively rooting out spies and the killing began.

There was no directive about interrogations. He knew from experience that if they were only tortured they wouldn't say anything, he said later. He told prisoners that they would be released if they talked. It was a lie, but it worked. He said this with a smile, as if pleased by his own cunning. Duch received people from all over the country, except Ta Mok's zone. Ta Mok didn't bother interrogating his prisoners, Duch said contemptuously. He just killed them.

Despite Son Sen's request that he go regularly to Choeung Ek to ensure that the killing was being carried out properly he claimed he only went once – he had no stomach for it. This wasn't true. Several guards at the execution site recalled Duch making regular visits to watch the killing. He leaned back, confessions in hand, and stared into the distance. A mother with her toddler wandered past on the road in front of us. 'We had instructions from the party on how to kill them, but we didn't use bullets,' Duch told Nate. 'Usually we slit their throats. We killed them like chickens.'

He then told us something that had never been formally established before: the Khmer Rouge had planned the mass murder. 'Whoever was arrested must die. It was the rule of our party,' he said – a calculated part of realising Pol Pot's vision and not the product of some wild savagery. The order had been issued as early as 1971 as a verbal instruction from the Higher Organisation. 'S-21 had no right to arrest anybody. We had the responsibility to interrogate and give the confessions to the central committee of the party,' Duch continued. All the prisoners sent to him had to be executed, without exception, Duch later told officials. 'Even children. This was the policy, the orders. No-one could leave S-21 alive.'

He now began to name names. He established the chain of command and responsibility for the killings. 'The first was Pol Pot, the second was Nuon Chea, the third Ta Mok.' Pol Pot had never directly ordered the killings, Duch said, bringing his glasses down on his knee for emphasis. Nuon Chea was principally responsible, but it was the Higher Organisation that had made the decisions and issued orders. 'I tried to understand the punishment and orders to kill,' he said. 'I have great difficulty in my life thinking that the people who died did nothing wrong.' He looked at the ground for a moment, an almost wistful look in his eyes. 'I am so sorry. The people who died were good people. There were many men who were innocent.' His attitude contrasted sharply with the arrogance and grudging apologies offered by other former Khmer Rouge leaders. Possibly it contained genuine remorse.

It had been Duch's idea to have the prisoners photographed on arrival. He did it to protect himself in case they escaped, making it easier to track the prisoner down. However, no-one did escape. On an earlier visit,

Duch had picked up my Leica and began playing with it. 'Very good,' he said, 'very expensive.'

'My friend Bizot will be happy to know that I have changed my ideas, my ideology,' he grinned. François Bizot was a French ethnologist who was arrested in 1971 with two Khmer assistants. He remains the only Westerner to have survived an encounter with Comrade Duch. Duch had overseen the executions of several other foreigners, including Canadians, Americans, Australians and one Briton. 'Nuon Chea ordered that the foreigners be killed and their bodies burned, so no bones were left,' he said. 'Only the Europeans were burned. I remember well the Englishman. He was very polite.'

This was John Dewhurst, a 25-year-old teacher who was captured by the Khmer Rouge in 1978 in the Gulf of Thailand while on holiday. His handwritten confession survived and reads, 'My name is John Dawson Dewhurst, a British citizen. I am a CIA agent who officially works as a teacher in Japan. I was born in Newcastle-on-Tyne on October 2nd 1952. My father was a CIA agent whose cover was headmaster of Benton Road secondary school.' It goes on to say that he was recruited, at the age of twelve, by a friend of his father's, who was a 'Captain in the CIA Newcastle district'. The foreigners were held for a month, during which they were tortured with electric shocks administered by the chief interrogator, Comrade Chan. Pol Pot decided to release Bizot, explained Duch, but the two assistants were executed.

It wasn't until his former friends and comrades began to arrive at the gates of S-21 that Duch began to suspect the method of arrest was arbitrary. First it had been Ke Kim Huot, his old teacher; then Vorn Vet, who had given him the job as commandant at M-13; then came Chhay

Kim Hour, who had recommended Duch to the party in 1967. After Kim Hour's arrival, he began to harbour real doubts. He became depressed, he said, and spent more and more time with the artists and painters. These were prisoners who had been put to work producing pictures and busts of Pol Pot.

The internal purges reached such a peak that by late 1978, the prison was full, he recalled. By then, Nuon Chea had replaced Son Sen. It was Nuon Chea who communicated with the other prisons and it was to him that Duch reported. As Nate would report, 300 Khmer Rouge soldiers were arrested and brought to S-21. When Duch asked Nuon Chea what to do with them, he was told not to bother interrogating them, just to kill them. And he did.

In 1979, when the Vietnamese took Phnom Penh, Duch had been the last Khmer Rouge to leave the city. He was later reprimanded by Nuon Chea for not destroying all the documents. He called Duch a fool. Nuon Chea had already rebuked Duch on several occasions. He believed it was a matter of time before the purges came round to him. Nuon Chea was conceited and self-important, unlike his former boss, Son Sen, with whom Duch would spend hours on the phone. Son Sen never visited S-21, said Duch, but he was impressed with Duch's work. This too was a lie. According to Nhem Ein and other former staff Son Sen had visited regularly. Duch was protecting the memory of his former boss. It is almost certain that Son Sen had saved him from Nuon Chea's wrath.

'After my experience in life I decided that I must give my spirit to God,' said Duch. He compared his life to St Paul's. Paul, who 'was above his brethren in intellect and influence', had been granted permission from the high

priests to hunt down and persecute Christians. Paul later
repented and was baptised, becoming one of Christ's most
ardent disciples, but continued to refer to himself as 'the
chief of sinners'.

'I think my biography is something like Paul's,' said Duch
with a faint smile. 'I am here. Whatever happens to me
now that you have come it is God's will.'

Suddenly, Duch lowered his voice and the atmosphere
changed. 'Does anyone know of this? That you are here?
That you know who I am?' His voice turned to a husky
whisper. We replied that only we knew. 'They will be
angry if they know,' he said. 'You must leave now.' Was
this was a friendly caution or a threat? The situation was
impossible to gauge. Even if he had, as he said, changed
his ways, we were still deep in a Khmer Rouge zone more
than two hours from the nearest town. Duch's protector
was in control of the area and, as far as we knew, Duch
could still order people to silence us if he felt threatened.

Just at that moment, a UN LandCruiser pulled up opposite us. We decided to travel out in convoy with it. We
said an abrupt goodbye and shook hands. As the car pulled
away I turned to see him remove his ARC T-shirt and step
into his shack.

When the story of his discovery and confession
appeared in the *Far Eastern Economic Review* and on
television, Duch disappeared. For several days there was
speculation by journalists and human-rights workers about
his whereabouts. Rumours spread that he had been assassinated on the orders of the leaders in 'retirement'.
Amnesty International issued a statement calling on the
Cambodian government to protect him. Concerns arose
about the security of UN and other workers in the area.
Once again, renewed conflict seemed a distinct threat.

Then I learned that Duch had given himself up to the authorities. He was flown by helicopter to Phnom Penh and to a high-security prison in the capital to be formally charged.

CHAPTER 20

The Quest for Justice

DUCH ENDED UP in the same military detention centre as Ta Mok, in the Tuol Sleng district of Phnom Penh, a five-minute walk from the prison that he once ran. He was charged under the 1994 law outlawing the Khmer Rouge.

In 1997, just before the coup, the two co-Prime Ministers, Hun Sen and Prince Rannaridh, asked the United Nations to set up a tribunal to try former Khmer Rouge leaders. With the subsequent political turmoil, this process had stalled. But now, with Duch's discovery, pressure was stepped up once again to bring those leaders who had defected to account.

Duch's re-emergence and subsequent revelations stunned people all over the country, particularly those who had worked with him. 'We are in a state of shock frankly,' said an ARC official. 'He was our best worker, highly respected in the community, clearly very intelligent and dedicated to helping the refugees.'

Back in Phkoam village, Duch's former neighbours

refused to believe the news. Even when I told them he had confessed of his own free will, they gave me sceptical looks. They were a wary lot, used to propaganda from one side or another. Several of his friends believed that if he hadn't followed the Organisation's orders, he too would have been killed. 'He never did anything bad, never created trouble,' said one villager. 'He should be released.'

Not everyone shared this view. When I showed my own photograph of Duch to another woman, she muttered, 'Criminal', before handing it back to me.

The American Refugee Committee then issued a statement effectively washing their hands of the episode. 'ARC does not know, and has no way of determining, past identities of individual members of refugee communities in any of the refugee camps on the Thai-Cambodian border.'

As an organisation ARC had come into existence during the border crisis of 1979 and knew the situation well. In the decade following the Vietnamese invasion, when the West and China supported the Khmer Rouge coalition, almost half of the funding for the border relief operation came from the United States Government. This money was available for work on the border, but not inside the country. Despite their 'apolitical' status, the ARC, like many American organisations on the border in the 1980s, followed what their political paymasters in Washington advised. Most relief agencies were discouraged from asking who was ultimately benefiting from this humanitarian effort. It was either take the money and play the game, or risk closing down altogether.

For the most part, this cynical manipulation of aid was accepted. Humanitarian intervention became a substitute for political action. Although occasional protests were made, most aid workers saw their work in strictly humanitarian terms. Anything beyond it was political and therefore beyond their remit. How these groups and organisations were able to preserve this neutrality in such an environment was nothing short of miraculous.

For the more politically aware, it wasn't a clear-cut argument. These aid workers understood that the refugees were prisoners of the factions, and became frustrated with the polarisation of the Cold War. Many accused the aid programme of assisting the wrong side of the conflict and aiding the Khmer Rouge.

It occurred to me that to work in Phnom Penh, which had its own complications, was an easier moral position to take. To work on the border was increasingly difficult to defend with all the obvious contradictions of assisting the Khmer Rouge and the war effort. Those with a more questioning and political reading, who took the moral weight of the border and all its injustice on board, were forced to question everything, including their own moral beliefs.

'We saved a hell of a lot of people's lives,' said Rob Burrows, Deputy Director of the United Nations Border Relief Operation. It's hard to fault these kinds of arguments. It is a language that reflects urgency and dedication, of a tough and uncompromising stance of apparent selflessness – all the attributes we have come to associate with aid workers. But it is also a language that deflects a closer scrutiny. Despite appearances many aid organisations have become defined by an establishment they appear to be free of, reliant as many are for government funding. As one former worker for ARC told me, 'Everything we do is political.'

As an organisation ARC would have known they were dealing with the Khmer Rouge. They would have known

that those with an education were cadres; people of influence and power. And ARC was using this relationship to
help the refugees. The people of Samlaut probably didn't
know that Duch had presided over Tuol Sleng, but it is
possible that they knew he had been in the secret police.
Many referred to him as Duch – not Hang Pin. They certainly
knew that he had been close to the leadership – Ta Sanh
had been Pol Pot's stronghold for several years.

When Burrows heard the news of Duch working for the
ARC he was relieved. The first thought that occurred to
him was, 'Thank God UNHCR didn't hire him.' My own
photograph of Duch that had appeared in the papers
showed him wearing his ARC T-shirt. 'I was thinking,' said
Burrows, "Jesus Christ, what if that had been a UNHCR T-
shirt?" It would have meant that we were idiots or worse.'

One former ARC director, Bob Medrala, wasn't surprised
by the revelations and didn't feel there was anything to be
ashamed of. 'If you've got people who look like they care,
who are smart, they become your workers – it's easy for
that to have happened,' he told me. There were plenty of
unsavoury characters on the border, Medrala added. They
were the survivors.

One afternoon in Phnom Penh, I went to see Duch's lawyer
with Sokheang. Kar Savuth kept a large python in his
garden. It sat lazily in a cage it had long outgrown. Its
coils were the thickness of a man's torso and were folded
like tyres stacked upon one another. Kar Savuth had kept
it since the Vietnamese arrived in 1979, when he saved it
from being killed by people who wanted to eat it. The
children called it *Chamroeun* which, in Khmer, means prosperous.

Kar Savuth had been appointed Duch's lawyer by the

government. With his stiff grey Chinese top, thick-rimmed spectacles and receding hairline, Kar Savuth reminded me a little of Kim Jong Il, the reclusive leader of North Korea. We sat in the shade of his garden, not far from Chamroeun's cage, the lawyer's gold Rolex occasionally glinting in the sun. His daughter served water and soft drinks. He pulled out his rather slim file on Duch.

Taking out a gold pen he began scanning the documents. 'During the Pol Pot regime we had to do what we were assigned to do,' he began in tired tones without looking up. 'If we didn't do it, they would have killed us.' He then outlined the basis of Duch's case.

Although Duch had been commandant of the prison, the lawyer said, he had never personally killed anybody. That had been the job of the guards. He had been cheated by the revolution and by Pol Pot and it was under the orders of his superiors that the killing was carried out. 'Even the executioners weren't guilty,' he said. Why?

'Because they were ordered to kill the prisoners. They were ordered from the top. If they didn't kill, they would be killed.' He leaned back, resting his elbows on his seat. 'That is why,' he concluded, 'Duch is innocent.'

I quoted Duch's admission that he had personally killed the remaining prisoners on Nuon Chea's orders. I also told him what Ein had told me about the beating of Sri the cook. Duch may not have killed him personally, but he certainly participated in beatings and in torture. Kar Savuth shifted in his seat. He seemed genuinely surprised.

'That's wrong,' he said, shaking his head. 'Duch's duties were only to read the confessions for Son Sen, because above Duch was Son Sen. Above Son Sen, there was Nuon Chea, and above Nuon Chea, there was Pol Pot.' He stopped to mull over what I had just told him, then leaned forward, a worried look on his face. 'I've never heard him say things like that,' he said.

I asked Kar Savuth whether, if there was a trial, Duch would be freed. 'Just bring in somebody who's still alive and ask if anybody saw Duch kill prisoners. Nobody saw him kill prisoners,' he said, looking more confident.

In 1961, Adolf Eichmann, who was being tried for his part in the European holocaust, told the court that he was 'just following orders'. It is the standard defence of mass murderers and torturers, from Bosnia to Rwanda, that it was a job, just like any other. When the table is turned, the guilty either deny their involvement completely, readily identify with their victims as lesser victims, or create elaborate and complex arguments designed to muddy the clarity of moral responsibility. In some cases they even continue to attack the veracity of their victims' claims.

If Duch were ever to face a court it is almost certain that his defence would rest on this one point: that he was following orders and if he hadn't, he too would have been killed – the Organisation would be ultimately to blame. And perhaps, to a certain extent, it was true. What real choices did any of the staff have if the only other option was death?

If no-one testified that they had witnessed Duch carry out a killing on his own initiative, I wondered, could Duch get off on a technicality?

After meeting the lawyer Sokheang and I returned to Amleang, where Duch's first prison was, to find someone who could confirm that Duch actually had killed with his own hands. Ham In, the survivor from M-13, had mentioned one of Duch's former bodyguards, who lived near the old prison.

Now forty-nine, Chan Voeun looked at one of the pictures

of Duch that I had taken. 'He hasn't changed much,' he said. He spoke with a deep voice, his hair was short and curly and his furrowed brow betrayed his anxiety. What seemed like the entire village had crowded around us, curious at the foreigner in their village. Voeun was building a new house when we arrived and nervously fingered a hatchet in his hands as we introduced ourselves.

Did he ever see Duch kill anyone personally and not simply give the order?

'I saw him kill one person with his gun,' he replied. 'It was after he interrogated a man for two or three days and he didn't confess. Duch took him outside and tied his hands and shot him in the chest three times. He died instantly.' Voeun said he wasn't the only witness; there were at least six others. He told us that Duch later killed three other bodyguards. 'If he interrogated them and he wasn't satisfied with their answers he would kill them himself,' said Voeun. 'He killed *a lot* of people.'

Sokheang has investigated scores of political murders, but never has anyone been charged. There were more than a hundred extra-judicial killings during the 1997 coup alone, many of which he investigated with his colleagues. One photograph from the time showed a body face down in a ditch. The flesh from the knees down had been scraped away to reveal the tibia, fibula and foot bones. It was as though the man had been dipped in acid. A local official on the scene had volunteered that perhaps it was a suicide.

Cambodia is a society plagued by violence. One of the most disturbing aspects of this 'culture of impunity' is the emergence of 'people's courts', where lynch mobs routinely beat people to death acting as police, judiciary and executioner. It is a measure of the frustration and rage of a people who have never known any form of social justice. Many believe this is one of the most enduring legacies of Khmer Rouge rule.

Decades of violence have compounded to create a shattered society where normality is a thin veneer. It has left people bereft of the ability to respond to those around them and, as a result, people have tremendous difficulty in trusting one another. Added to this is the fatalism inherent in Khmer Buddhism, where people feel unable to effect anything approaching positive change. This belief in a preordained life, where the individual is powerless to act, is deeply rooted. 'It undermines people's ability to have initiative, to speak up, to dare to work together, to trust each other, to cooperate,' Ellen Minotti, a social worker in Phnom Penh, told me. 'All over the country there is a deep anger at the injustice.' No-one believes in the ability of those in authority to act in a responsible way. Many believe that if there is a Khmer Rouge tribunal, it might unravel the fragile peace that exists and prove to be both politically and personally destabilising.

Few young Khmers have any real understanding of what took place under the Khmer Rouge. In the standard history textbook for students of fifteen years old, six lines out of seventy-nine pages referred to Pol Pot and the Khmer Rouge. The rest was devoted to the glories of the Khmer empire and the various wars with Cambodia's traditional foes: the Thais and the Vietnamese.

'We must not ask Duch and other Khmer Rouge *why*,' Ho had told me. 'There is no reason *why*.' I asked him to explain. 'Every day someone hates somebody. They invented many reasons to kill people. They were all excuses and lies. And they will only shirk responsibility. Khmer people do not have the powers of self-criticism, it's one of the more negative aspects of Khmer culture. In our culture it's always the faults of others. It's the classic characteristic of a society in decline – it was Cambodians killing Cambodians.' *Why* is an accusatory term that can offend. *How* by contrast invites people to look at situations and invites understanding. When I talked with former Khmer Rouge from Tuol Sleng and elsewhere I did my best to avoid using why. It put people on their guard and in some cases they would clam up altogether. People kill one another all the time all over the world; the crucial thing is to understand what led them at that moment to do such a thing. Ho believed that by understanding the stages of how Cambodia as a society could produce such a cataclysm, people would be able to learn from the past and move on.

'The most important thing is to know *how* the people were killed, not *why* – that is why a trial is important.'

But how do you persuade people that having a tribunal is worth it? In Cambodia the record of broken political promises and betrayals far outweighs the promises kept. People are scared that they will go through all that pain for nothing or actually put themselves in danger. Cambodia, said Minotti, is still not a safe place to be.

Sokheang told me that working in human rights now was a logical extension to him joining the Khmer Rouge in Paris. 'With this work, I can help save lives.' He sees his human-rights work as a way to address the social injustices all around him. His experiences have also left their mark psychologically and he suffers from acute insomnia, headaches and stomach pains. His doctor has told him that there is nothing physically wrong with him. Sokheang's large assortment of pills he knows are to relieve the symptoms, not the cause. But Sokheang is in a privileged position working in the human-rights world. He can channel much of this energy into his work and it provides him with something like a support structure.

Not long ago Sokheang's brother, Ly, made a trip back to the area where the family had been sent during the Khmer Rouge. He learned from the locals that the man who had killed their three brothers was still living nearby. They offered to take Ly to see him. 'I didn't dare,' he said, 'otherwise it would've brought me back to the past, twenty years ago.'

Sokheang, on the other hand, wanted to return and confront him. He wanted to find out what exactly had happened and then file a complaint if a tribunal ever convened.

His brother thought it would be pointless and that it would only reawaken painful memories. The family was also afraid of retribution. Sokheang, not wishing to argue, let the subject go. 'They were living together at that time and I feel that they may have suffered more than me, because I was away.'

Why did he want to confront this man, I asked. 'Because a crime is a crime. There is no time limit for you to complain even twenty, thirty, fifty years on if you know that man killed your brothers. It can also serve as a lesson for future generations, to prevent it from happening again. This is the main reason.'

Ly didn't believe the trial should be restricted to the surviving Khmer Rouge leaders. 'If they want to have an international tribunal they have to try *all* the people who committed crimes,' he said.

Across the country, nearly everyone I spoke to, including people who had worked at Tuol Sleng, believed surviving Khmer Rouge leaders should be put on trial – at least in principle. 'I want them killed for what they did,' one woman from Samlaut told me. 'Separating loved ones, arresting people – I don't want just a trial. I want to eat them.'

Although the negotiations to set up a tribunal had been dragging on for years, and despite the violence, Minotti found cause for optimism. She told of how some Khmers she knew talked about meeting up for a family reunion although they weren't exactly family. They had been together during the Khmer Rouge period, and helped each other, and had survived together. Now their ties were unbreakable.

'What I'm amazed at,' she said, 'is why the good people are good, because I don't see any reinforcement for people to be good, for being incorrupt, for not stealing and not cheating. And there are a *lot* of people who are good. It's just stunning to me.'

One organisation that has been trying to provide a critical understanding of the Khmer Rouge period is the Cambodian Documentation Centre, based in Phnom Penh. The centre was established in 1995 by Yale University's Cambodian Genocide Program to facilitate training and field research in Cambodia. It was created for the purpose of collecting as much data on the Khmer Rouge period as possible and has amassed hundreds of thousands of documents, including the confessions and photographs from Tuol Sleng. Should a trial of Khmer Rouge leaders convene the centre will provide much of the evidence. The ultimate aim is for the centre to become a permanent, autonomous institute open to the general public for educational purposes. It is an extraordinary undertaking. One morning I went to meet the director. Chhang Youk, now in his forties, was immaculately turned out in a tie and shirt, streaks of grey running through his hair. Behind his desk sat reams of documents and files on shelves that dwarfed him. His offices have become one of the first ports of call for foreign journalists and he is routinely quoted in the local and international press.

Youk had fled Cambodia as a refugee after the Khmer Rouge were ousted. He later settled in the United States and studied political science in Texas before working with the Dallas police force in the crime-prevention unit before being selected to head the Cambodian Documentation Centre. Youk has a young staff of archivists and researchers, most of whom were children during Khmer Rouge rule. As we sat in his cool, polished offices, they could be seen in the background busily cataloguing, storing, copying and numbering. It is a slow process as new material keeps coming to light. One of the most important undertakings has been the production of a magazine in English and in Khmer called *Searching for the Truth*, which is distributed all over the country. In it scholars and eyewitnesses provide their analysis and tell their stories. As a result, the centre receives new information as more eyewitnesses come forward. While I was there, a former survivor from S-21 thought to have died suddenly re-emerged. It is a long process of investigating a past that they hope will never be repeated.

Youk believed the future was bright. 'It's a new generation now,' he said confidently. He seemed to believe that a trial was simply a question of time. Almost 200 countries unanimously adopted the agreement between the government and the UN to establish a Khmer Rouge tribunal. He talked of having Cambodians write their own history and expected something similar to a South African-style Truth and Reconciliation Commission in conjunction with a tribunal, with public forums for debate and discussion in villages.

The US Government had been the first to fund the centre with a grant of over a million dollars. I often wondered whether it was healthy to have as the principal backer for all this crucial research a government that had played a role in bringing the perpetrators of the murder to power. 'One has to be pragmatic,' said Youk. The US interest in all this, he believed, was to somehow make amends for the past.

I wanted to believe what he was saying, but found little reason for the optimism he espoused. The tribunal, if it was to convene, would only concentrate on the Khmer Rouge years between 1975–9. Only five of the original Khmer Rouge standing committee were still alive and they were old and, in some cases, sick men. Duch had been in prison for several years now. The US meanwhile continued to deploy their B-52s in Afghanistan, perhaps even using the very planes that had unleashed their deadly cargo on Cambodia.

Youk believed that the centre was a crucial stepping-stone to putting an end to the violence and lawlessness. The tribunal would also stop the Khmer Rouge period being used as a yardstick to measure the country's abysmal human-rights record. 'It will be a lesson for the younger generation to learn that if you commit the crime of genocide or a crime against humanity or anybody, it doesn't matter how long it takes, people will be after you.'

Not everyone believed in a trial. In Sopheap was still a believer in the revolution when I first met him. He had been Ieng Sary's personal secretary when the Khmer Rouge had been in power. During the 1980s, he was a diplomat for the Khmer Rouge, based in Cairo, and had been close to Pol Pot before the ailing leader died. He had been well aware of the killings under the Khmer Rouge. He described himself as 'a good Khmer Rouge'. He hadn't defected or changed sides, he said. He had surrendered.

He didn't see the need for a trial and didn't understand why only the Khmer Rouge should be held to account and not, for example, the United States. 'I don't believe it's for justice,' he said contemptuously.

He told me how Khieu Samphan, the former head of state under Pol Pot, was regarded by Cambodians as a gentle man. Although he belonged to the hierarchy, he didn't kill anybody, he said. 'Putting this man in court when others were responsible for killing people – what kind of justice is that?'

So who then did he believe should go on trial?

'I'm not a lawyer or a historian,' he said, shrugging his shoulders. 'You see, all these people know nothing about the structure, even me.'

Several of In Sopheap's siblings were killed during the purges, while he himself was implicated on at least six occasions by friends and comrades taken to S-21. 'Ieng Sary told me,' he said. And it was Ieng Sary who had saved him. 'It's very dangerous to have your personal secretary in prison.' He told me that he knew for certain that one brother, In Sophann, had been taken to S-21. I gave him a copy of his brother's confession. It was the first time he had seen it.

His eyes ran back and forth, while his finger ran down the pages. After some time he looked up and raised his eyebrows. 'How can Pol Pot or Ieng Sary take this as something of a confession? There's nothing here.' His brother's death, he said, was a result of internal conflicts within the regime; he was the victim of a power struggle.

'I cannot accuse Pol Pot of bringing my brother to the prison. I cannot even accuse Mr Duch of taking my brother to the prison.' He refused to accuse the leadership of any wrongdoing, 'because it was very anonymous'.

As someone who had stayed in the Khmer Rouge right until the end and was still a supporter, did he feel in any way responsibile for the millions who had died, I asked. 'During my work as ambassador I never defended the killing.'

'But you didn't condemn it either.'

'I didn't have all the elements to judge. Concretely, what evidence do I have?' I looked at the confession on the table beneath his elbow.

It was a game which he would not or could not see beyond. Instead he chose to see the excesses of the Khmer Rouge period in the abstract, as though what happened had nothing to do with him. And this is what had enabled the Khmer Rouge to murder and kill without conscience. They could hide behind a piece of machinery, deaf to the screams of the people caught up in its grinding cogs.

In Sopheap had supported the revolution all of his adult life. To turn against it now would be too much and perhaps he knew it. Duch had his Christianity, a new structure to be able to face his past. In Sopheap had nothing.

'There should be a trial,' said Sokheang back at his home. 'Everybody agrees with that.'

So why did people like In Sopheap have such difficulty acknowledging their responsibility, I asked.

There were two ways in which it worked, depending on the rank, he said. He gave the example of a recent riot in Phnom Penh which had been organised, most likely by Prime Minister Hun Sen, to look as though it was a spontaneous outburst of anger. The police stood by and watched as a foreign embassy was ransacked and torched. When asked why they didn't intervene, the police said they hadn't been given any orders to stop it. And no minister resigned. 'If this had happened in France or in England or in America,' said Sokheang, 'at least the minister in charge of security would have resigned immediately. But here, nobody took responsibility. The Khmer Rouge used the same tactics to explain what had happened. They used to say that any decision of the party was a collective decision. The decision did not come from any one individual.' That way they weren't accountable, hiding as they did behind the faceless Organisation, and could believe the claim, possibly quite genuinely, that they were innocent of any wrongdoing. Much like the executions that had taken place in Sihanouk's day, the idea of giving out one blank cartridge could absolve them of all guilt as long as there was even the smallest possibility that they weren't responsible.

I reminded Sokheang that Ieng Sary had once said, 'Let history be the judge.'

'This is nonsense,' said Sokheang. 'As I said before, a crime is a crime, regardless of whether you killed one man, two men or three people or you killed a hundred people.' He stopped for a moment, lost in thought. 'I feel that I was responsible,' he continued looking beyond the railing and into the darkness, 'because I think that some of my friends who joined the movement and were killed later, joined because of my influence.'

How many of them were killed, I asked.

'Several dozen,' he said. Then, 'Less than a hundred.'

In February 2002, Ke Pauk died of liver complaints. A former Khmer Rouge zone secretary, Ke Pauk had defected to the government in 1998 and was given the rank of brigadier-general in the Cambodian army. Involved in the massive purges of the Eastern Zone, he was considered one of the main candidates to be tried for genocide, war crimes and crimes against humanity. It was Ke Pauk who had sent Duch's brothers-in-law to Phnom Penh.

It was a bad omen for the advocates of justice as the negotiations for a tribunal of Khmer Rouge ground wearily along. Time was beginning to run out.

On a cool December morning in 2002, I dropped by Phnom Penh's Municipal Court, where a former Khmer Rouge commander was being tried. A large crowd of bored-looking Khmer and foreign journalists milled about outside, awaiting news of the proceedings. Overweight Cambodian policemen in motorbike helmets swaggered around with AK-47s and an air of self-importance. Nothing much was happening and the longer I chatted with people the greater the feeling that the verdict would be delayed still further. I was told that Nuon Chea, or Brother No 2, had arrived to testify. I looked through the window at the assembled shadows inside, but couldn't see him.

Sam Bith, the sixty-nine-year-old former commander, was being tried for ordering the 1994 kidnapping and murder of three backpackers; a Briton, a Frenchman and an Australian. They had been travelling on a train that was attacked by Khmer Rouge guerrillas and taken hostage on their way to Kampot in the south. Ten Cambodians were also killed in the attack. The backpackers were executed weeks after, when negotiations for their release and the payment of a ransom broke down. Their bodies were later found in shallow graves. Their Achilles tendons had been severed to prevent them from escaping. Later, Sam Bith had defected to the government side and was promoted to the rank of general. The British, French and Australian governments pressured the Cambodian Government to have him arrested. Briefly, Cambodia was a story again.

It was then announced that Sam Bith was unwell and that the case would be postponed until the following day. The assembled journalists groaned and gathered their gear, then crammed around the courtroom door, ready for Sam Bith. I kept an eye out for Nuon Chea.

When the doors finally opened there was a scramble of lenses to get a shot of Sam Bith. A van had drawn alongside as a mass of hands and bodies shepherded him into the back. Out of the corner of my eye, I noticed that another LandCruiser was making for a different gate. I broke from the crowd and ran to follow it out into a busy main street, the large shadow of an elderly man pressed against the frosted window. But it was too late. Nuon Chea had disappeared into Phnom Penh's busy traffic.

The following week it was announced that Sam Bith had been found guilty of murder, kidnapping, membership of an armed group, robbery, terrorism and destroying public property. He was sentenced to life in prison and ordered, with another former Khmer Rouge commander, to pay fifty million riels (about £7,700) to each of the Khmer families. He had been represented by Duch's lawyer, Kar Savuth.

The news was regarded as a triumph. 'I'm delighted,' said the British ambassador, who described the verdict as a major step 'towards justice for the families of the three young men'. The ruling was described as 'a milestone' by the press. No mention was made of the ten Cambodians who lost their lives.

Most Cambodians I spoke to were unimpressed with the verdict, believing the case was an isolated example and the result of pressure from three Western governments, all of them major donors to Cambodia's national development programme. As Sokheang told me, 'We wanted to please the embassies.'

Sam Bith was led away to prison dismissing the verdict as 'unjust'. Nuon Chea returned home a free man.

CHAPTER 21

Living with the Past

I FOLLOWED THE woman along the path that squeezed between a jumble of tightly packed dwellings. Smoke from cooking fires was severed by blades of light that cut through the alley. Small children ran about. She showed me the way through the main room of the house. It was dark and musty inside. A thin white body lay stretched out on the tiled floor under a mosquito net. A television set blared away in the corner. I tiptoed around, careful not to disturb anything as she led me through the gloom into the kitchen beyond. Suddenly I stumbled. As my eyes became accustomed to the dark I could see a drop of about seven inches where the tiles had sunk. The bodies had been removed several years before, she said, but despite their best efforts the floor continued to sink.

The woman's name was Dy Vibol, and her house stood on what had once been the open area behind Tuol Sleng. Before the execution ground had been moved to Choeung Ek, many of the important prisoners were disposed of in graves here. I remembered looking over the area some years before, thinking that no-one would ever build on it, let alone live there. Now it was crammed with an assortment of wooden houses.

Dy Vibol was a large matronly woman with a kindly face. She had lived here for several years with her husband, their five children and her brother and sister. Her husband, a policeman, was rarely at home. It was a small wooden building with blue doors sheltered by a nearby palm. Tuol Sleng loomed behind.

'I realised when I moved into this area that the hollows in the earth were mass graves,' she told me. 'The one my house was built on must have been a big one because it keeps sinking.' She gave a nervous laugh.

Despite the overcrowding, there was a conspicuously open area next to Dy Vibol's home. When the owners began building, she explained, one family member had become ill and died. It had remained vacant ever since, too blighted by bad luck to build on. The bones had yet to be removed. When I asked Dy Vibol why she didn't live somewhere else she laughed. They couldn't afford to.

I later asked Sokheang how a generally superstitious people, who believed in forest spirits, ghouls and magic, could live on a mass grave and not be afraid. His reply: you get used to it. Or as another man who lived near Dy Vibol told me, 'What happened here was nothing to do with us. We suffered too.'

Like a pack of cards Sokheang doled them out: photographs of a wedding, a funeral, babies, a school outing, pictures of friends and relatives. 'Survived, dead, dead, survived, disappeared, dead, disappeared, survived, dead,' he said as he placed them in quick succession on the table.

This brother, said Sokheang, pointing to a smiling young

man, always liked having his picture taken. Another photograph showed a group of young men before the gate of
Kompong Thom Lycée. 'This is a portrait of one of my
teachers,' he said, showing a man with a youthful face. 'I
was very close to him. He was a good man – a progressive. He was executed because he told them he was a
professor.' He handed me another photograph: a picnic
beside a river, young men and women with dazzling smiles.
Amid one group was a stocky young Sokheang next to his
two brothers who had been killed. Then he came to a
group photograph of twenty-seven classmates. He paused
for a moment, his forehead creased in concentration. 'Only
three survived.'

The photographs, taken in Kompong Thom, depicted a
vanished world – a world before Pol Pot. They were the
only undisrupted continuum with the past. Like the
photographs of Tuol Sleng these pictures were reminders
of something that had been irrevocably lost. Sokheang's
mother had risked her life by clutching on to them during
the Khmer Rouge – they would have betrayed the family's
'bourgeois' background. While they represented what had
been lost, they were a reminder of what might have been.
Looking at the photographs it is almost as though Sokheang
and the surviving members of his family are exiles in their
own country; home has become a memory, a place in the
mind.

All photography is about death: photographs immortalise
their subjects. Like the photographs of the condemned in
Tuol Sleng, they are both proof of lives lived and lives
extinguished. Sokheang's photographs were so touchingly
ordinary they looked as though they could have been taken
only last year. But there is Sokheang's story, his narrative
and his explanation. Without it, they are just innocent

family pictures. Only for Sokheang and his family is the chasm between seeing and knowing bridged.

It occurred to me that if we only remember the destruction through the photographs at Tuol Sleng we are remembering a small part of the devastation. Sokheang's photographs transgress this and it is not only the victims that are recalled as people who were murdered, but also of a whole way of life that was murdered with them; they have become another tragic testimony to the totality of the destruction. But they are also a celebration of a life that can be replicated, of a life that refuses to die.

Sokheang knew his family had suffered greater hardships than he had done. He had joined the revolution of his own free will. They had endured a calamity they had no control over. 'When I arrived home after the Khmer Rouge, after twenty-two years,' he said looking at the photographs spread out before him, 'when I think about the suffering that my family endured, I knew that they suffered a *lot*. Of course, having been separated for a very long time, the family wasn't as close as before.' He had led a more privileged life under the Khmer Rouge and he felt guilty. 'Even though I lived through the Pol Pot regime; they were in the cooperatives.' His family had been forced to work hard in constant fear of their lives. 'And when I arrived back, they said nothing,' he said, putting the photographs carefully back in the bag.

Several years ago, a friend of Sokheang's who now lives in Paris proposed that the survivors from his group come together to erect a *stupa* in memory of the people they knew had been executed. Some of Sokheang's surviving friends had since become wealthy and held positions in the government. A few of them see the construction of a memorial as a sensitive issue, since there are many former

Khmer Rouge in the current administration. However, Sokheang remains undeterred. 'We are more than sixty years old now, so it's up to each person to decide. I don't care. People like Ho, who share the same ideas as me, we have remained close,' he said. 'I never abandon old friends.'

Friendship and loyalty were all-important to Sokheang and for me he was a true intellectual. He and I once became embroiled in a heated discussion on a car journey from Battambang to the outskirts of Phnom Penh, a drive of just over five hours. When we arrived in the city, he slapped me on the back and told me we could disagree, a teasing grin on his face. After all, he said, we were friends. Not many people I knew could debate so heatedly nor so frankly. And that was what made Sokheang so different. He was open to new ideas and he didn't allow his intellectual beliefs to get in the way of his core values. He once told me, 'you have the right to believe what you want, but do not forget that we are friends.' He was referring to comrades who had since joined different political parties or moved away from politics altogether. 'If they say that capitalism is good, that's their problem,' he said with a grin. 'And sometimes we would have passionate discussions about that. But when it's finished, it's finished. We have a coffee together, go to the cinema together, but still I keep my opinions and they keep theirs . . . I still consider them my friends.'

Trust was the point from which the Khmer Rouge had departed so radically. All their relationships were governed by fear. As In Sopheap had said about his own boss, Ieng Sary, it was dangerous to have your own secretary in prison. And in the case of Duch, he had taken in his old comrades, tortured them and killed them.

*   *   *

Several years after Duch's arrest, I asked his lawyer, Kar Savuth, how Duch felt about being arrested and held in prison when so many others were walking free. Duch was angry, he said. 'He said it was because of you that he was put in jail.'

Again I began to wonder if his remorse had been genuine, or just an elaborate smokescreen. If his conversion to Christianity was a lie or simply an attempt to avoid arrest. Before his conversion, Duch had become depressed as a result, it seemed, of his wife's death – not for his role in the murder of thousands.

Khieu Samphan told *Le Monde* in 2004 that Duch was not a torturer by temperament, but by conviction; that he saw his work as an interrogator as an unpleasant but necessary job in the service of a great revolution. But having talked with former interrogators, executioners and survivors, all the evidence, I found, pointed to the contrary. He not only carried out his duties with conviction, but he enjoyed it.

He displayed the same diligence with S-21's bureaucracy that he had with his studies. As a mathematician he found the mapping-out of conspiratorial frameworks intellectually pleasing. As a teacher he revelled in the position of total power he commanded over his subordinates and got a perverse thrill toying with prisoners in the correspondence and during interrogations.

However, Pastor Lapel was convinced that Duch's conversion was genuine. He saw it as proof of the power of forgiveness.

'It's the real thing,' he said. 'It's hard to believe him with this background, but you can see that it bore fruit.' Telling the truth, he said, was central to the Christian way of life and the confession of sins was the first step towards deliverance. 'After all,' he said, 'one of God's words is "forgiveness".' And this was a key difference between Buddhism and Christianity.

The Buddhist ritual of confession, the *Patimokkha*, was only similar to the Christian practice by its acknowledgement of sins committed. It did not release the sinner of his bad karma. Buddha had not delivered people from guilt or purged their sins and he never offered cures for disease or affliction. Everyone was responsible for their own state of affairs, and were bound by the karmic law of cause and effect. This cycle of death and rebirth, known as *Samsara*, was represented by an ever-turning wheel. The only way to break this cycle of reincarnation was by making merit through a series of penances and rituals and gradually paying back the debt, cancelling out the bad karma. Giving to monks in the early mornings was the most obvious example of this. This process could go on for many incarnations. There was little hope of immediate salvation from a recently committed sin.

Christianity, by contrast, could absolve believers from their guilt here, now, in this lifetime. It provided people with a release from the karmic forces they believed governed their lives. Lapel told me of a trip he had made to Anlong Veng where he had baptised eighty-four people in one day, all former Khmer Rouge and their families. Some of the commanders later became lay pastors. A lot of the people have blood on their hands up there, I ventured.

'Oh, definitely,' he laughed. 'Buddhism is in crisis here. Christianity is simple, easy to understand and untainted by the corruption of the *Sangha* that has been largely discredited. It's a corruption that is perhaps not publicly acknowledged but is privately.'

In Khmer Buddhism, good karma, like respect, is something that can be bought. For example, a gangster who who has enriched himself through violent crime can cancel out the bad karma by building a new pagoda, erecting *stupas* and buying gifts for the monks. By participating in festivals and providing presents he could also buy back respect from the villagers. All this would raise his standing in the next life.

'I'm very careful when I come to Cambodia,' said Lapel. 'I don't come with *loie* – money. I come with love.' All he offered, he said, was spiritual guidance and the simple belief that if you confess you can be forgiven.

Buddhism in Cambodia is essentially a passive philosophy. It concentrates on abstaining from evil, rather than urging people to do good works for the benefit of others. In Khmer Buddhism most penances and merit-making are carried out by ritual. One Khmer friend, disillusioned by Buddhism, told me how his grandmother gave all her money to the temple to feed and clothe monks as well as to construct a *stupa*. This didn't make sense to him when so many people were poor. He said it was one of the main reasons he became a Christian.

A survivor of the Khmer Rouge himself, Pastor Lapel had become a Christian during their control. He told me how two Khmer Rouge guards had come for him one night when he was sick, and when they saw his ivory crucifix, they let him be. He believes it saved his life. He was later baptised in a border refugee camp and then moved to the United States.

On one return visit, Lapel and his family went to Tuol Sleng. There they found his father-in-law's photograph on the wall, then a cousin's. She had been a science professor before the war and, like Sokheang and many others, supported the revolution. Like Duch, she had been impris-

oned by Sihanouk's police. After being released she joined
the Khmer Rouge.

'I couldn't believe it,' said Lapel of the photograph on
the wall. Did he feel angry towards Duch? 'Oh yeah,' he
said quietly. I asked if he could ever forgive Duch. There
was a long pause. 'Yes,' he said finally. 'If I met him now
I would say, "I love you. I hate what you have done."
When I gave my commitment to the Lord, I knew some
people I met were former Khmer Rouge. I've probably
shared Christ with the people who killed my parents. But
in Cambodia we're here to reconcile.'

And despite seeing his own relatives' pictures at Tuol
Sleng, he remained convinced. 'It's hard to believe that a
person, a mass murderer, a killer can suddenly claim that
he is a good person,' Lapel continued. 'But I believe him.'

As the negotiations for a trial continued between the United
Nations and the Cambodian Government, Duch remained
locked up.

Since Sokheang's return from the border, he had worked
for UNTAC with a French colleague, as an interpreter and
analyst. They often crossed contested areas and Khmer
Rouge territory. It was gruelling work and often extremely
dangerous. After attacks they interviewed people in hospitals and investigated secret government prisons. When
UNTAC departed Sokheang began working for a human-
rights organisation.

Sokheang had some knowledge of Duch's case and had
plenty of experience visiting prisoners as a human-rights
worker. I asked him if he believed Duch had really wanted
to tell the truth.

'Before, I believe he really wanted to talk,' he said. But
now, he doubted he would tell the truth. 'Being a pris-

oner,' he said, 'there is a lot of pressure, psychologically and from his lawyer, politically. When I knew that Duch had been chief of S-21, I hated him for what he did. For me, a revolution is to save people, to cleanse through education. Violence will only lead to more violence, and it will become a vicious circle. Duch said that the decision to kill people was not his. He said that his task was only to get confessions. This is true, but only up to a point. He wasn't a decision maker, but he could make suggestions.' Sokheang said that Duch really believed in the revolution, and if he hadn't followed the orders he too would have been in trouble. 'This is not to excuse him, not at all, but I think he believed fully that the revolution should be carried out in that manner. As they used to say, "you cannot make an omelette without breaking eggs." Anyway, for me it's absolutely unacceptable. Duch did that with conviction.' He turned and switched off the light. 'They treated people like animals.'

In 2003, I returned to Anlong Veng for the last time. What was once a collection of pitiful shacks and a single dusty trail was now a town with a thriving market, a karaoke-lounge brothel, several schoolhouses and a hospital.

Local commanders and entrepreneurs were hoping to promote Anlong Veng as a tourist destination. Escorted by a Mr Lee, I was taken to see the 'sights' such as the *Sala* where Pol Pot had been tried, the remains of his house and his grave. On the way up the Dangrek range I noticed that a burnt-out tank I had seen before had been carted off. I later saw it in a war museum in Siem Reap.

Mr Lee had been close to Pol Pot but I wasn't quite sure of his position. Although a friendly man he was evasive when I asked. Earlier he had tried to sell me old photographs of Sihanouk's visit to the Khmer Rouge liberated areas in 1973. They had somehow survived the damp and the war, although white ants had enjoyed a small feast. Back in the car he had told me that Pol Pot had died of natural causes and not suicide as some had claimed.

In 1997, the Americans had been trying to negotiate his transfer to Thailand in order to spirit the ailing leader away to be tried. I couldn't understand why. Pol Pot in the dock would risk having him pointing fingers in all sorts of uncomfortable directions. It was difficult to see who would have wanted him on trial. The UN, the Thais, the US, the British, the Singaporeans, the Vietnamese, the Chinese, the Thais, the Malaysians had all helped the Khmer Rouge at one time or another. And for the Khmer Rouge themselves, he had become a liability, since it was his name that had become associated with the terror almost to the exclusion of anyone else's. His sudden death seemed so terribly convenient. Convenient, that is, for just about everyone involved except for the victims.

Mr Lee had no doubt as to the cause of death. Pol Pot had Hodgkin's disease, had suffered a stroke and been on oxygen for several years. His body had been cremated before an official autopsy could be conducted, although the Thai military had taken fingerprints and photographed his teeth. The Thai prime minister at the time had told journalists to stop the speculation: Pol Pot had died of natural causes. There had been heavy shelling at the time and he couldn't get a fresh supply of oxygen, which would have come from Thailand, a mere fifteen-minute stroll up the hill.

After passing the defaced stone statues of Khmer Rouge soldiers on the slope, we arrived at the summit of the mountain. Next to a checkpoint where a group of police

and soldiers were playing cards, Mr Lee showed me where
'The People's Tribunal of Anlong Veng' had convened to
denounce Pol Pot. All that remained of the *Sala* were some
posts that protruded from the long grass. Nearby a small
blue sign read, 'This place will be reserved as a tourist
sight – The Ministry of Tourism.'

We then carried on along the top of the range, looking
over the vast expanse of rapidly shrinking jungle below. Pillars
of smoke rose from bush fires into the sky. On the way Mr
Lee pointed out where Son Sen and his family had been
murdered and further on showed us the *Sala* where Ta Mok
had been taken into custody. I asked Mr Lee who had arrested
him. 'Don't say arrest,' he said, a hurt expression on his face.
'In order to stop the fighting he came from his house in
Thailand to his house on the border and agreed to hand
himself over.' Ta Mok had sacrificed himself for his people.

The house where Pol Pot spent his last few days no
longer stood. The wood had been too valuable. All that
remained was a broken toilet bowl that lay on its side in
the weeds, together with some discarded bottles. His grave,
or more accurately the spot where his body had been
cremated, was now covered with a rusty corrugated-iron
roof, presumably to keep the rain from washing away what
little was left. There were a bizarre collection of oddments
scattered about: a rusty beer can, a few empty bottles of
Red Bull and some bits of rubber tyre. Someone had been
paying their respects to his spirit, judging by the can of
incense stubs.

It was a beautiful spot. The sun shone through the trees
and the grasses heaved and swayed all around us. It seemed
a peaceful end for the man nominally held responsible for
the violent deaths of so many of his own people.

Crouching, Mr Lee pointed out bits of charred bone to

me with a piece of bamboo that he had picked up on the path. Some people had taken bits of bone away with them as souvenirs he told me. 'Makes me sad,' he said, as he poked away.

I went back to Tuol Sleng. Directly opposite the gates of the museum there was now a restaurant. The Boddhi Tree was situated next to what had been the infirmary for the prisoners who were treated before being sent back for further interrogation. In a garden of potted plants and terracotta tiles visitors to the museum sat on silk cushions and ordered their marinated chicken fillets served with steamed asparagus. I glanced at the menu where 'the philosophy' of The Boddhi Tree was spelled out.

'Set in a stylish house,' The Boddhi Tree's continuing aim, it read, was 'to create a more meaningful life-fulfilling, social and business community development experience'. The restaurant had been one of the locations used for inter-rogations. No doubt many of the faces that now stared back from the walls of the museum had been tortured, some of them to death, in that very garden.

In one of the buildings in Tuol Sleng, a new tiled toilet with gleaming white urinals had been installed. Benches had been placed at intervals in the shade of the palms outside. Upstairs an auditorium played a film. Everything, it seemed, had been rearranged, this time for the tourists.

In November 2001, plans were announced for the former bases and hideouts of the Khmer Rouge to be made into tourist attractions. Anlong Veng, last stronghold of Pol Pot, was, said the Minister for Tourism, 'both beautiful and historic', and he outlined his vision of the area as a tourist resort. Plans to build a hotel, casino and duty-free shop a few hundred yards from Pol Pot's grave are said to be underway.

Meanwhile, just down the road from Tuol Sleng, Duch was entering his fifth year in detention waiting for his day in court. I had asked the relevant authorities for permission to meet with him on numerous occasions. But, each time, my requests were met with silence.

CHAPTER 22

Lessons from an Empty Schoolhouse

THERE IS A story of a repentant killer called Angulimala, who became one of the Buddha's most devoted followers.

An excellent student, Angulimala was deeply resented by his other classmates for his successes at school, and for the favour shown to him by the teacher. His classmates then contrived tricks to convince the teacher of Angulimala's deceitful nature. One night they stood outside the teacher's window so that the teacher would overhear them. 'Angulimala is going to get rid of the teacher,' one of them said. 'His father knows the king, so it shouldn't be difficult,' said another. Later they planted a fake letter from Angulimala to his father so that the teacher would read it. It confirmed Angulimala's intention to have the teacher removed. Just as they planned, the teacher banished Angulimala, telling him not to return until he had collected the index finger of a thousand people. Disgraced as an outcast, he fled to the forest. There, distraught, Angulimala didn't know what to do. He became convinced that the only way to be able to return was to follow the teacher's instruction. After killing the first victim, it became easier. Before long Angulimala had become a well-known killer who terrorised the population. Then one day Buddha arrived. Against the wishes of the king and the local people, he decided to walk through the forests of Savvathi where Angulimala was known to be.

Angulimala spotted the Buddha first. He had already collected 999 fingers and was determined to make Buddha's the last. Then he could return to his studies. As he stalked the Buddha, the Buddha always seemed to be the same distance from him. He then ran but still the Buddha was walking at the same distance and speed. Exasperated, he called out, 'STOP!' and the Buddha turned to face him.

'I have stopped, Angulimala. It is *you* that have not stopped,' said Buddha.

The Buddha told him of the great suffering his ambition had caused and the terror his name inspired. Angulimala, realising the error of his ways, asked the Buddha for help. Buddha then took him in as a monk and taught him the Dharma. He then became one of the Buddha's most faithful monks.

Since Duch's incarceration, and after following his journey through the country, I couldn't help feeling I was tracing the life of someone who had long since died. People, including his own family, would often talk about him in the past tense.

In the hours I spent with his mother and sister, it didn't seem fair to ask them what they thought about his confession. But I did ask his sister, Kim Hiep, if she had ever found out what happened to her husband. She said she had asked Duch in 1997. He had replied that he didn't know.

Duch's daughter Ky Siew Kim remembered Duch as a good father. 'I feel sad when he is far away from us like this – then we felt we had some protection. Now, I feel alone.'

It was at times like this, several years after Duch's imprisonment, that I began to question my own role in his incarceration and what purpose it had served other than to shut him up. By seeking out Duch, confronting him and then publishing the contents of his confession with his picture, I had naïvely believed that the truth about the killings would be made known, that a real justice would be forthcoming and other former Khmer Rouge brought to account. Instead the only Khmer Rouge who had confessed, the very person who was willing to provide the world with an explanation, had been muzzled from telling the truth, possibly for ever. And I had been instrumental in that gagging.

When I began to clear my mountain of newspaper cuttings on Cambodia, I came across a photograph of Nuon Chea taken just after his surrender to the Cambodian Government. What held my attention was what looked like a Parker pen clipped on to his shirt pocket. Previously, when Pol Pot had given one of his last interviews, it was not his predictable denials of mass murder that had intrigued me. It had been a tube of Pringles which sat on the table before the interview. The evil that the Khmer Rouge had come to represent in our collective minds was not at the end of some malarial river deep in a dark primordial jungle. Mass murderers enjoy Pringles, too. These details don't bring us closer to them. They bring them closer to us.

As I write this, Duch is still in prison awaiting trial. He

remains a heavy smoker. He is given three meals of meat, vegetables and rice a day and has reportedly put on weight. He is isolated from other inmates. His cell is spartan, with a fan, several books, a bed and a bowl for a toilet. I've heard he has also tried to spread the word of God among other prisoners.

Down the road Tuol Sleng continues to be visited by streams of tourists. I returned one more time. As I wandered down the corridors past Chan Kim Srun and her baby, past the picture of John Dewhurst, I wondered what the final lesson from all this killing was.

Over the years, the more I looked at the photographs, the more distracted I became by detail; the periphery of the photographs, such as a padlock on a door, or cracked plaster behind a prisoner, became the focus of my attention. The photographs became interesting not for what they showed, but rather for what they concealed. Their meaning continued to elude me as though they were a secret code from the past. I began searching for clues, something out of the ordinary, a small part that might reveal something of the whole of S-21.

On one of my last visits to the museum I brought pictures of prisoners from the archive, hoping to find the exact spot where they had been taken. One of them had distinct marks on the walls and several numbers sprayed behind a terrified-looking prisoner. On the wall next to another, the smear of a hand could be seen. It appeared in several of the mug shots.

I went upstairs along the balconies. I went to the next building. I could find neither the numbers nor the smeared handprint. They had been painted over. Instead I found graffiti where some tourists had scrawled messages in some of the rooms. 'Don't let shit like this *ever* happen again,' wrote Wayne in 2000. Among these messages, I noticed that someone with very neat handwriting had written in chalk on the walls of several rooms, high up near the ceiling. They were mathematic equations as though some lessons had been taking place. My eye followed them around the rooms as if they were yet another clue.

When I first visited Tuol Sleng, fifteen years ago, it had shocked and terrified me. The photographs and the horror depicted instilled in me a sense of purpose. I returned to the UK and lobbied MPs, held exhibitions, joined protests and campaigns. Today, that urgency has given way to inertia, to an overwhelming feeling of helplessness at the enormity of what happened. There are times when I find myself wondering if it happened at all. Now looking back as I took pictures of the pictures at the museum, I realised I was participating in another person's sufferings and vulnerability and exploiting their memory still further and for much more nebulous reasons. And they couldn't answer back. None of those who instigated this horror have ever been held accountable. If we can't respond to the overwhelming evidence in the form of photographs of the condemned, what does that say about us? What does it say about photography? All I am left with are the faces that adorn the walls of empty buildings.

In October 2004, after seven years of negotiations, the Cambodian Government ratified an agreement with the UN to try surviving leaders of the Khmer Rouge. Human-rights organisations had consistently raised concerns that such a tribunal would be subject to political manipulation. If a trial does convene, like Rwanda and the Hague trials, it is likely to go on for a long time yet. And only between seven to ten former Khmer Rouge are expected to be tried, including Duch.

For most Cambodians however, talk of justice means little in their daily struggle to survive in what has been one long trail of suffering. As they overcome their problems in a country still reeling from the effects of a protracted war, they have more pressing needs. After all, it has been over two decades since the Khmer Rouge genocide was exposed and made known to the world.

Above my desk in Bangkok hangs the mug shot of Chan Kim Srun with her baby on the day they arrived at Tuol Sleng in 1978. It was the picture that had haunted me as a teenager and again when I first set foot in the prison in 1989. The pictures I took of Duch are safely in my drawer. Although I was nervous when I took them, they are incredibly sharp. And if I look closely I can just make out my own silhouette in the reflection in his eyes. I look at Kim Srun's as she looks back at her tormentors and I see nothing.

Afterword

IN JULY 2006, Duch was transferred from the military prison in Phnom Penh to a holding centre at the Khmer Rouge tribunal on the outskirts of the city. Known as the Extraordinary Chambers of the Courts of Cambodia, the UN-backed court was established to try surviving members of the Khmer Rouge. Duch was joined by four others; Noun Chea, or Brother Number 2, Khieu Samphan, the former Khmer Rouge head of state, Ieng Sary, the former Khmer Rouge foreign minister and his wife Ieng Thirith. Ta Mok, alias 'the butcher', died in custody. Duch was charged with murder, torture, war crimes and crimes against humanity. He was the first to go on trial.

Not long after Duch's transfer, I caught my first glimpse of him in eight years. The large buildings where the tribunal is housed are part of a military headquarters. Set behind imposing walls, next to the main road behind a deep ditch, the signs announcing the tribunal were easy to overlook. Amid tight security uniformed guards man two entrances; one for tribunal people and the other for everyone else.

Inside the compound, and next to the courthouse, was a statue depicting Cambodian justice in the form of a man pointing a finger, wielding a club. Behind it, was the walled compound where Duch and the other former Khmer Rouge were kept.

As the first Khmer Rouge in a courtroom, Duch's pre-trial hearing was held amidst much media fanfare. The door of the courtroom was flung open and a frenzy of elbowing photographers burst through to get a shot of him. There he sat in the dock, illuminated by the flashes of the world's press. Visibly greying, he looked startled by the wave of shoving photographers, his eyes flickering to the side as if unable to face the jostling melee. I held my camera above my head and tried, rather half-heartedly, to get a picture of him. He didn't move.

This tribunal is one of the most complicated of its kind and is fraught with difficulties. It is made up of a mixture of international and local investigators and judges, with Cambodians in the majority. It continues to be plagued by allegations of political interference, corruption and a lack of transparency.

It is hard to see what this complex and expensive business will mean to ordinary Cambodians. According to one survey, more than three quarters of the population have little or no knowledge of the court. Only five people are to be held accountable for the deaths of 1.7 million. What will people think when a handful of old people go on trial in far away Phnom Penh and the killer of their relatives continues to live freely in a nearby village? As the head of Duch's defence team told me, 'There will be many people who will be disappointed.'

Duch may well be the only former Khmer Rouge to be brought in front of the tribunal. The other four are elderly and infirm and may not live long enough to face trial. An attempt to widen the net and include other former Khmer Rouge was met with resistance from the Cambodian side. Many believe the delays are a deliberate attempt by prime minister Hun Sen to protect former Khmer Rouge in his government and to limit revelations of involvement with the Khmer Rouge that could prove embarrassing to China. Allegations of corruption have also threatened to de-rail the process entirely.

Since meeting Duch in 1999, I continued to wonder about the sincerity of his confession and whether, if he was ever was to face a court, he would tell the truth. Like a tired news report I've replayed the moment he confessed over and over in my mind. The memory of that encounter has since been replaced by a series of photographs of him talking, as if they belong to someone else's recollection. Was it genuine remorse? Would he tell the truth after all the years of unlawful incarceration?

Some have speculated that Duch's psychological make-up made him pre-disposed to torture and kill, that it came easily to him. At the end of his indictment there was a psychological assessment. In a few short sentences he was described as fastidious, conscientious and 'control oriented.' Even in custody, it read, he continued to seek recognition from authority and that he had developed 'powerful defence mechanisms, especially through splitting and denial.' Perhaps most interesting of all, his imagination was, it read, 'limited in scope, as is his ability to put himself in other people's shoes.'

I've often wondered what the killers at places like S-21 did in order to survive, both physically and mentally. Clearly, to disconnect from the killing and prove to the leadership that you were committed was central. But what if the only way to survive was to actually enjoy the work, to completely throw oneself in and take pleasure in the horror, would that make you more guilty?

Despite the passage of time, and in the lead up to his trial, Duch remained true to his confession back in 1999. According to members of his defence team, he consistently recognised his responsibility for the crimes committed at S-21 and has willingly assisted in the investigation. When the court took him back to Tuol Sleng and the mass graves at Choeung Ek, he wept openly. 'I ask for your forgiveness,' he told some of his former victims. 'I know that you cannot forgive me, but I ask you to leave me the hope that you might.' He also verbally attacked one former guard who had always maintained he executed one or two people, contradicting him, saying the former guard was among the most zealous, killing hundreds.

It has taken thirty years to bring the Khmer Rouge to account for their crimes. The process of indicting war crimes suspects and bringing them to trial in UN-backed courts is painfully slow. In March 2009, while Duch waited for his trial to begin, the International Criminal Court issued the first-ever arrest warrant for a head of state, Sudanese president Omar al-Bashir. He joins Slobodan Milosevic of Yugoslavia, Charles Taylor of Liberia, and Jean Kambanda of Rwanda as heads of state subject to international justice for their alleged crimes. Charging people while they are still in a position to inflict further suffering has to be an important development.

When I stumbled upon Duch, all those years ago, it was a chance encounter; a small accidental part of something far larger. I never thought for a moment that I'd be called a witness to his trial and for many years it looked like he would never have his day in court. Whether his contrition was real or not, is impossible to say with any certainty. But the possibility is there. He is the only Khmer Rouge who has publicly acknowledged his responsibility, apologised and asked to be forgiven. For me, it's important to believe that people can change. To think otherwise is to embrace what the Khmer Rouge believed: that people were beyond redemption and must be killed.

Postscript

O N 26th July, 2010, after seventy-seven days in court, Duch became the first ever Khmer Rouge to be tried and convicted in an international tribunal. He was found guilty of war crimes and crimes against humanity and sentenced to a total of thirty-five years in prison. Prosecutors had sought a forty-year sentence but, because of mitigating circumstances – time already served in prison, his willingness to assist the court, his stated remorse and his repeated apologies to the victims throughout the trial – his sentence was reduced to nineteen years. If he serves the total, he will be released in 2029 at the age of eighty-six. His defence lawyer has announced that he will appeal.

Many Cambodians saw the verdict as a betrayal. They were angered that a man who ordered the killing of so many thousands of people should be sentenced to a mere nineteen years. 'He tricked everybody,' said Chum Mey as he wiped tears from his eyes. 'I was a victim during the Khmer Rouge, and now I'm a victim again.' One woman whose parents were murdered by the Khmer Rouge warned that 'no one is going to have the energy to look at the second case.'

But how do you measure the damage and pain inflicted by men like Duch? 'We can never give what they have lost,' said Judge Cartwright. 'A sentence can only be symbolic.' Co-prosecutor Chea Leang said that, at the very least, the judgement 'finally represents credible legal acknowledgement of the Khmer Rouge's criminal policies.'

But is that enough? The reaction to the verdict high-lighted the chasm between two worlds; that of the theory of Western justice and the real experience of emotional loss. To many it seemed wrong that Duch should receive a fair trial when none of his victims did but, as one Cambodian journalist wrote, 'Justice should never be vindictive.'

                                        Nic Dunlop, July 2010

Bibliography/Notes on Sources

I have listed only sources that were particularly useful as well as a select bibliography for further reading. I relied on numerous translations from Tuol Sleng Museum; many were supplied by Stephen Heder. Much of the rest of the material comes from magazines and newspapers as well as a number of confidential debriefing notes and documents, some of them passed on anonymously. The *Phnom Penh Post* was a particularly valuable source of information as was *Searching for the Truth*, the magazine of the Documentation Centre of Cambodia.

Ashe, Var Hong, *From Phnom Penh to Paradise* (Hodder and Stoughton, London, 1988)

Ayres, David M., *Anatomy of a Crisis: Education Development and the State in Cambodia 1953–1998* (University of Hawaii Press, Hawaii, 2000)

Barron, John & Anthony Paul, *Peace With Horror* (Hodder and Stoughton, London, 1977)

Becker, Elizabeth, *When the War Was Over* (Simon and Schuster, New York, 1986)

Bizot, François, *The Gate* (Harvill Press, London, 2003)

Burchett, Wilfred, *The China, Cambodia, Vietnam Triangle* (Zed Press, London, 1981)

————, *Mekong Upstream* (Seven Seas Books, Berlin, 1959)

Chanda, Nayan, *Brother Enemy: The War after the War* (Harcourt Brace Jovanovich, San Diego, New York London, 1986)

Chandler, David, *Voices from S-21: Terror and History in Pol Pot's Secret Prison* (University of California Press, 1999)

————, *A History of Cambodia* (Silkworm Books, Chiang Mai, 1998)

————, *Brother Number One: A Political Biography of Pol Pot* (Westview Press, 1999)

————, *Facing the Cambodian Past* (Silkworm Books, Chiang Mai, 1996)

Chhoung, Tauch, *Battambang during the Time of the Lord Governor* (Phnom Penh, 1974)

Davies, Paul & Nic Dunlop *War of the Mines* (Pluto Press, London, 1994)

Doyle, Michael W., *UN Peacekeeping in Cambodia: UNTAC's Civil Mandate* (Lynne Rienner Publishers, Boulder, London, 1995)

Ea, Meng-Try & Sorya Sim, *Victims and Perpetrators? Testimony of Young Khmer Rouge Comrades* (Documentation Centre of Cambodia, Phnom Penh, 2001)

Ebihara, May M., Carol A. Mortland, Judy Ledgerwood, *Cambodian Culture since 1975: Homeland and Exile* (Cornell University Press, Ithaca and London, 1994)

Etcheson, Craig, *The Rise and Demise of Democratic Kampuchea* (Westview Press, 1984)

Evans, Grant & Kelvin, Rowley, *Red Brotherhood at War* (Verso, London, 1984)

Fawcett, Brian, *Cambodia: A Book for People Who Find Television Too Slow* (Penguin Books, London, 1989)

Harrel-Bond, B.E., *Imposing Aid: Emergency Assistance to Refugees* (Oxford University Press, Oxford, 1986)

Jackson, Karl (ed.), *Cambodia 1975–1978: Rendezvous with Death* (Princeton University Press, Princeton, 1989)

Jennar, Raoul, *Les clès du Cambodge* (Maisonneuve and Larose, Paris, 1995)

Kiernan, Ben and Chanthou Boua (eds.), *Peasants and Politics in Kampuchea 1942–1981* (Zed Press, London, 1982)

Kiernan, Ben, *The Pol Pot Regime: Race, Power, and Genocide in Cambodia Under the Khmer Rouge 1975–79* (Yale University Press, New Haven and London, 2002)

———, *How Pol Pot Came to Power: A History of Communism in Kampuchea* (Verso, London, 1985)

———, (ed.), 'Genocide and Democracy in Cambodia', Yale University Southeast Asia Studies, 1993.

LeShan, Lawrence, *The Psychology of War: Comprehending its Mystique and its Madness* (Helios Press, New York, 2002)

Lewis Herman, Judith, *Trauma and Recovery: from Domestic Abuse to Political Terror* (Pandora, London, 2001)

Mason, Linda and Roger Brown, *Rice, Rivalry, and Politics: Managing Cambodian Relief* (University of Notre Dame Press, 1983)

May, Someth, *Cambodian Witness* (Faber & Faber, London, 1986)

Monier-Williams, M., *Buddhism in its Connexion with Brahminism and Hinduism and its Contrast with Christianity* (Munshiram Manoharlal publishers, Delhi, 1995)

Mysliwiec, Eva, *Punishing the Poor: The International Isolation of Kampuchea* (Oxfam, Oxford, 1988)

Nee, Meas with Joan Healy, *Towards Restoring Life: Cambodian Villages* (JSRC, Phnom Penh, 1995)

Ngor, Haing S. and Roger Warner, *Surviving the Killing Fields* (Chatto and Windus, London, 1987)

Osborne, Milton, *Sihanouk: Prince of Light, Prince of Darkness* (Silkworm Books, Chiang Mai, 1994)

————, *Before Kampuchea: Preludes to Tragedy* (Allen & Unwin, Sydney, 1979)

Paskin Carrison, Muriel & the Venerable Kong Chhean *Cambodian Stories from the Gatiloke*, (Tuttle Publishing, Boston, Rutland and Tokyo, 1987)

Philpotts, Robert, *Reporting Angkor: Chou Ta-Kuan in Cambodia, 1296–97*, (Blackwater Press)

Photo Archive Group, The, *The Killing Fields* (Twin Palms Press, Santa Fe, 1996)

Picq, Laurence, *Beyond the Horizon: Five Years with the Khmer Rouge* (St Martin's Press, New York, 1989)

Pilger, John Anthony Barnett, *Aftermath: The Struggle of Cambodia and Vietnam* (New Statesman, London, 1982)

Pilger, John, *Heroes* (Pan Books, London, Sydney and Auckland, 1989)

————, *Distant Voices*, (Vintage, London, 1994)

Ponchaud, François, *Cambodia: Year Zero* (Penguin Books, London, 1978)

Reynell, Josephine, *Political Pawns: Refugees on the Thai-Kampuchean border* (Refugee Studies Programme, Oxford, 1989)

Robinson, Courtland W., *Terms of Refuge: The Indochinese Exodus and the International Response* (Zed Press, London and New York, 1998)

Shawcross, William, *Sideshow: Kissinger, Nixon and the Destruction of Cambodia* (Simon & Schuster, New York, 1979)

————, *The Quality of Mercy: Cambodia, Holocaust and Modern Conscience* (André Deutsch, London, 1984)

Sheehy, Gail, *Spirit of Survival* (Bantam Press, London, 1987)

Szymusiak, Moylda, *The Stones Cry Out: A Cambodian Childhood 1975–1980* (Jonathan Cape, London, 1984)

Thion, Serge, *Watching Cambodia* (White Lotus Press, Bangkok, 1993)

Ung, Bunheang and Martin Stuart-Fox, *The Murderous Revolution* (Alternative Publishing Cooperative Limited, Australia, 1985)

Vannak, Huy, *The Khmer Rouge Division 703: From Victory to Self-destruction* (Documentation Centre of Cambodia, Phnom Penh, 2003)

Vickery, Michael, *Cambodia 1975–82* (South End Press, Sydney, 1985)

Weschler, Lawrence, *A Miracle, A Universe: Settling Accounts with Torturers* (University of Chicago Press, Chicago, 1998)

Yathay, Pin, *Stay Alive, My Son* (Bloomsbury, London, 1987)

Reports, articles, periodicals and essays:

Amnesty International, *Kampuchea: Political Imprisonment and Torture* (London, June 1987)

Asia Watch, *Cambodia: Human Rights Before and After the Elections* (Human Rights Watch Vol. 5 No. 10 May 1993)

Human Rights Watch/Asia, Human Rights Watch Arms project, *Cambodia at War* (New York, 1995)

Asia Watch/Physicians for Human Rights, *Landmines in Cambodia: The Cowards' War* (New York, 1991)

Bull, David, *The Poverty of Diplomacy* (Oxfam, Oxford, 1983)

Falconer, Bruce, *Murder by the State* (*Atlantic Monthly*, November 2003)

Hawk, David, *Tuol Sleng Extermination Centre*, Index on Censorship, (London, 1986)

Healy, Joan, *Towards Understanding*, unpublished essay (1992)

Heder, Stephen and Brian D. Tittemore, *Seven Candidates for Prosecution: Accountability for the Crimes of the Khmer Rouge* (War Crimes Research Office, American University, June 2001)

Heder, Stephen, *Justice for Cambodia?* Talk to the School of Oriental and African Studies (University of London, November 2002)

Hughes, Rachel, *The Abject Artefacts of Memory: Photographs from Cambodia's Genocide* (Media, Culture & Society, Sage Publications, London and Delhi, 2003)

Jackson, Tony, *Just Waiting to Die? Cambodian Refugees in Thailand* (Report by Oxfam, 1987)

Maat, Bob, *The Weight of These Sad Times, End of Mission Report on the Thai-Cambodian Border* (UNBRO 1989)

————, *The 'Major Disruption' at Samet, Christmas 1984* (Jesuit Refugee Service, Occasional Papers)

Niland, Norah, *The Politics of Suffering: The Thai-Cambodian Border: A Case Study on the Use and Abuse of Humanitarian Assistance* (University of Dublin, Centre for Peace Studies, Irish School of Ecumenics, November 1991)

Payne, Carole, *Deathwork: Unbearable Witness* (School for Studies in Art and Culture, Carelton University, Ottawa, October 2000)

Thye Trebay, Guy, *Killing Fields of Vision* (*Village Voice*, New York, May 1997)

United Nations, *Kampuchean Humanitarian Assistance Programmes: The International Community's Response* (New York, 1986)

————, *United Nations Transitional Authority in Cambodia*, (UN report, December 1993)

UNBRO report, *Displacement and Survival* (Bangkok, December 1994)

UN Secretary-General report, *Financing of the United Nations Advance Mission in Cambodia, Financing of United Nations Transitional Authority in Cambodia* (7 May 1992)

GLOSSARY

Cambodia – is a French corruption of Kampuchea.

Cyclo – a peddle-powered tricycle taxi with a seat in the front found mainly in Phnom Penh.

Dharma – the Buddhist Scriptures.

Kampuchea – is the Khmer name for Cambodia, a derivative from the Sanskrit 'Kambuja', the name of a tribe in India from whom the Khmers are thought to have originated.

Khmer – Cambodia's indigenous dominant ethnic group.

Krama – is a traditional Khmer scarf used to shield people from the sun, a hammock, a sarong used also to carry things.

Maquis – the name given to the underground French resistance that fought against German occupation in World War Two, also used to describe the Khmer Rouge clandestine liberated areas in the lead-up to their takeover.

Pagoda – a Buddhist temple building used for worship which houses a large Buddha statue and where ceremonies and rituals are held.

Phnom – a hill or a mountain.

Sala – is an open building usually found on the edge of villages

or in the grounds of a temple, used for meetings and ceremonies.

Sangha – the Buddhist monastic order.

Sompeah – traditional Cambodian greeting where palms are placed
together as in prayer. It also denotes respect, depending on
how high the hands are held. The higher the gesture, the
more respect is being shown.

Stupa – a Buddhist shrine used to house relics or the remains
of relatives who have been cremated, similar to the shape of
a bell.

Ta – 'Ta' as in Ta Mok means 'Grandpa'. An honorific title for
anyone of that age or any man of middle age and above –
a status superior. It is a term that emphasises respect rather
than affection.

Wat – a Buddhist temple or monastery.